SAVING
OUR SKIN

A Surgeon's Story of Tenacity,
Adventure and Giving Back

PERRY ROBINS, MD
with JULIE BAIN

RIVER GROVE
BOOKS

This book is a memoir reflecting the author's present recollections of experiences over time. Its story and its words are the author's alone. Some details and characteristics may be changed, some events may be compressed and some dialogue may be re-created.

The information given here is not intended as a substitute for any professional medical advice. It is provided for entertainment purposes only. If you suspect that you or someone you know has a medical problem, you should seek competent medical help.

Published by River Grove Books
Austin, TX
www.rivergrovebooks.com

Distributed by River Grove Books

Design and composition by Greenleaf Book Group and Sheila Parr
Cover design by Greenleaf Book Group and Sheila Parr
Cover image: ©Shutterstock / eltoro69

Publisher's Cataloging-in-Publication data is available.

Print ISBN: 978-1-63299-240-6

eBook ISBN: 978-1-63299-241-3

First Edition

For Marcia, the love of my life,
who taught me that it's never too late to find your soul mate.

Contents

INTRODUCTION

A Roast or a Toast?

Measuring my life in one-liners.

I f you're lucky enough to have reached a certain age and level of achievement, inevitably someone organizes a roast. What the people who show up have to say about you is sure to be honest, revealing and enlightening. Wouldn't that make anyone nervous?

For me, this happened in San Francisco on a chilly evening in March 2009, with gusty winds making the boats anchored in the bay bob and sway like tipsy sailors. I was feeling a little off-balance myself. Many colleagues and friends from several countries were in town for the annual meeting of the American Academy of Dermatology. Some had mentored me, and some were those I had taught to become surgeons. My son and daughter had even flown across the country for the occasion. We were gathered at Gastagnola's restaurant at Fisherman's Wharf to feast on butter-drenched Dungeness crab and sourdough bread—and to put me in the crosshairs.

I was 78 and had recently decided to stop practicing medicine—not that I was losing my skills as a skin cancer surgeon. My hands were still steady as a rock, and despite my efforts to cut back, demand for my services was high and my office staff in New York City kept filling my schedule.

Why would anyone care enough to roast a dermatologic surgeon, you might ask? It's not like being a movie star (although I've removed skin cancers from quite a few of those). But I did create a bit of a revolution in my field by showing dermatologists they could also be surgeons, which was unheard of at the time. I devoted myself to teaching and promoting a new type of surgery (later called Mohs, for the name of its inventor) that evolved to become the gold standard in treating many skin cancers. I also decided to fight the long-held notion that tanning was healthy and spread the word that it leads to skin cancer. Believe me, there was a lot of resistance to those ideas back in the 1960s and '70s.

I infuriated some people, won some over, gained supporters and ultimately succeeded. I personally performed about 47,000 skin cancer surgeries during my 40-plus of practice (yes, we kept track of them all, starting with computer punch cards back in the early days). I taught in nearly 50 countries and in four languages. I spread the message about sun protection and skin cancer around the globe, saved lives and made a difference.

I loved my work and my patients, and I seemed to run into them everywhere, not just in New York but also at the Parthenon in Athens, at the Vatican and in the lobby of a hotel in Baden-Baden near the Black Forest of Germany, where a woman asked if she could dispense with her upcoming visit to my office and just show me her suspicious mole right there. I would miss those daily connections, but I felt ready to slow down a little. After a lifetime of not-so-successful relationships, I had finally met the love of my life, Marcia Robbins-Wilf. I was lucky enough to have my health, my kids and grandchildren nearby, lots of friends in many countries, passion for travel and plenty of money, so why not have some fun?

Having already packed up my office full of plaques, awards and memories at NYU Medical Center in New York City, where I had been affiliated since my training in 1964 and had been chief of Mohs surgery since 1972, I then made the big decision to sell my private practice. It was also the 30th anniversary of The Skin Cancer Foundation, the charitable organization I had founded in 1979 to educate physicians and the public about skin cancer. All, apparently, a good excuse to roast me. Yes, I was feeling a little nervous about being the center of such attention—especially among people so highly skilled with scalpels. Were they going to skin me alive? But while I (like most surgeons) have a healthy ego, I also have a fairly clear-eyed awareness of my strengths and weaknesses, so I thought, *Bring it on.*

Of those who stood at the podium, a few lobbed softball jokes, such as Leonard Goldberg, MD, who came from South Africa to train with me at NYU in 1979 and was now a successful Houston dermatologic surgeon. He recalled me often buying him lunch at the hospital cafeteria in those days, then eating off his plate when I had finished wolfing down my own meal first. Well, sure. What hungry hospital chief would have the patience to wait for a slow-eating trainee?

Dr. Goldberg also shared, "Once you learned how to make money, you also learned how to *lose* money." *Yes, that's true,* I thought. Like the medical journal I started that bled in the red for nearly 20 years. It also built awareness and credibility for the new medical specialty of dermatologic surgery that I helped to create. And yes, eventually I sold it and made a few shekels.

Then there were the many other entrepreneurial efforts I attempted, including importing cashmere suits from Hong Kong, opening a restaurant in Paris and investing in real estate development and even an airline start-up. Hey, sometimes those efforts worked; sometimes I didn't have the right partners to make them happen. Sometimes my ideas were just, dare I say it, ahead of their time. And, yes, occasionally I lost my shirt. Sometimes losing my shirt helped somebody who needed it more than I did. No matter what, I learned a few things along the way!

I did some good with my money, too, and I talked to my medical students about the importance of giving back as well. Dr. Goldberg acknowledged that when he said, "Perry taught me to be a surgeon, and my destiny was altered forever. He also taught me how to be positive and generous and to use money to help others."

When my son, Lawrence, had his turn at the podium, he cracked that his speech would be longer than my second marriage. Can't say he was wrong. He'd had some major ups and downs in his 39 years, but I was touched he was there for me. Lawrence is smart and charismatic, and he made some very funny fat jokes. I know, I know—I've never met a food I didn't like.

Elizabeth, my kind-hearted daughter, poignantly pointed out that I had been a father figure to so many people in my life, perhaps thinking, at times, more so than to my own children. *Ouch.* But she said, generously, "My brother and I have shared him for the past 30-some years. We know there was enough of him to share. He is a great, huge man—literally and figuratively. He is a bundle of spirit, love, energy and happiness."

Alfred W. Kopf, MD, who had recently retired as a professor of dermatology at NYU Medical Center and the number two person in the Department of Dermatology, told a story about the first employee of the Foundation, who consistently mispronounced the word melanoma as "megalanoma" but then correctly diagnosed himself as having one when, annoyed, I gave him a research book to study up on it. We saved his life. As Kopf was not usually a comic storyteller, I was impressed that he elicited a good laugh out of the mispronunciation part.

Then he paused and became more serious. "I pondered endlessly to try to come up with some faults. But I came up with this," he said, showing a blank screen on his PowerPoint presentation. He continued, "There's nothing wrong with this great contributor to dermatology and dermatologic surgery—with his fundraising skills, brilliant ideals, passion for communication and education in a lifelong pursuit of decreasing the mortality and morbidity of patients suffering with cancers of the skin. Thanks, Perry, for your generosity, leadership and endurance. God bless you for all that you have done."

Now isn't this a great way for me to tell you about me without having to do the bragging myself? And to make you smile over the fact that only a physician would use the words "mortality and morbidity" in a roast (or toast)!

Believe me, though, the feeling is mutual. For being one of my earliest supporters, Al Kopf is my hero, and I owe him more than he can possibly imagine. Not just for my successes in medicine but for teaching me how to be a mensch.

The final speaker was Deborah S. Sarnoff, MD, a New York City dermatologic surgeon who spent a year training with me in 1985 and '86. I consider her one of the best and brightest of all the students I've known. She did a hilarious Catskills-worthy impression of a Jewish mother boasting about me.

She fired off a few zingers laced with Yiddish. Then she said, "My son, he's trained more than 70 doctors, all over the world, and they've gone on to train others. Fred Mohs may have invented Mohs surgery, but my son, he *promoted* Mohs surgery. He put Mohs surgery on the map. He devotes his life to teaching and helping others." She ended with these words: "He never let anything stop him and he never learned the meaning of the word *no*."

Well, she's right about that, I thought. I hope my real mother would have been proud of me. Sadly, she died in 1961 of complications from diabetes. She was kind, generous and giving, and she never raised her voice in anger. She was my role model and my greatest inspiration.

I laughed and shed a few tears throughout the roast and felt lucky to have gotten away with my skin intact. When I stood up at the end to say a few words, I blurted out, "I have a confession to make: All those things they said tonight were true!" That got a big laugh. But then I said something that I meant from the bottom of my heart: "What makes life worthwhile is having wonderful friends." That's certainly one measure of a man, right?

Here's the thing about being roasted by wonderful people who know you well: They have a way of handing you the themes of your life to ponder, for better or worse. Did I always yearn for money because of my tough childhood when it was scarce? Check. Did I overcome obstacles from an early age? Check. Both my parents worked, and so did I. I didn't do well in school because I worked long hours, had no time to study and I fell asleep in class. I had dyslexia. I was bullied for being Jewish. I never thought I'd go to college because no one in my family ever had. But somehow I did— and then went on to achieve more than I ever dreamed. I'm proud of that. Could I have been present more for my own two kids when they were young? Check.

My daughter, Elizabeth, said, "You know the expression 'Just do it?' That completely epitomizes my father and has been a valuable lesson since I was a little girl. You want to start a business? Just do it! Too many people are paralyzed by fear, overthinking things. He just does it. I love that about him."

But just doing it is not the entire story. These are troubled times, and it seems as if stepping on others while focusing only on yourself is a viable way to get ahead. I honestly feel, though, that you can achieve success while being a good person, sticking to what you believe in, doing the right thing and giving back. By being a mensch. I think my stories can help others, too. Hey, I've got a million of 'em! That's why I decided to write this book.

My son, Lawrence, also said that I never let fear stop me from turning my dreams into reality. My hope is that I can inspire you to do the same.

CHAPTER 1

Hard Work in Newark

Tough lessons from my ancestors and the
Not So Great Depression.

Timing is everything, especially when it comes to making money. Let's just say the timing was off for much of my family history. My grandfather and namesake, Pherris Robins, was a promising artist who emigrated from Lithuania in the 1880s to escape Czarist persecution of the Jewish people. (What had probably been "Rabinovich" in Russia became "Robins" in America.) He settled in Newark, New Jersey, where he and his cousin opened a furniture store. My grandfather died before the shop became profitable, and I'm sorry I never knew him. The cousin moved the furniture company to Millburn, New Jersey, and it became a local success, but my grandmother never received a dime from it. She and her three boys and two girls had to make their own way.

My maternal grandparents had equally bad luck. My grandfather died in an accident, leaving behind his wife and three daughters, who moved from Massachusetts to the Lower East Side of New York City to try to make a living. Grandma Markowitz often told the story of the day the Labor Department came to vet the conditions of a clothing factory where Esther (who would become my mother) and her two sisters worked. At the time, they were well underage, and they hid in a big sewing machine to avoid being seen by the labor inspectors.

By the 1920s, though, New York and New Jersey were booming, and the Robins boys had big hopes and dreams. Lewis and his two older brothers, William and Jack, became interested in real estate and started buying land in the Bronx, where many Russian Jewish immigrants were settling. They made some money, and when Lewis Robins married Esther Markowitz, it seemed like prosperity was unshakable.

My older sister, Irene, came along in 1926. Newark Airport opened two years later and quickly became the world's busiest commercial hub, attracting more business to the area. (That airport would spark my interest in learning to fly as well as my passion for travel.) Also in 1928, construction began on the Chrysler Building, that glittering symbol of Art Deco prosperity across the Hudson (and just a few blocks from where I would practice medicine for nearly half a century).

The stock market crash of October 1929 changed everything, and the country plunged into the Great Depression. I made my entrance into the world just eight months later, on June 14, 1930. My timing was not good.

During the Depression years, my father and uncles struggled to pay the taxes on the land they owned and eventually lost it all. That was disheartening for my father, who lost a lot of his drive because of it. I think it took the wind out of his sails. He later ran a gasoline station on Bloomfield Avenue in Montclair, but times were tough and my parents didn't have much money.

THE NICKNAME GAME

While my given name is "Pherris," after my paternal grandfather, it never stuck, and I soon became known as "Perry." When my mother first registered me for school in Newark, the principal suggested

she officially change my name, as Pherris was unusual and he thought the children would make fun of it (and, no doubt, bully me for it). To this day, my diplomas and passports say either Perry Pherris Robins or Pherris Perry Robins.

My other nickname was triggered by my hair. When I was a toddler, I'm told, I had gorgeous golden-blond curls. People would comment on my hair so often, my mother was reluctant to cut it. As a result, my uncles insisted on calling me "Patricia" until I got a haircut. After I finally received a haircut, they shortened the name to "Pat." It stuck, and for many years my nickname was Pat. One day while in college, my roommate went to fetch the mail. He laughed when he handed me a postcard addressed to "Dear Pat." In fact, I recently received an email from a distant relative that began with "Dear Pat." Some habits die hard. The grand irony, of course, is that not only did my hair darken as I grew up, but I also lost most of it far earlier than I would have liked. But as I often say, it doesn't matter, as grass doesn't grow on a busy street!

My mother was a very caring and kind person, warm and affectionate, and she made do with what she had. Not only did she look after her own immediate family, but she also tended to my father's two brothers and two sisters who moved in with us. She cooked, kept a tight control on the household chores and worked in a bakery to earn extra money. She worked extremely hard. I learned later that to save money on our food budget, she often just ate the free cake at the bakery and skimped on the healthier foods during meals at home to leave more for the rest of us. That certainly contributed to her developing type 2 diabetes.

My father, who was younger than my mother, was a good-looking hunk with a golden voice. He adored music and loved to sing. He was a great storyteller and could expertly mimic people. When he talked, everyone listened. I realized from a pretty young age, though, that my parents were completely mismatched. I don't want to say my father was lazy. He was conscientious and did his job. He did the best he could, but he didn't have the joie de vivre or the spirit that my mother had. She was full of energy and loved to travel and entertain. He was a homebody, happy just to nap on the couch. As the Depression slogged on, I imagine that many of my mother's dreams were dashed, too. My parents argued all the time. They should have gotten divorced, unequivocally. But in those days you didn't get divorced. You couldn't afford to.

I knew there were troubles at home, but I don't recall that it affected me that much. Still, when I was in about the third grade, the principal at my school became concerned. I was tall for my age, and so super skinny that my ribs stuck out. I wasn't applying myself in class, and I was not motivated in my lessons. I remember that the principal called my parents and wanted to know if we had enough money and enough to eat. My parents said they were fine. He also wanted to know if there were arguments or family problems at home. My parents said no. Let's face it: The Depression was not a time when people aired their dirty laundry in public. Nor did parents often ask about their kids' well-being. They had bigger problems to worry about.

It's true that I wasn't a good student and didn't really care about learning until quite a bit later, but I also had dyslexia. I eventually learned how to work with it, but I have trouble even today. I cannot read a long speech as I tend to stumble a bit. Luckily, I learned to think on my feet and became pretty adept at public speaking anyway.

A LESSON IN ENTREPRENEURSHIP

This photo triggers one of my earliest memories. When I was 5 or 6, walking home from school, I saw a man with a pony not far from our house. Of course, I was enchanted by it. The man asked if I'd  like to sit on the pony. I said, "Gee, that sounds like fun. I'd like to!" He helped me up into the saddle, then he took some photographs and asked where I lived. I pointed to our house on the corner. A few days later he was knocking at the door of our home, asking my parents if they wanted to purchase the photographs he'd taken of me. They were furious with me and reluctant to buy the photos because of limited funds, but they purchased a couple of the pictures anyway. I think I got a spanking for it. Today anyone would be wary of a stranger trying to lure a child. But I think it might have been an early lesson for me in the power of entrepreneurship!

While times were tough during the Depression, I remember many good things about my childhood. For one, my dog, Queenie, was always there for me. When I was a baby, the owner of the bakery where my mother worked gave her a beautiful German shepherd puppy (after the bakery owner's 3-year-old left the puppy in the refrigerator on a hot day "because it was perspiring"). The puppy survived the ordeal, became completely protective of me and wouldn't let anyone near me in my baby carriage. Once when my aunt tried to pick me up, Queenie bit her on the arm. Still, everyone loved that dog, who was with us for many years. I've been lucky to have quite a few great dogs in my life.

We lived in a house in Newark, a few blocks from Weequahic Park, and on the weekends my Uncle Jack would take me for walks around the lake. My other uncle, Bill, was self-educated, an avid reader and very intelligent. He taught me a lot as I was growing up and, in some ways, became more of a father to me than my father himself.

I was close with my aunts and uncles, and with my sister, Irene (although we'd fight sometimes, like when I'd steal a piece of cake and blame it on her). There were lots of kids in the neighborhood to play with, although most of them were not Jewish, and a few bad apples occasionally taunted me about it, or tried to beat me up. It seemed so unfair, too, because even though my parents were both raised in religious Jewish families, we never belonged to a synagogue or temple.

Yes, we observed some traditions, especially while my maternal grandmother was still alive. Friends and relatives would come on Friday nights for a big dinner, and we would lock the doors as a symbol of the security of being together and keeping out intrusions. I loved those evenings, and one of my fondest early memories was that on Friday nights, my grandmother would bake a special small challah bread, just for me.

We would use the special dishes for Passover, too, but when my grandmother died, that stopped. We'd still get together with all the family for Rosh Hashanah and Yom Kippur. We didn't go to synagogue, but my mother would say, "You're not supposed to eat," so we'd fast for half a day—although it's supposed to be the whole day.

I remember how thrilling it was the first time I was told that I didn't have to go to school because it was a Jewish holiday. I was so excited I went out and told the other kids in the neighborhood they didn't have to go to school, either. A few tried it and got caught. When their parents found out I was their cause for unsanctioned truancy (as most of the neighborhood kids were not Jewish), I'm pretty sure I got a spanking.

As for my bar mitzvah, it was uninspiring. I never went to Hebrew school, so about a month before I turned 13 my parents decided I should do something. They hired a rabbi who taught me to pronounce the words phonetically, and I read it the best I could off a sheet of paper. That was my entire Jewish education.

The one thing I did throw myself into wholeheartedly in those years was hard work—and from an early age. When I was 8 or 9, I'd go to the gas station with my dad and uncle on Saturdays and help change and fix tires. If I was a good boy and did well, I got to sit in the rumble seat of the Ford and we'd drive down to an ice cream parlor in Newark called Sloppy Dave's for a maple walnut sundae. To motivate me, my father or uncle would say, "Perry, if you're not going to work, you're not going to get your sundae." So I would work! I guess that kick-started the work ethic I learned from my mother as well as my lifelong love affair with good food—especially ice cream.

My parents often said, "The harder you work, the luckier you'll be." I definitely wanted to make them proud. I also had a bicycle route delivering copies of *Ladies' Home Journal* and *Liberty* magazine, with its tagline "A Weekly for Everybody." Yes, those publications were heavy, but when I was in grammar school, I was taller and stronger than most kids. As a result, I was also assigned the humiliating task of having to carry a neighbor girl's accordion to school and back, because it was too big and heavy for her. Can you picture that? Let's just say I wasn't cool. And I hated having to wait for her, as she was seldom on time. I'd say, "Come on! Come on! We're going to be late for school! I'll be in detention." While I wasn't a good student then, at least I was obedient and did my best to follow the rules.

When I was about 11, I started working as a busboy at Preakness Hills Country Club. That was my first glimpse of true luxury. It looked like *The Great Gatsby* come to life. I wondered if I would ever be wealthy enough to join a country club. (Now I belong to three.) That job was not easy. I was lugging food and dishes back and forth, always hearing, "Hurry up! Clean the table! Here! Get the mop! Wipe up the floor!" I couldn't move fast enough.

My work didn't stop in the summers. It just changed. When the school year ended, my parents sent me to my aunt's farm up in Montville, New Jersey, where I spent the days as free labor, picking corn, peppers and tomatoes. I liked being in the country, though, especially when I could end the day by jumping into the local swimming hole. And I have such vivid memories of the hotel *kochalein* (translated from Yiddish as "cook for yourself") during those years. This was a tradition going back to the turn of the 20th century, in which Jewish farmers rented rooms to Jewish immigrants who wanted to get out of the city in the summer. My aunt rented out six or seven bedrooms, and all the families had kids. There was an army of kids, which was fun for me. The huge garage, which usually stored tractors and hay machines, would be fixed up for kitchens, with a stove, icebox and table where the families would eat their meals. The iceman would make deliveries each day.

I remember one guy, short and fat, who worked for the city of New York, was funny and loved to tell jokes. I remember another family who were devout Communists, and they'd sit around in the evening and try to brainwash me. "Russia's going to defeat the Germans and help the world," they'd say. My aunt would get angry and say, "If you dare mention one more word about Russia to my nephew, I'm going to ask you people to leave." Back then I didn't even know where Russia was.

I had no idea we'd move to that rural area of northern New Jersey when I was 14, and my life would change in so many ways. But in those years I'd return to Newark before school started.

Besides working in the bakery, my mother had formed a partnership with a caterer called Clinton Manor. They rented a restaurant in the Mosque Theater, which was the opera house of Newark. (Today it's called Newark Symphony Hall.) The restaurant also catered the concessions, so when the opera performances were on, my father and I would help out and sell lemonade at intermission. When everyone went back to their seats, I got to sit in the back row for the rest of the performance. My father loved classical music, and this was my first chance to experience it live. I don't think we even had a record player in those days. I was squirmy at first but learned to love listening to the music. I remember one of my favorite singers was Lily Pons. I worry that kids today don't have any exposure to classical music and that it's a dying art in this country.

At home, my father liked to listen to classical music on the big radio in the living room. And I couldn't wait to hear my favorite radio shows, too, like *Tom Mix* and *The Lone Ranger*. I'll never forget the excitement of lying on the floor and hearing those introductory words that included, "Return with us now to those thrilling days of yesteryear," and ended with the rousing "Hi-Yo, Silver! Away!" It gave me the chills. I also loved the radio show *Let's Pretend*, in which actors performed classic fairy tales, such as *The Arabian Nights* or *Rumpelstiltskin*. It was great to escape into those stories. But my most memorable radio moment was that Sunday afternoon, December 7, 1941, when the program was interrupted to announce the attack on Pearl Harbor.

THE SOUND OF MY CHILDHOOD

When I was a child, I loved hearing my father hum or sing his favorite songs. He especially loved classical music, and while I didn't know the names of his favorites when I was very young, they were

imprinted in my memory. Later I learned that one he often hummed was "Humoresque," that well-known tune by Antonín Dvořák. But his very favorite was Jules Massenet's "Méditation de Thaïs." You'd probably recognize it if you heard it.

My son, Lawrence, who has worked in the entertainment industry, is friends with the violinist Joshua Bell. A few years ago Lawrence helped him organize an event at his apartment, to which I was also invited. At the end, Joshua thanked everyone for coming and said he wanted to end with a tribute to Lawrence Robins, for all he had done. Purely by coincidence, he started playing the Massenet piece that my father always sang, and it brought tears to my eyes.

Thanks to Lawrence's connections, Joshua played at The Skin Cancer Foundation Gala in 2014 (above) as a volunteer without charge. Sting sang, too, as a personal favor to Lawrence. It was one of our most memorable events ever!

Once the war started, Uncle Bill was called to service in the Navy as a Seabee. He became a chief petty officer and was stationed in the Aleutian Islands, where he fought to remove Japanese forces that had seized two U.S.–owned islands there. Uncle Jack was drafted into the Army but remained stateside. My father, who was over the draft age at that time, went into defense work for the Pennsylvania Railroad—a job he would continue until taking a disability retirement 20 years later.

While my father was working for the railroad, he had a Polish supervisor who, when he discovered my father was Jewish, perpetually gave him the night shift. More than a few times, my father told me you had to be very, very special to get ahead in this world, and even more so if you were Jewish. It was the first time he tried to instill in me an understanding of what it meant to have Jewish roots. I was too young to really understand what was happening with Hitler's rise to power, but it gave me an inkling nevertheless of what anti-Semitism means.

Even though the war helped to kick-start the economy again, times were still hard because of shortages and rationing. My father didn't want to spend a lot of money on gas, so we didn't drive very far. We hardly ever went out for dinner, but I fondly remember a Sunday night ritual, when our whole family would jaunt to downtown Newark to a Chinese restaurant. I loved escaping to the movies on Saturdays to see westerns. I remember how outraged I was when admission was raised from 10 to 11 cents—highway robbery! Our big treat, though, was to drive to Newark Airport, park by the gate and watch the planes land and take off. It was always exciting and impressive to me, and it sparked a longing in me to spread my wings and fly and see new places.

Soon I was making my own model airplanes out of balsa wood in the kitchen at home. I loved trying to build fighter planes like the ones being used in the war, then you could wind the propeller with a rubber band and let it fly! Sadly, I never had a chance to get on an actual airplane and fly until years later, when I was in the Army.

While I would hear news about the war on the radio, and knew enough to be frightened of Nazis, my mother sheltered me from most of the harsh realities. I have only fond and warm memories of her. She was the biggest inspiration of my life, and I like to think that I inherited her personality, ambition and optimism. She was so generous, not only with her own family but with many others. One of my favorite stories about her is one I only learned at her funeral in 1961, after she died of complications from diabetes.

At the service, the principal from a Newark school stood up and told us that one snowy day back in the early '40s, two children came to school wearing only paper shoes. He knew that my mother was the secretary for a women's organization, so he called and asked, "Do you think your organization can afford to buy these kids some shoes?" She replied, "I don't know about the organization, but I will." She went to the school, picked up the kids, took them to a shoe store and bought each of them two pairs of shoes. And she never told anyone. At the funeral, the principal said, "After that, there was no question that every time we needed something, I'd call Mrs. Robins and she would never say no."

I was so touched by that story, especially because she never needed any credit for her good works. She was very modest. I have deep reverence and love for my mother because of that. I'm so grateful she lived long enough to see me graduate from medical school and begin my internship in New Jersey. I wanted to be like her, and I wanted her to be proud of me.

One of my own first steps into the "giving back" realm was when I was about 13 and I heard about a charitable fraternal organization called the Knights of Pythias. Remember the ancient story of Damon and Pythias, loyal friends bonded by brotherhood and each willing to die to save the other's life? The organization, founded during the Civil War, was inspired by that story and its spirit of friendship and benevolence.

I heard about it through Dr. Nathan Grossman, a dentist who was married to my father's sister and was very active in the organization. He said, "Hey, you know, Perry, they want to start a junior order for kids to become involved." It was similar to the Masons, which also had a junior order. He asked me to invite some of my friends to his lodge. They would sponsor us and arrange for a place to meet and someone to direct us. I recruited a bunch of my Newark pals to help form the organization and, since they all knew me but not each other, they voted me as president.

We did some small good works and even decided to inaugurate a new chapter in New Rochelle, New York. That's where I met a girl named Wendy Siegel, and I was completely felled by her charm and beauty. She was my big heartthrob on Webster Avenue. (It's funny how I remember that address.) We went up there by train, and for the next three weeks I couldn't get her out of my mind.

I wanted to be with her, but it was nearly impossible for me to get to New Rochelle from New Jersey, especially at my age. Anyway, we started the new chapter, but then it all fell apart when I learned that my family was leaving Newark and moving to the country near where my aunt's farm was. There was my bad timing again, as my first taste of leadership and my first crush were nipped in the bud.

CHAPTER 2

Down on the Farm

Even more exhausting hard work,
country-style.

For years my father had admired a 50-acre spread in Montville, New Jersey, adjacent to the farm my mother's sister and husband owned. Once the showpiece of a Civil War veteran, the rolling acreage contained orchards of apple, peach and pear trees and a 19th century house filled with paintings and antiques. When the owner died in 1943, my father went to pay his respects. The veteran's sister had inherited the property, which was about 15 miles northwest of where we lived in Newark, and told my father she would be open to selling it. The price of $5,000 seemed enormous, but my father and his brothers thought that if they pooled all their resources, they could buy it together.

It didn't go as planned, however. Just a day or two before my father was to take title to the property, the sister went to bed that night not knowing a stove burner had been left on. Maybe a curtain fluttered too near the burner, or someone carelessly tossed a dish towel on it, but something sparked a fire, the flames spread and the place burned fast. Because the house sat on the border of two towns, when the call came in the two fire departments argued about whose responsibility it was. By the time firefighters showed up, it was too late to save anything. Nothing was left except bricks and the bare foundation.

I hated to see my father's dream of living in that historic house go up in smoke. We made the best of it, though. The owner reduced the price to $3,000, and my father and his two brothers (who had both finished their military service) decided to put their do-it-your-self skills to good use and build a new house. Because of the war, it was very difficult to get building materials. They managed to find used lumber and started construction on a three-bedroom Cape Cod–style home. They worked mostly on weekends, and relatives and friends helped when they could. My uncles had been working as tile setters, and I remember stripping previously used tile so we could have fancy tile showers in our bathrooms.

In June 1944, about a week after President Roosevelt delivered his emotional D-Day prayer, "Let Our Hearts Be Stout," on the radio, I blew out the 14 candles on my birthday cake. I had nursed my wounds over the loss of my first love and had recently gradu-ated from grammar school, the tallest kid in my eighth-grade class. Now I was looking forward to summer. In July, as the Battle of Normandy started to turn the tide of the war, we prepared to leave Newark for our new life in the country.

I thought our new house, which was built on stilts, was great. (Years later, with the help of a jeep and some equipment, my father and uncles were able to put in a proper foundation.) As for the burned-out structure, rumor had it that the original owner had pre-viously hidden or buried money in the walls and foundation. You can imagine how that sparked my imagination. Consequently, on numerous occasions my father and I chipped away at the bricks and foundation to see if we could locate the buried treasure, with no success. Over the years, we continued our periodic searches but always came up empty-handed.

I had fun exploring my new territory. A dozen cedar trees embraced the entrance to the farm, and there was an artesian well where people came to collect water for its fantastic taste. A river flowed through the property, where we could swim and fish off a bridge, and in the springtime, when our beautiful dogwood tree was in bloom, we collected carp in the swamp areas. I got to mingle with an assortment of animals, including goats, ponies, horses, cows and rabbits, plus a collection of dogs, big and small.

In those days, Montville was a small rural community of mostly farmers. Our next-door neighbor raised dairy cows and another neighbor had a chicken hatchery where she raised baby chicks. My mother's sister and brother-in-law did the farming on our property as well as their own, growing vegetables for local markets. We raised chickens, and every morning I had to feed them and collect the eggs, which my father sold to his colleagues and friends at work.

During the summer my uncle taught me how to front-load the harvested vegetables onto the trucks to be taken to the market. He taught me to drive the tractors when my feet could barely reach the pedals. We had about 60 apple trees, and every fall we would pick the apples and take them to the local cider mill. For a bushel of apples, we received credit for three and a half gallons of cider that would be pressed for us. Around Thanksgiving we sold our gallons of cider to a local supermarket.

On Sundays, when the weather was nice, we grilled hot dogs, hamburgers or chicken in our big outdoor fireplace. Friends and relatives found their way to the Robins farm to enjoy the feast. They'd come in their new cars and bring cakes and I'd think they were so rich! It was my father's pride and joy to be the chef.

OUR ROCKEFELLER CENTER TREE

One day a man drove up to our house and said, "I've been looking at the trees on your property, and there is one tree I would like to buy." He said he'd pay $75 for it, which was a fortune in those days. My

father (left, with my mother) came out to negotiate with the man and said for that price he would sell him a few hundred trees. The man said no, he only wanted one. He would come back in the wintertime when the ground was frozen to harvest it and take it away on a trailer.

Asked why the man was so eager to buy this one tree, the workers with him said, "Don't you know where the tree is going?" I said, "To his home?" They said it was going to Fifth Avenue and Rockefeller Center. We were bowled over, but no, it wasn't *that* tree. Not the Christmas tree. Instead, it matched the type of flowering trees that were planted along the Promenade in the 1940s. Still, I said, "My gosh, if I'd known that, we would've charged more!" I remembered this story about 30 years later, when I organized a fundraiser for The Skin Cancer Foundation at the skating rink at Rockefeller Center. We might have grown our seed money within view of my family's tree, still growing there.

Our land was adjacent to a summer resort town called Lake Hiawatha. I had friends there, and I would sometimes ride my bike over to visit. One day I borrowed a rowboat and was peacefully paddling around near the shore when I heard a boy yell, "Hey, you don't belong here!" Then he tipped over my boat and I fell overboard. When I rubbed the water out of my eyes and looked around, there was a kid about my height with a big smile on his face. His name was Buddy Shenkin. He was from the Bronx, his parents were divorced and his mom had gotten the Lake Hiawatha bungalow in the settlement. We became best friends from that instant. People thought we were brothers. In many ways he was like a brother, and we stayed good friends until his death in 2015 (even though he once tried to talk me out of going to medical school).

My farm life sounds idyllic, doesn't it? It *was* when I had spare time, but that became an increasingly rare commodity. Most Sundays, for example, my job was to try to tame the acres of New Jersey's finest weeds with a 12-inch lawn mower. It felt like a futile task to keep up with it, at least until the snows came—or until my father finally broke down and bought the tractor he'd always wanted, so he could cut the grass "like a gentleman farmer."

There was an endless supply of chores that needed to be done, and my father didn't have the energy that my mother did. She must have been frustrated at times with the drudgery of her daily life and not being able to get out much. My sister, Irene, had graduated from high school and took a job as a draftsperson at CBS, so she wasn't home often to help out. While my father still commuted to his railroad job in Newark, my mother had given up her job in the bakery there and probably missed her friends, her women's organization and the activities of the city.

She and my father often spoke Yiddish when they didn't want kids to understand what they were saying. Maybe they used it to hide their disagreements, too, I'm not sure. But I learned a few helpful phrases along the way. I know I was sometimes a *fresser,* someone who gulps down food too fast, like a dog. And my mother, who made beautiful birthday cakes, was a *balabusta,* someone who is talented in the kitchen or a good homemaker (although she was also so much more). And she knew how to get me to obey her. *"Ich hob dich in bod"* was interpreted in my family as: "Ah, I have you helpless," or literally, "I have you in the bathtub."

My mother loved to go for car rides in the country, but she seldom even got to do that. We'd always beg my father to take us, but he would usually say, "No, no, we'll stay home" and then lie on the couch. Boy, did I love it on the rare occasions we'd head out on the steep road that led up to High Point, about 1,800 feet above sea level. My father had bought a used Franklin cheap from a family in Montclair, and that old Franklin would jerk-jerk-jerk all the way to the top. But I was so proud, saying, "Look at us! We're beating all the other cars!" That was big excitement for me. Once I started high school, though, playtime became even more scarce.

While there was a high school closer to the farm, in Boonton, my parents decided I should go to high school in Caldwell, partly because friends and relatives from Newark were in that area and partly because it was considered a better school. Not that I had magically become a good student—at least not yet. In fact, I had a tough time of it in those days.

I had to get up very early every morning to feed the chickens and collect the eggs. Then I walked or hitchhiked a mile and a half to the school bus, which took me another five miles to the high school. After classes, I worked at a hardware store for two or three hours. Then I'd take the local bus back to the town of Pinebrook and walk the rest of the way home. I'd often fall asleep at the dinner table. It was worse in the winter, when it was cold and dark. I remember trudging home one evening after a snowstorm, when one of my galoshes came off and was lost for good.

I never had time to try out for sports. I didn't attend high school dances or do much dating then, as I didn't have spending money and transportation was difficult. I could have slept through all my classes. It wasn't that they were so boring; I was just exhausted. I often fell asleep on the bus, too. Reading was difficult for me because of my dyslexia, I was too tired to study, I seldom did my homework and yet, somehow, I got by with a C average. I must have listened at least some of the time!

The hardware store where I worked after school was called Gosman Brothers, but it was a woman who ran it. She had inherited the business when her father died and decided to take it on. Ruth was probably in her mid-40s, single, bright, attractive and articulate. She saw some things in me that I had never recognized. She said I was creative and a dreamer—"always full of ideas." Between customers, instead of being ambitious and straightening out the racks or sweeping the floor, I would sit on the counter and just stare into space. Ruth noticed and asked, "What are you doing?" I said, "Well, I was thinking how you could remodel this store and make it beautiful and have more customers. Or maybe you could advertise."

Gus, one of the employees, was extremely handy. He could fix anything, and he took the time to teach me, too. I learned about a lot of things in that store, from nails and plumbing parts to tools and shotguns. That's when I discovered I was good with my hands and at figuring out how things worked, skills that would come in handy later. Gus and Ruth would occasionally tease me a little, like when they told me (as a southpaw) that I needed a left-handed monkey wrench. I was a little naive, but they were very gentle with me.

I was working there on the day in April 1945 that President Roosevelt died. People kept coming into the store, saying, "What's going to happen to this country? Where are we going? Will Truman be able to handle it?" Just about a month later, before I finished ninth grade, it was VE Day. Then, before I started 10th grade, the war was over.

I probably worked harder than most teenage boys, but I hadn't yet figured out who I was beyond that. I was passive, gullible and cooperative. When my boss or my parents said, "Do it," I didn't question it. I just did it. Those traits probably could have led me into trouble, like the night toward the end of high school when, after seeing a movie in a neighboring town, my friends decided to steal some hubcaps. I could easily have gone along with them, but I'm glad I didn't. They were caught by the police. The next morning, I had to drive to the police station to bring them home, and I was very relieved it wasn't my parents coming to bail me out.

THE DRINKING GAME

One day a gentleman pulled up to our house with a wife and baby in the car. He said to me, "I understand you sell wine." I said, "Of course not. What gave you that idea?" "Well, a neighbor told us that you do. We appreciate good wine and would like to buy some. Do you have any wine at all?"

I said, "As a matter fact, we do. We have elderberry trees, and my father presses the berries, and we use it for the Jewish holiday. We've never sold any. However, I will let you taste it if you'd like."

My father came out and asked the man why he was there. He said, "I'm with the ABC, Alcoholic Beverage Control. Your neighbor [who was feuding with my father] told us that you sold wine." "Absolutely not," my father replied. "I will give you a sample from the gallon that we make for our own use."

The man asked if he could check our property, went into the barn and found an old still. My father said he had no idea it was there and swore he'd never used it. The agent said, "I have to fine you $20 because you need a permit to make wine for personal use."

That must have been painful for my father, who didn't have $20 to spare. And, in fact, he rarely drank. One time at a wedding, though, he was tipsy. My mother refused to ride home with him, so we went home with someone else.

continued

I almost never drank alcohol, either, once I was of legal age, because when I did go out on a date I would have barely enough money to pay for the food. And given a choice between food or alcohol, I would always choose food! I never did become much of a drinker.

I was also grateful for the guidance that my Uncle Bill, who lived with us, provided during those years. He was the one who taught me the facts of life. He also taught me how to drive and let me use his jeep. And he encouraged me to do something with my life. While no one in my family had gone to college, Bill was very intelligent and had educated himself by reading a lot. But he was turned down for an important job at the United Nations, even though he passed the aptitude test. His lack of a degree was part of it, but being Jewish probably didn't help. He often told me that being Jewish, I would end up working the night shift like my father if I didn't study harder and get a good education. He told me he knew I could get better grades if I tried, and that I could even be the first in my family to go to college. He kept nudging me, and eventually I started to think maybe I could do it.

My senior year, I cut back on feeding the chickens and collecting the eggs. I cut my hours at the hardware store. My uncle would drive me to the school bus to reduce my commuting time and give me more hours to study and sleep. I got almost all A's that year, good enough to get me accepted to the University of Maryland, the least expensive school on the East Coast. But I still wasn't entirely convinced I wanted to study that much. When I graduated from high school in 1948, I put my books on the floor and said to my parents, "I hereby take an oath never to open the books again." They said, "OK, if you don't want to go to college, then you have to move out." That was probably the final nudge I needed. I said, "No, I'll go to college."

REVENGE AT THE
HIGH SCHOOL REUNION

I went to one high school reunion; I think it was the 30th. The senior class president came over to me and didn't recognize me. He had to look at my name tag. I never really liked the guy. He asked, "Perry, what do you do?" I decided to just say, "I got a job in a hospital." He kind of sneered and said, "Aw, I never thought you'd amount to much." He probably thought I was washing the floors. Then he asked, "Tell me, have you ever been in touch with Jerry Robbins?" We used to ride the school bus together. His father was a painter. He was a social butterfly, short and wiry, and everybody loved him. Of course, I was always sleeping on the bus. I said, "No, I've lost contact with him." He said, "Oh, he is a famous surgeon who operates on patients from all over the world. Really, he's published many articles and books, he's lectured in many countries and speaks several languages." I said, "Then maybe I should get in touch with him." He said, "Well, what would you have in common with him?" He said he'd learned all this because his boss had recently been a patient. I knew where he worked, and I said, "Wait a minute, is your boss Hymie Shulman?" He said, "Yeah, how did you know?" I said, "I'm the one who operated on him, putz. I'm your Dr. Robins!" I have to admit, that felt good.

CHAPTER 3

Hitting the Books

Me, a scholar? I don't think so!

The University of Maryland, in College Park just northeast of Washington, D.C., looked beautiful when I arrived in the fall of '48. Of course, I hadn't visited any college campuses before arriving there, so my perspective was not exactly worldly.

I had assumed I'd go to Rutgers or somewhere close to home, but UMD was cheaper than the schools in New Jersey, and that was the deciding factor. Because my father worked for the Pennsylvania Railroad, I was eligible for free transportation to Washington, D.C., and then had just a short bus ride. So there I was—low on cash, skeptical, an uninspired student, but also enchanted with the Georgian-style buildings and flowers everywhere. Maybe this wouldn't be so bad after all.

Thanks to the GI Bill, enrollment at the university had more than doubled since the end of the war to about 10,000, so the majority of students had to live off campus. I was a freshman from out of state, so there was no room for me in the dormitories. I rented a tiny furnished basement room close to campus. It had an improvised shower made from a pipe coming out of the ceiling with a curtain around it. I was on my own for the first time, and yes, it was a little scary.

The gullible, obedient child in me wasn't sure what to do at first. I had no idea what I wanted to study or even *if* I wanted to study. But the early leadership skills I'd glimpsed in myself from organizing the Knights of Pythias chapter in Newark gave me an idea. Just weeks after arriving, I started a political party to run for freshman class president. I met and recruited some other students to serve as vice president, secretary and treasurer. We came up with a great motto. "Don't be a square in the Freshman Circle: Vote for Perry Robins!" I knew a student taking flying lessons and even talked him into dropping my promotional flyers onto campus from a small airplane. I was confident we would win.

Here's what I didn't count on: My opponent, Norm, promised everyone a big beer party if he was elected. I lost by about half a dozen votes. After his slim victory, Norm did throw the beer party, many students showed up and it was quite a ruckus. Because of that, he was expelled, and his vice president was installed. That was the beginning and end of my career in politics.

MY BRUSH WITH RICHES

My mother had a wealthy cousin who lived in Washington, D.C., and she thought it would be beneficial for me to get to know his family. Morris Cafritz had emigrated with his family (like my own grandfather's family) from Lithuania when he was a young boy. They settled in Georgetown, where he worked in his father's grocery store. After college and law school, Morris became a real estate developer. He met the gorgeous, much younger (and not Jewish) Gwendolyn Detre de Surany, from Budapest. They married in 1929. He made millions, and in 1948 they created the Morris and Gwendolyn Cafritz

continued

Foundation to support many local charities. He worked nonstop, and she became legendary for her extravagant parties attended by Washington's elite.

Soon after beginning my freshman year at the University of Maryland, I dutifully showed up at the Cafritz mansion on Foxhall Road, where I was bowled over by the servants, the grounds overlooking the city and the unabashed luxury of it all. Gwendolyn was charming but brusque as she told me about her three boys. Calvin, her oldest, was just a year or two younger than me. They were in school but she promised that she would invite me for dinner soon to meet them. Let's just say I'm still waiting for that invitation. I never heard from her again or met the rest of the family.

I remember thinking at the time that their life must have been perfect and that it would have been fun to get to know those boys. I only learned much later that Morris died of a heart attack in 1964, and that there were many rumors about Gwendolyn's drinking and the boys' estrangement from her, including a tumultuous lawsuit after her death in 1988. Filed by her middle and youngest sons, Carter and Conrad, the suit contested her will, in which she left the bulk of the estate to her charitable foundation. All those riches couldn't buy harmony or happiness, but in 1948 I sure thought they looked good.

In my second year at UMD I moved into a dormitory, which made me feel much more a part of campus life. Remembering how much I'd enjoyed the brotherly bonds of the Knights of Pythias fraternal organization, I visited several campus fraternities, but then decided not to join because I still thought I might end up transferring to a school closer to home. I guess I hadn't asserted my independence from my family and the farm yet.

I began dating a young lady who was training to be a guidance counselor. She suggested I take her one-day exam that would reveal my aptitudes and interests. I was skeptical, but the questions were fun to answer. Two days later I was completely surprised when she showed me the results and said I could do anything I wanted, and do it well, if I put my mind to it. She also said I was fascinating. No one had ever said anything like that to me, and honestly, I figured she was exaggerating and just being kind because she was attracted to me.

Still, those test results may have planted the tiniest seed. My parents certainly tried to push some ambition into me, saying, "Why don't you major in something that might be useful?" I had been considering a course in business administration or maybe science. I had to choose, so I decided to major in chemistry just to please them. I still had no idea what I wanted to do.

Coincidentally, I had a roommate, Morty Fox, from the eastern shore of Maryland, who was premed. All he ever did was study, study, study. That was a turnoff for me, as I had no desire to work that hard or to be a doctor. In fact, I had never even been to a doctor in my life.

I did get a kick out of tormenting Morty, though. In my psychology class, we learned about the power of suggestion, which was a whole new world to me. With a couple of friends in the dorm we planned to test it out on my hapless roommate. One morning when he awoke I said, "Morty, you don't look very well. Do you feel all right?" He said he felt fine. He went to the shower room and a couple of my co-conspirators said, "Morty, you look terrible! Are you OK?" After the third or fourth fellow made similar comments, Morty said, "I think I'm going back to sleep." We loved our new-found scientific knowledge and power.

While I was doing my best to pay attention in my classes, I also spent a lot of time thinking about how to make pocket money so I wouldn't have to write home for additional funds to support my budding social life. I saw an ad for a company in Elmira, New

York, promising anyone could make extra money selling Christmas cards. My entrepreneurial instincts kicked in. I bought a bunch of the cards, recruited a few students to sell them for me, saying I'd go 50-50 with them. When they sold out, I ordered more. That went well, so I soon branched out into business cards and student ID cards. Then I wondered if we might be able to get some white bucks, the shoes then at their peak of popularity with male college students. I did acquire a small supply of the most common sizes, although it was tough to keep enough inventory due to the lack of storage space in the dorm. My little pilot operation thrived, and we also sold nylon stockings and personalized stationery on commission. I made enough money that I didn't have to ask my parents for help anymore. That made me happy.

During the summers, when I was home in New Jersey, I came up with more entrepreneurial schemes to test my salesmanship. These included going door to door with a photographer and offering to take pictures of the children or the family. Then (remembering my long-ago pony photos that my parents felt obligated to buy), we would come back with the proofs, give one to the family for free and try to sell more. I was good at that. My sister, Irene, had gotten married, and I worked with her husband, Abraham, to sell people large meat deliveries. With a certain level of purchase, the customer would get a free freezer to store it in. That worked for a while, at least until people realized how long it would take to use all that frozen meat.

Back at school with a little cash in my pocket, my confidence around women rose a notch, although my lack of a car was a drawback. I met a nice girl from Philly on the train my junior year. I arranged to visit her there and took her to dinner at Old Original Bookbinder's seafood restaurant, famous for its lobster. That was impressive enough to convince her to come to Maryland for my junior prom.

I was excited and went to great pains to make sure she had a place to stay in one of the sorority houses. I had a friend, Bob Damm, who owned a taxi, so I went in his cab to pick her up at the train station, but when she arrived at the sorority house, they said they were overbooked for the prom weekend and she couldn't stay there. Although I couldn't afford it, I reserved a hotel room for her near the train station. Something about the whole experience spooked her, though. Maybe it was an inkling of my own raging-hormone fantasies about being alone with her in a hotel room, since I was still a virgin. Or maybe it was her stockbroker father; who knows? By the time I went to the hotel to pick her up, she had left and taken a train home to Philly, and my lusty prom dreams evaporated. I can still hear Nat King Cole's velvety vocals taunting me in the song that played constantly on the radio that year: "Too Young."

Army ROTC training was compulsory during my first two years of school. It mostly consisted of wearing a uniform and marching around with guns. It was not very exciting, and we didn't learn anything useful. Before my junior year, I elected to sign up for the advanced ROTC program, as it would enable me to receive a commission when I graduated and—even better—get paid a small stipend every month. But I heard stories about how the graduates of this ROTC program were being sent to Korea, where the regular soldiers hated them because the college whippersnappers knew nothing about military warfare.

Then I learned that Glenn L. Martin, founder of the eponymous aircraft manufacturing company (known today as Lockheed Martin), was giving the university millions of dollars to change the Army ROTC program to an Air Force ROTC program. Those who wanted to continue with Army ROTC had to go to another campus, and those who didn't want to leave or join the new Air Force ROTC could be excused. Being pragmatic and wanting to save my skin, I decided that with the Korean War going on it would be best to postpone going into the military as long as possible.

*My father and mother were over the moon to see me
in a cap and gown—with a college degree!*

Instead I hit the books, and I never did transfer to a school closer to home. I did pretty well academically, all things considered, and in June 1952 I became the first college graduate in my family. My parents were so proud and hopeful for my future. I still wasn't so sure.

CHAPTER 4

Wheeler Dealer in the Army

Pushing my luck, until a miracle
assignment in Japan saves my skin.

College graduation meant my draft deferment expired. Since I didn't know what I wanted to do anyway, I figured I might as well let the Army pay me while I tried to figure it out. My options were two years as a private or three years as an officer. Some of my friends thought it would be foolish not to go in as an officer and take a three-year commission. However, I heard that by accepting a commission you were subject to being in the reserves for the rest of your life. (I was fortunate that I didn't accept a commission, because those who did were the first to be called when the Vietnam War broke out. They went right into battle.)

I rode a bus to the recruitment center, where an interviewer asked me what I did in civilian life. I told him I had a bachelor's degree in chemistry, and with typical military logic, he said, "Fantastic, you can drive a chemical truck." So, I was shipped to Fort Eustis, Virginia, the transportation training center for the Army.

On my third day in the service, I got sick. When my fever spiked to more than 104 degrees and I was shaking and incoherent, I was admitted to the military hospital on base. It seems hard to believe now, but at 22, I'd never even been to see a doctor except for my Army physical, so you can imagine what a scary experience this was for me. For the next 24 hours, my condition didn't improve, and I was scheduled to be transferred to a larger military hospital. Before that happened, though, my fever broke and I started to feel better.

The day before I was discharged from the hospital, the medical officer I'd gotten to know a little asked me if I'd like to become a medical corpsman and work in the hospital. I asked him what would be the advantages of that. He told me I wouldn't have to go through basic training, for one thing. And when you work in the hospital, he said, "You get steak every night and ice cream with every meal." That clinched it. I said, "When do I start?" I never did learn to drive a chemical truck. It makes me laugh now to think that the nudge that changed the course of my life, and maybe even *saved* my life, was motivated by ice cream!

The next day, I reported for duty at the hospital and was assigned to work the night shift in the emergency room. I'd like to say I learned something about medicine there, but really, six days a week, from midnight to 7 AM, I mostly just slept. There were very few patients. I got to know the corpsman who worked the shift before me, also six days a week, and we decided that it wasn't fair that we only had one day off a week. (Nurses covered the shifts on Sundays.)

I decided to complain to the captain. As a brand-new private, this might not have been a very bright idea, but he agreed to assign a third corpsman to our shifts. Then I had an even better idea: I said, "Why don't we all do double shifts two days a week, and then we'll have the rest of the days off?" Somehow we got away with it. I guess I wasn't a typical private!

SCIENTIFIC EXPERIMENTS ON THE SIDE

Now that I was no longer in school, I started to miss learning. Fort Eustis was close to the College of William and Mary, so now that I had more free time, I decided to apply for graduate school in the biology department. I was accepted into a fellowship program that was working to solve the severe destruction of young oysters in the Chesapeake Bay oyster beds. An aggressive type of snail was drilling into the soft shells of the oysters and killing them.

I loved having this real-world problem to work on. So every weekday I went to the fishery biology laboratory at Gloucester Point from 8 to 3. I would first stop at the docks and pick up a bushel of oysters, which made a fine breakfast, lunch, dinner or all three (although I could still eat dinner at the base).

We performed experiments and learned a lot about the effects of salinity, for example: Fresh water was coming down to the Chesapeake Bay and salt water was coming from the ocean. By moving the oyster fields closer to the fresh water and thus reducing the salinity of their surroundings, we found that the snails became less active. We discovered we could also slow down the predatory snails by lowering the oyster beds to deeper waters. They were less aggressive when there was light by the oyster beds, however, so we threw old oyster shells back into the water, where they reflected more sunlight.

Because of all this, we were quite successful in reducing the mortality of the oysters. I loved this feeling of discovery and accomplishment, but I didn't sign up for a second semester for one reason: I couldn't afford the tuition. (I still love oysters, though.)

I wanted to make more money. I had lucked out so far in my military career by negotiating better hours and squeezing in some graduate school, so I decided to keep pushing my luck. I found a part-time job selling air conditioners and freezers at Sears Roebuck in Newport News. Of course, I didn't tell the manager I was in the Army. After being there about a month, the boss told me I had to work late so he could take his wife to the hospital. He walked out the front door, then I walked out the back door. I had to get back for muster roll call that evening on post or I would have been reported AWOL. I guess he saw me leave, because the next day he fired me.

Undeterred, a few days later I found a job with an insurance company, collecting from about 100 people who were paying a dollar a week for their policies. Always looking for economies of scale, I found that I could minimize my trips to visit the families by offering them a free pair of nylons if they would pay for four weeks at a time. That was working well until the insurance company, which needed to bond me, checked my bogus references. For example, it took a lot of chutzpah, but I had included the local mayor on my list. When they asked him about my character, at first he said he didn't know me. But when they told him I said I voted for him, he said, "Oh he's a great guy!"

Upon checking my second reference, however, which affirmed that I had lived in Newport News for the past five years, it didn't go so well. They tracked my background and contacted the postmaster in tiny Pinebrook, New Jersey, where I grew up and asked if he could recall a Perry Robins. He said, "Hell yes! I saw him a month ago when he was here to visit his parents. He's in the Army somewhere down in Virginia." They found out I was U.S. government property, and I was canned.

You'd think I would have been properly chastened by all this, but somehow I thought I could keep testing my limits. Or maybe I thought I was made of Teflon. Because I'd been making extra money, I offered to pay my colleagues $20 to cover my shifts so I could go home to New Jersey for two weeks. I figured nobody would miss me. When one of the guys I was paying to work for me showed up late for my shift, though, people started asking, "Where's Robins?" Luckily one of my friends knew where I was and called me at home. I drove like hell all night from New Jersey to Virginia. I even brought my mom with me to help keep me awake. Of course, she fell asleep immediately, while fear and adrenaline kept me going.

Fortunately, my friends covered for me, and I wasn't reported AWOL. Still, the captain was not pleased with my less than full attention to duty and said, "I'm so disappointed in you! What you did is not in the spirit of the military. I'm putting you on the next ship to Korea." That got my attention. It was 1953, no peace treaty had yet been signed, and many thousands of servicemen had been killed in action there.

Thank goodness I had a few friends in influential places. The captain's secretary, who could have been the inspiration for Radar O'Reilly in *M*A*S*H*, was one of them. He knew how to work the system. "Don't worry, Perry," he said. "I have to cut your orders to go to Fort Lewis near Seattle, where you'd be deployed to Korea. But your records might go astray to, say, Camp Kilmer in New Jersey. When you get to Seattle, your records won't be there, and it will take a couple of weeks before they'll issue a new file. You have less than nine months left in the military, so with some luck, maybe the delays will save your ass."

I was still worried, of course, but was glad I could go home for a few days to see my parents before starting my new "adventure." I was excited about flying to Seattle, though, as it would be my first time on a commercial airplane and my first trip west.

It seems so young and innocent now, but I called all my friends and told them, "I get to fly! I'm flying to Seattle!" I promised my family that I'd call collect to let them know I'd arrived safely, but then would hang up so they wouldn't have to pay for the long-distance call. I had a window seat on the plane, and as I gazed down at our country unfolding below, I thought, *Wow, I can't believe Uncle Sam is paying for my ticket. What a lifetime experience to say that I'm flying in a plane.* It was exciting, but I was also nervous about what might lie ahead.

When I arrived at Fort Lewis, I reported to the Embarkation Center. Sure enough, they didn't have my records, and the sergeant told me to come back in a few days. Two days later I returned, and he told me, "We still don't have your records. Come back in a few days."

I waited. I went to the USO Club. I hitchhiked to do some sightseeing. I visited beautiful Mount Rainier, and thumbed a ride to Mount Hood in Portland, Oregon. While it was thrilling to see some of the Pacific Northwest for the first time, I soon ran out of money and was bored.

A week, two weeks, three weeks went by, and the sergeant said, "Well, you're almost within your final nine months, and you won't be eligible to go overseas much longer. But I see there's an opening for a corpsman at Tokyo Army Hospital. I can put you on the ship today."

I felt sort of dazed and said something like, "Tokyo? I don't know . . . ." He looked at me and said, "Are you crazy? That's the best duty in the world! I've been there. They have hot and cold running women. The food is great. It's wonderful over there. I'll cut the orders right now." I agreed to be at the port at 4 AM, where I boarded the *SS Patrick Henry.* The transport ship, filled with 2,000 GIs, departed at about 5 AM. Soon I heard that the ship wasn't going to Japan. It was going straight to Korea.

I said, "No, it's going to Japan." They said, "No, you're on the wrong boat." I said, "No, this is it. They told me the *SS Patrick Henry.* They said to be here at 4 in the morning. I have these orders." They said no, I was mistaken, the sergeant was mistaken. *Bum luck,* I thought. *You win some; you lose some.* I was scared. While I'd been sleeping in the ER and selling refrigerators at Sears, these soldiers had been preparing for combat and how to stay alive. I hadn't even been through basic training.

To make matters worse, the weather was terrible. A storm hit, and the boat began to shake, rattle and roll—and never stopped. Some of the GIs were so sick they couldn't get up, and we had to tie them down to keep them from being thrown out of their bunks by the movement of the ship. I discovered that I have good equilibrium, and I never got seasick during that whole terrible trip across. I was glad I could help a lot of the guys who were sick.

About 10 days later, the ship stopped to refuel—in Yokohama, Japan! I heard a list of 10 names called, and fortuitously, mine was one of them. We disembarked and headed toward a railroad car, which I assumed would take us into Tokyo. Then an Air Force captain called out, "Robins! Robins! Come with me." He put me in a jeep, and I asked, "What's happening?"

He said, "I need corpsmen at Tachikawa Air Force Base who can also drive ambulances. I see you went to transportation school in Fort Eustis, Virginia." I said, "Yes, but I never became a truck driver." He said, "Let's go. We have burn patients being flown in from Korea that we need to treat. We'll teach you how to drive an ambulance."

I thought about the 2,000 soldiers left on the SS Patrick Henry who were destined for Korea and wondered what would happen to them. I felt bad for them but relieved for me, thinking I was probably the least-prepared-for-combat private in the U.S. Army.

I was assigned to the captain's unit at the air base with the ambulance drivers. I learned fast. We started receiving GIs who had been burned in a fire. We drove many of them from Tachikawa south to Yokosuka, a naval base that had a better-equipped burn unit. We transported other patients who'd been evacuated from Pusan to military hospitals. Many needed their wounds taken care of. The first time I saw big war wounds and needed to change dressings, I was fine and never felt shocked or woozy. I felt that

I had enough experience to help these people. That boosted my confidence, and theirs.

"Private Robins reporting for duty!" at Tachikawa air base in Japan, 1953.
I had no idea what to expect.

I didn't have time to get nervous or homesick. Everything was new and fascinating. While Allied occupation of Japan had ended just a few months earlier, the Japanese people were still very much affected by it. Many had surrendered their emotions, their feelings, their ways of thinking. Some were obsequious to Americans. Others desperately needed money. My first impression was that the Japanese cars, trucks and railroad cars were tiny compared with American ones. But the farm boy in me was amazed at the size of the fruits and vegetables. Those peaches, tomatoes, grapes, cucumbers and peppers were all enormous. I heard they used human manure in the fields. I guess it worked.

After a few weeks at Tachikawa air base, things calmed down a bit. I was surprised when the captain said, "You don't belong here. You're very bright. I can send you on to Tokyo Army Hospital now if you want to go." I said, "Absolutely!"

The next morning a jeep driver took me to the hospital, where I got the best assignment I could have imagined: to work each morning in the pediatric clinic for babies and children of military families, and to attend school in the afternoons to learn Japanese. I couldn't believe my good luck. I worked with one doctor, Donald Strominger, MD, from Barnes Jewish Hospital in St. Louis. He was a born teacher and a wonderful mentor. We bonded immediately. He took me under his wing and taught me how to read X-rays, examine the kids and provide tender loving care to the children. He loved to teach, and I enjoyed working with him. I truly loved helping the babies and young kids, seeing them deathly ill one day and bouncing bundles of joy the next. I thought, *My gosh, what is more gratifying than the warm glow you feel when helping someone?*

The parents were wonderful, too. They would bring a pie to the clinic to show their appreciation, or make pasta with meatballs, saying, "We thought you would like something homemade." I'd never experienced anything like it. It was so rewarding and gratifying. Not only was it a good life, but I would say it was also my saving grace. It changed everything.

Not that I became a perfect angel who followed all the rules! For the first few months I lived in the barracks at Grant Heights, in the northwestern part of Tokyo. Built in the 1940s, it provided housing for military personnel assigned to different posts in the area. And I decided I needed some company there. A pet monkey seemed like the perfect entertainment!

ME AND MY MONKEY

One of the families we treated in the clinic was rotating back to the States. They had a small monkey and asked me if I would like to have him. I said, "Yes, why not?" It would be fun and it didn't cost anything.

They said he didn't eat much and gave me a list of what to feed him.

I took him back to the barracks and mostly kept him on a long chain. All the other GIs enjoyed playing with him. One day, however, even though we put a diaper on him, he removed it and made a mess. The sergeant in charge said, "Robins, get rid of that monkey! It's against regulations."

I took the monkey to the fire station, where Japanese firemen were working for the military. They were thrilled to have the monkey. I went to visit him every day before or after work, even though he didn't know me from beans. After about a week there, though, the monkey got loose and set off all the fire alarms. All hell broke loose because they didn't know if there really was a fire. They said I had to take back the monkey.

I put an ad in the local military paper saying, "Monkey for sale, $50, well trained." The next day at the clinic, five people called me about it. They asked, "What can the monkey do?" I said, "Well, it will take a little time for him to get used to your voice." But of course, the monkey couldn't do a thing. The first caller bought him for $50. That was good money, but I was sorry to see the monkey go.

Without my pet monkey, I felt like I had a hole in my social life. I had made some attempts at dating, but there wasn't any privacy on the base. And I was still a virgin, which was weighing heavily on me. Of course, sex was widely available—for a price. There was so much poverty there, and women had to do what they could to survive.

We would change our payment scrip for Japanese currency in front of the Ernie Pyle theater in the Ginza District. (Its name was temporarily changed from Takarazuka Theater during the Occupation years, while it was used as a theater for Allied military personnel.) Dozens of young women would be lined up near the theater soliciting the guys. The ladies would reach out, grab the soldiers' pants and open the zipper, saying, "You take me home? If I make you happy, you pay me." There was a lot of that going on. I resisted, though, since I was, and am, a romantic at heart. I wanted my first time to have some meaning.

A further deterrent, though, was the rampant spread of sexually transmitted diseases. As part of my job at the clinic I was called upon to help a lot of the local GIs who contracted gonorrhea, which accounted for about 75 percent of all STDs during the Korean War. Yes, I gave many, many injections of penicillin. One grateful sergeant that I treated was in charge of transportation and told me, "Perry, don't worry; when you're due to go home, I'll arrange for you to fly back to the States, rather than go in a transport ship."

I was busy and loved what I was doing, so I didn't push my luck by trying to add in a part-time job or moneymaking scheme like I had back in Virginia. I did, however, save some scratch another way. Chase Chemical Company of New Jersey had provided cases and cases of vitamins to the military, and it was our job to dispense them to the Japanese staff who worked for us. I also found out they were like liquid gold. I'd give some to a cab driver or the person behind the counter at the bakery, and they wouldn't charge me. Hey, I was doing my job to distribute the vitamins! I was having such a good experience in Japan that in 1954 I decided to extend my service for a few months to finish out some of my reserve time.

I had heard about a sergeant who had to sell a shack he owned in a nearby village. He had been caught selling truck tires to the Japanese—directly off trucks that he didn't own. He was sentenced to the stockade. Since I had managed to save a little money, I decided to splurge and buy the shack for about $100. I was excited about my first investment in real estate. I also fantasized about its potential as a love nest.

The one-bedroom shack was supplied with blankets, dishes, pots and pans, chairs, a table and one Japanese girlfriend the previous owner had to leave behind. She was a dental assistant at the clinic, young and beautiful, and she cried and cried and cried. She had lived with this sergeant for a long time, and he had promised to marry her. Her life changed abruptly when he was arrested. No way would I take advantage of her grief. I felt terrible for her and gave her $20 to take the train to go back home to her village.

That's me in the middle, with my Japanese girlfriend, Riko, and a fellow soldier.

When she moved out, she told me about her friend Riko, who was looking for a place to live. I agreed to meet her, and when I did, I thought she was gorgeous and adorable, so I agreed to let her stay with me. She was a great person, good natured, and she taught me a lot of Japanese. She taught me a few other things, too.

Yes, Riko-san had a little more experience in the art of love than I did. I was 24 and so naive, I didn't even know how to do it! But she was a good teacher, so I made up for lost time. I had finally shed the burden of my virginity. And it wasn't just for kicks. We genuinely cared about each other and had a fun and loving relationship.

I had become friends with a fellow who was a baker in the commissary. He also had a Japanese girlfriend—and a car. The four of us had a great time taking road trips and exploring on our time off. Army gas was only 10 or 11 cents a gallon, and we took full advantage of it. One of our trips was to Mount Fuji. I say I climbed Mount Fuji, but really we just went as far as the mules would take us.

I have wonderful memories of that time: the food, the countryside and the people. Riko was such a good person, and she stayed with me for about six months until my tour of duty was up. She wanted to come back to the States with me, but that was not possible. It was heartbreaking to leave her behind, and I did what I could to help her. I gave her some money and left her the shack as well. I cried as we said goodbye.

When it was time to leave Tokyo, my mentor, Dr. Strominger, said, "Perry Robins, if you don't become a pediatrician, I'm going to haunt you for the rest of your life. You've got the smarts, you've got the personality. You're a natural pediatrician." I had never imagined I could go to medical school, and it didn't seem realistic for someone like me. But I said I'd try.

As promised, the sergeant I had treated arranged for me to fly back to the States. I was the only enlisted man on the plane; all the others were officers. They asked me who I knew to get such a fancy ride home. I said, "Mr. Penicillin!"

We landed at an Air Force base in Honolulu, and I was told it would be 24 hours before they could put me on another flight to Fort Dix, New Jersey. I thought if 24 hours is good, what's wrong with 72 hours? I felt they wouldn't miss me if I did some sightseeing and spent some time visiting Hawaii.

I was discharged in October 1954, and I had no idea what I would do next. But the words of my mentor kept echoing in my head: "Perry Robins, if you don't become a pediatrician, I'm going to haunt you for the rest of your life. It will absolutely be a disaster if you don't go into medicine." I had promised, "OK, I'll give it my best shot." I had to figure out a way to make it happen.

CHAPTER 5

Chasing a New Dream

*If I want to become a pediatrician,
I have to expand my horizons.*

It felt good to be back on the farm in New Jersey that autumn of '54. The trees in the orchard were turning to fall colors. The dogs jumped with joy to see me. My mother welcomed me home with one of her beautiful cakes, and my father, as always, was happy to have my help with much-needed chores. My best friend, Buddy Shenkin, had gotten married, and we caught up over our favorite pizza at the Reservoir Tavern in Boonton as all-American girl Doris Day sang on the jukebox. It all felt familiar and comforting, but I had changed. My years in the military had given me confidence, a wider perspective and a sense of purpose. I wanted to be a pediatrician. As my mother said, "What took you so long? We always thought you would be a great doctor!"

No matter how much I wanted it, though, getting into medical school wasn't going to be easy. I was at a disadvantage for several reasons: 1. New Jersey did not yet have a medical school. 2. Very few state universities would accept New Jersey students unless they were outstanding, and my high school and college grades were not. 3. I had almost no money. And 4. I hadn't taken the MCAT exam.

Despite all that, I wrote to some medical schools in other states for applications. I got replies suggesting that I study, take the MCAT and reapply in another year.

I knew that if I didn't start medical school right away, I might get sidetracked from my promise and my dream. But I didn't see any alternative—yet. I had to make a living, so I started looking for a job. I thought it would be smart to stay in the medical arena, so I applied at several pharmaceutical companies to be a sales rep. After my first interview, at Pfizer, they said they would hire me. However, after training me, they would have to send me out into the hinterlands because they wouldn't place new employees in tough areas like the metropolitan New York area. I told them I wasn't willing to relocate, as I'd been away from home for such a long time. As a result, I didn't get the job. I had the same experience with Roche and Lederle.

I tried a different direction when I interviewed for a job at Otto H. York Industries, selling oil refinery products. Mr. York, a chemical engineer, asked me and several other candidates how I would like to be compensated. He said, "We can put you on a straight salary, a salary and commission, or a straight commission." I chose a straight commission, saying, "If I'm not bringing in the money, you're not going to keep me on. But if I am earning the money, my gosh, I want to keep it all!" I may have displayed more confidence than was warranted, because I got the job. It was all wrong for me, though. I had little training as a salesperson and even less knowledge of the oil industry. We were selling special pads to refineries that would allow the oil to flow into the cracking towers at a higher speed, and the complex operations required math that was way over my head.

After a few weeks, Mr. York said, "Perry, I'm sorry; I have to let you go. The crew tells me that you're not experienced enough to bring in contracts." I said, "Please, Mr. York. I have a couple of sales pending, and some of the more experienced guys will tutor me. Please, just give me a little more time to prove I can do it." When he relented and agreed to give me another chance, I said, "Thank you, Mr. York. I think I would like to quit. I would never want it to be known that I was fired."

If I'd been successful at the job, it might have dissuaded me from the doctor path. But this setback just made me more determined than ever to go to medical school—sooner rather than later. My family was supportive, but my friend Buddy was a naysayer, emphatic about trying to talk me out of it. "It's such hard work. You're going to be an old man before you graduate. It's not worth it," he said. His advice was to get a job and work my way up in a company. I valued my friend's opinions, but on this I disagreed with him totally. I had loved working in medicine in Tokyo; it wasn't just about making money. And I was only 24 years old and knew I had lots of years ahead of me.

When a friend told me that I might be able to apply to medical schools in Europe without taking the MCAT, I felt like the lights had just come on in a dark place and I could finally see my path ahead. I immediately wrote to a couple of universities in France and Belgium. It was a long shot, but since I had learned a little French in school, I figured it was worth a try.

While I was waiting and weighing my options, the charming young lady I was dating, named Sylvia, introduced me to a friend whose husband was a chemical engineer at B.F. Goodrich Company. He was involved with a new plastic that could be used to make garden hoses. He was going to leave the company to start this new business, and we decided to work on it together. We had just started to look for investors and a factory when I learned about an opportunity to go to Europe for free, where I'd be able to apply to medical schools in person. I decided I had to break up the partnership, as well as my relationship with Sylvia, and go for it. I lost touch with Sylvia but I learned that the chemical engineer stayed with B.F. Goodrich for many years. In fact, I heard from him again a decade later.

YOU'RE AN IMPOSTER!

About 10 years after the garden hose venture, I was making an appearance on the *Today* show with Barbara Walters, talking about skin cancer, sun protection and sunscreens. I returned to my office after the show and started seeing patients. I received a phone call from the chemical engineer I had considered going into business with a decade earlier. "Perry," he said, "what the hell are you doing? You are an imposter! You never went to medical school! It was just a few years ago we were looking for a factory to make garden hoses. Why are you doing this? Have you gone off your rocker? Please stop it. You're going to get arrested and get into trouble!" I told him that a lot of years had passed and yes, I had gone to medical school. Yes, I did a residency, then a fellowship and, yes, I have a great practice treating skin cancer!

My parents wanted to do anything they could to help me get into a medical school. They didn't have much money, but they did have some good contacts. My father had a friend who had sold him tires when he ran the gas station. This friend had two sons who were studying medicine, one in Brussels, Belgium, and the other at Leiden University in the Netherlands. Their father told them that an American kid might come to visit and to learn from their experience. *But how to get there?* I was extremely fortunate that one of my mother's good friends knew a Greek family who ran a shipping company. They transported coal from Newport News, Virginia, to the Netherlands. They agreed to ship me to Rotterdam along with the coal. I decided that once there, I could visit some schools and apply in person.

I packed my suitcases. On a bright Sunday morning in the summer of '55, my father drove me about 400 miles down to Newport News. We looked at the small freighter moored there, then looked at each other. My father said, "Do you really want to do this? If you're scared or if you just don't want to go, you don't have to." I said, "No, no, no. I'm fine." I thought, *What do I have to lose? Full steam ahead!*

I boarded the ship and met the captain, who showed me to a surprisingly nice berth (with no coal in sight). He told me that no one else spoke English except the radio operator and an elderly English woman returning to Europe after working as a nanny in the States for many years. I thought she would be a nice companion to talk to during the trip. Unfortunately, she had romantic ideas, and that was not very appealing to me. So I decided to take the opportunity to learn Greek from some of the crew. The radio operators started writing out words for me every day. I learned 20, 30, 40 words, and soon we were doing sentences.

After we were at sea for three days, a hurricane started forming in our path, so we turned around and made the three-day return trip to Newport News. Once we got underway again, I had another 10 days to practice my Greek. There was absolutely nothing else to do, so by the time we arrived in the Netherlands, I could speak some Greek. I didn't know I could learn anything that quickly!

In Rotterdam, we anchored in the harbor so the crew could unload the coal, and a little water taxi picked me up to take me to the dock. Ever the farm boy, my first impression was of produce, just as it had been in Japan. A fruit vendor was selling apples and oranges. I was hungry and wanted to buy some. He looked at his watch and said, "Sorry, I'm closed. I only have a license to work until 6, and it's 10 minutes after." I said, "Can I 'steal' one, but slip you the money?" He said no. I tried to barter something. No go. I finally gave up when I was distracted by seeing people walking with wooden shoes and thought, *Oh my gosh, it's just like in the storybooks.* But I soon learned, to my disappointment, that wooden shoes were only worn on the dock where it was wet, or by fishermen or farmers.

I took a train down to Brussels to visit the son of my father's friend, who was studying medicine there. I stayed with him for a while to see how quickly I could improve my French. While my mastery of Greek on the freighter seemed miraculous, my improvement *en français* was not exactly *rapide.* Of course, there were more distractions in Belgium than there were at sea—including *les belles femmes* and *beaucoup de pâtisseries.* When I interviewed at the medical school in Brussels, I learned that unless you were truly fluent in French, it would be very difficult to pass the exams. I also heard that one professor particularly didn't like Americans. So that was out.

I hitchhiked to Paris. It was my first visit, and I was in awe. As for medical schools there, I learned that they were so competitive that large numbers of students were weeded out each year and only a tiny percentage of enrollees graduated. Not being fluent in French would make it extremely difficult to be one of the few. While I stayed there, though, I discovered the wonders of the student cafeteria, where we paid less than 15 cents for a great meal that included a bottle of wine.

Everyone was well-dressed in Paris. I did my best to fit in.

I met a chap named Percy who showed me the sights and the best places to eat for very little money. I walked everywhere. One day I was in the Latin Quarter, sitting on the steps at the Panthéon. An American couple came over and asked me in English, "Where is the Panthéon?" I had been working so hard to improve my French, and I didn't want to break the spell, so I said something in French. He looked at me and said, "Goddammit, isn't there anybody around here who speaks English?" I blurted out, in English, "You dumb bunny, if you open your eyes you'll see that you're standing right in front of it!"

Giving up on medical school in France, I took a quick trip over to England to see if I could get into an English medical school. I went to one of the schools, applied for entrance and was accepted—except that I had to get my credentials approved. Alas, they found that I was missing one semester of some ridiculous course required for admission; I think it was botany. I tried to sweet-talk my way out of it, but they were very stiff upper lip and unbending. I was starting to go into panic mode as I headed back to Brussels.

The guy I'd been staying with had decided to leave Brussels and transfer to Leiden University in the Netherlands, where he could be with his brother. He suggested I come up and apply there as well. I made my way up north of Rotterdam, to Leiden, and was bowled over by the 16th century university and Botanical Garden, even though I was too late for tulip season. I presented my college transcripts, had an interview and they said, "Your grades are not great, but we'll probably give you a chance. You'll hear from us in a few weeks. We start in October." This was great news, but I still didn't know how I was going to pay for it.

By coincidence, a possible solution came my way when I met a GI who told me that Heidelberg University in Germany was offering a few scholarships to American medical students, with free tuition. My first thought was, *Really, Germany? For this poor Jewish kid who grew up hearing about Nazis?* My second thought was, *And I don't speak a word of German!*

However, I could afford this program. I knew I had to pursue the opportunity. I packed my suitcase, asked my friends in Leiden to wish me good luck and took the train to Heidelberg. When we crossed into West Germany, several big, tall uniformed German officers entered the compartment where I was sitting, shouting *Achtung!* and other words I couldn't understand. I was terrified. Could they tell I was Jewish? I was shaking and thinking, *What the hell am I doing here?*

But, of course, they just wanted to check our passports. I handed mine to the officer. He smiled, and I think he said, "Welcome."

After leaving the train station, I searched for someone who could speak English. I asked a gentleman where the university was, expecting to find a typical campus. He looked at me and said, "There is no campus. This is not like an American university." Classes are held in buildings spread out across the city—some dating back to the 14ᵗʰ century. I ventured into one of the buildings and saw raised amphitheater-style classrooms like you see in old movies. I visited the majestic assembly hall as well as the *Studentenkarzer*, or student jail, where once upon a time, minor infractions could get you incarcerated.

I walked around and discovered how beautiful Heidelberg was, situated in a valley between two mountains that were covered with flowers and manicured trees. The fragrance from the flowers permeated the air. The city had escaped bombing during World War II, as there were no factories there. But in 1945, right before the end of the war, German troops used explosives to destroy three arches of the landmark Old Bridge that crosses the Neckar River, which flows through the city. The red sandstone bridge, built in the 18ᵗʰ century on the foundation of previous bridges dating back to the Middle Ages, is near the famous 14ᵗʰ century castle perched 300 feet above. The bridge, newly rebuilt, and the ruins of the castle glowed golden in the setting sun.

That night I stayed in a bed-and-breakfast in the center of town and tried to sleep. I knew that during Hitler's rise to power, Nazis burned down the synagogues in Heidelberg and deported its Jewish citizens to concentration camps. My brain was buzzing with thoughts like, *How did a Jewish kid from New Jersey end up here?* and *What makes me think I can be accepted into medical school at the oldest university in Germany, learn the language fast enough to do well and pass the exams needed to become a physician?* It seemed ridiculous and nearly impossible. Then I heard my Tokyo mentor Dr. Strominger's voice in my head, saying, "Perry Robins, if you don't become a pediatrician, I'm going to haunt you for the rest of your life."

So, the next morning I brought my transcripts and marched bravely into the university's admissions office. I was thrilled when I learned that the young woman interviewing me was Jewish. Her father was some bigwig in Germany and during the war had been able to hide the fact that his wife was Jewish. I mentioned that I spoke very little German, and even that was a big exaggeration. She said most of the *Oberärzte* (the young professors of medicine) did speak English, and for the first year they would help. "But after that, you must speak German," she said. She was very pro-American and admitted me on the spot. I couldn't believe it!

An expensive transatlantic call was out of the question, but I immediately posted a letter to my family saying how excited I was to accept this opportunity.

CHAPTER 6

Willkommen in Deutschland!

Really, medical school in Germany?
All I can say is, "Gesundheit ist besser
als Krankheit!"

The woman who had admitted me told me there were a few American students enrolled, but she warned me, "It's best you don't associate with them. Otherwise you'll make the mistake of speaking English all the time."

I took her advice and made up my mind right then that learning German was my top priority. This was my best chance to become a pediatrician, and I did not want to fail. I found a roommate who couldn't speak a word of English, and we communicated in French until I progressed a bit in my German. During those first weeks and months in Heidelberg, I devoted every effort, every second, to learning the language as rapidly as possible. I studied my tush off. I'm convinced that I owe much of my success to that early effort.

Knowing that I was Jewish, quite a few of the German students approached me and said, "We were misled. When your mother and father, aunt and uncle, teacher and principal tell you that Jews are bad, what do you believe? You believe it, and it wasn't until years later that I found out." One kid had been head of the *Hitlerjugend*, the Hitler Youth movement, and he actually cried. He said, "I can't believe my relatives told me such things when it was all lies." I was not expecting a reaction like this and was incredibly touched by it.

My lecture classes were in German, and attendance was not mandatory. But for the first six months I attended classes to see what they were like. And I bought the lecture notes, which were sometimes available in English, or I paid to have them translated to English. When we had a new professor in psychiatry from Munich, a couple of students drove down to Munich to buy his notes. I also studied from American textbooks, even when my German became good enough that I didn't need them anymore, just to double-check that I could say what I wanted to in German as well as in English.

It was not easy. I am not one of those people who has a natural aptitude for languages. I had studied French in high school and college, but I never did particularly well. I got C's. I wasn't interested in languages then. Yes, I had learned a lot of Greek on my trip over just because I was bored and didn't have anything else to do. This was different. It wasn't just conversational language I needed, but also scientific and medical terminology. It was excruciatingly hard work.

I was excited about the prospect of becoming a doctor, but I was also motivated by F-E-A-R. I was terrified of disgracing myself by not being successful after telling everybody I was going to medical school in Germany. Some of my friends had said, "You'll never make it. You will fail. You're wasting your time. You're kidding yourself. You're an ass for doing it." I wanted to prove them wrong. And I wanted my parents to be proud of me.

I was grateful for the tuition help, that's for sure. As for the costs of living there, I didn't know how I would manage it. The GI Bill awarded me $110 a month for 36 months. My sister, Irene, sent me $2 every week, and from time to time my parents sent a check for $100. At first I rented a cheap room in a garage, with the water and shower on the outside. After a few months I splurged on a room in an apartment building that was built for students, with communal toilets and a shower in the basement. It was a whopping $30 a month, but compared to where I'd been it felt like the Ritz.

When I went shopping in the local grocery store, the clerks there were amazed that a male medical student would shop and do his own cooking. If I was short of funds, they would always offer credit. I had saved some money from all my years of working in high school and college, but I wanted to hang on to it. I was extremely frugal and continued to save for what I desired most: a car.

That first year was very, very tough for me, and not just because of the language barrier. I had *so* much to learn. I spent the majority of my time sitting on my tush, frustrated—studying, eating, studying, eating. I was skinny as a rail growing up, but that had started to change when I was in the Army. The barracks were next to a bakery and my friends and I had gorged ourselves on the goodies. I can see in photos from that time that I went up a couple of sizes. But the big weight gain came in medical school. Food was calming and comforting. I've struggled with ups and downs ever since.

FOOD FIGHT

I often say I never met a food I didn't like, and it's mostly true. The only cuisine I don't care for is Indian food. I can tell you, my stomach doesn't like spices. I have a very sensitive stomach. In medical school, when I had some digestive problems, they arranged for me to

continued

go to the kitchen to get a special meal. In fact, I tried to date a dietitian there, but she wouldn't go out with Americans.

There is one German dish that I developed a passion for: roasted veal shank (*Kalbshaxen*). I have been back to Germany many times but can rarely find it. One restaurant in Munich near the Hofbräuhaus serves it. It's a portion for four people, but I just say, "Never mind that. Bring it on!"

Beyond the language hurdle, there were other firsts to overcome. I had seen major wounds in the military when I was transporting patients, but since I ended up in pediatrics in Tokyo, I never saw major surgery. So the first time we went into the operating room to observe surgery in medical school, I have to admit I was a little squeamish. My toes were tingling a bit. That got better over time. And in anatomy class, the first time I saw a cadaver was a big shock. Some of us made jokes to help squash the discomfort. In fact, I called the cadaver assigned to me "Marilyn Monroe." But we took our anatomy lessons seriously, and the dissection we learned was a big step forward in our medical education. I sure wasn't thinking of myself as surgeon material, though.

During my second year in Heidelberg, 1956 through '57, I started to feel more confident with the language and the discipline of being a medical student. Not only was I learning, but I was also doing *well*. I even figured out how to make time for a social life. My roommate and I decided to have a party. We lived next to a grocery store, where half a dozen beautiful young German girls worked. Naturally, we invited them to our party, but they never showed up. The next morning, I went to see what had happened, as they had promised to come. They told me that they had rung the doorbell, but the doorman wouldn't let them in. He said the boys were busy earning the prestigious title of "Herr Doktor" while these women were mere *Putzfrauen*, meaning too low-class for us.

Dating in Germany was quite different from how we did it back in the States. German friends often got together on weekends for dinner at home. On a typical Saturday night, we might make pasta together, and on Sunday we would walk in the woods and stop at a little café for coffee and apple pie. Of course, good German beer and wine were plentiful, but for many European students, drinking alcohol was an accompaniment to meals, not an activity unto itself. I never became much of a drinker, mainly because I had so little money. It just never became a habit. We didn't spend much, but we had lots of fun. In those first couple of years, I dated a few times, but I was too focused on my studies to form any serious attachment. And when I did have some time off, I preferred to travel.

Each spring, medical students were given two months off to work in a hospital as an extern. This gave me a chance to gain experience in the military hospitals in Germany, including the Army hospital in Landstuhl and the Air Force hospital in Wiesbaden. My previous experience in Tokyo gave me an advantage, and I was thrilled to work with the doctors and their veteran patients, with only an occasional thought about Nazis.

Europeans take a lot more vacations than Americans do, and medical school in Germany was no exception. We had many holidays, and two weeks off between semesters. So I started exploring whenever I could. I hitchhiked to Paris. It was mostly truckers who picked me up, and I loved to practice my French with the drivers. I'd write out questions in advance and grill them.

I also spent some time in Barcelona, where I teamed up with a couple from the States that I met there. He was an architect studying Gaudí. Together, we got to know every building, every apartment, every park Gaudí had conceived, especially the cathedral La Sagrada Família, which has been under construction since 1882 (but getting closer to completion now). We also went to Majorca together and found a place to stay with room and board for $3 a day.

I loved to travel. Every new place I visited stimulated my wanderlust even more, but I was tired of hitchhiking. And it limited my scope of exploration, so I decided to break the bank and use all my funds to buy a car. My parents dipped into their meager savings to help me, too. I chose a little silver-gray Peugeot 203, and I hitchhiked to Paris to pick it up at a showroom near the Arc de Triomphe. The sales manager said, "Do you need any fuel?" I said, "No, I'll get it at one of the local gas stations." I drove two blocks around the Arc de Triomphe at rush hour and promptly ran out of gas. Seriously, they sold cars with no gas in the tanks.

I had always wanted to see Denmark, so on our next school break, a friend and I drove the Peugeot up to Hamburg and up to the Baltic, then took the ferry across, because otherwise it's a long loop to go around to Copenhagen. It was beautiful, and so were all the tall blond-haired, blue-eyed people. Except on the very first day there, I met a stunning olive-skinned, dark-haired Danish girl named Elizabeth. She was charming, educated and sophisticated, and I was smitten.

I guess she thought I was interesting and funny. We teamed up and quickly became an item. She'd had a tragic life. Her father was a seaman who impregnated a Danish girl and then disappeared. Her mother died from some illness, so Elizabeth was left an orphan and adopted by a Danish family. The son of the woman who adopted her taunted and abused her, and got her pregnant. The mother forced the son to marry her, but eventually they divorced and she finally escaped from him. She became a teacher, then met another fellow, became pregnant and had another child. So when I met her, she had two young kids.

It was a conservative era (just a few years after Ingrid Bergman was labeled an "instrument of evil" for her affair with married Italian film director Roberto Rossellini and subsequent pregnancy), but who was I to judge? Elizabeth was bright and articulate, and we were crazy about each other. Every two weeks she'd come down to Heidelberg, and every two weeks I'd go up to Copenhagen. There were two ferry lines, one German and one Danish. The buffets on the latter were extraordinary, with 20 different kinds of fish. We always planned our trips so we could ride on the Danish boats. This continued for almost three years.

It was the most grown-up relationship I'd experienced, but it wasn't perfect. Elizabeth's best friend tried to poison our relationship by telling me things like, "She just wants to go to the States. She would marry any American she found, and you just happened to come along." That bothered me a little, but I didn't believe it.

Things finally fell apart between us, though, at a New Year's Eve party at the U.S. Army Officers' Club. An officer seated next to her kept encouraging her to drink, and she got a bit inebriated. It wasn't fun to watch. When it was time to leave, she wanted to stay longer. She said, "Go. The lieutenant will drive me home." She didn't return till about 4 AM, which I found inexcusable. I was heartbroken, but I also knew I needed to keep my eye on the ball, and I had a long road ahead of me before I could practice medicine in the States. So that ended the relationship. I figured it was for the best.

During my third year, I decided to do my externship in the States over the summer instead of in the spring, which would allow me to do some springtime traveling in Europe instead. *Pourquoi pas?* Yes, I suppose I could have just hunkered down and focused on my studies, but I was close to so many places I'd never been before. I couldn't pass up a chance to explore.

My friend and fellow student Klaus Giese, from Saarbrücken, a town west of Heidelberg on the border of France, decided to join me. He was very bright, interesting and knowledgeable. He also didn't speak a word of English, so I would have to focus on my German and French. He had always wanted to follow the route of Napoléon from Grenoble down to Cannes on the Mediterranean. Together we plotted a very ambitious itinerary. We mapped our route from Heidelberg, south through France to the Côte d'Azur on the Mediterranean, on to the major sites of Italy, down to Brindisi at the "heel" of the boot, then taking the ferry to Greece and after that, finishing our journey in Turkey—funds permitting, of course.

Checking the map before setting off in the Peugeot from Saarbrücken.

We had read Arthur Frommer's new best seller, *Europe on $5 a Day*, and we were going to try to duplicate his frugal ways. We each had about $150, and we hoped to make it last four or maybe even six weeks. We set off in the Peugeot as soon as classes ended in March 1958. And while the trip didn't go exactly the way we'd planned, it was epic and memorable nonetheless.

We stopped in Saarbrücken so I could meet Klaus' family and then headed into France. Within an hour we had to stop again; I was hungry. A baguette and some cheese did the trick. We traveled east to Strasbourg (pâté!) and then south through Burgundy and *la route des grands vins,* including Dijon and Beaune. Of course, the winemakers invited us into their stores to sample and buy the wines. Klaus was a connoisseur, so he wanted to stop often to taste, study and make pronouncements about the *terroir.* I did very little sampling, and even less buying. But I was happy to do the driving, as springtime was in full bloom, with flowers everywhere. It was gorgeous. I was also happy to just sit in a café, have a cup of coffee and see all the elegantly dressed people (and beautiful women!) walk by.

When we approached Grenoble, I was bowled over by the spiky, snow-covered Alps and the charming ski resort atmosphere. I loved seeing people walking around in their ski clothes, carrying their skis. It was so picturesque. I took hundreds of black and white photographs everywhere I went.

From there we visited many of the stops on La Route de Napoléon, as we meandered through the Rhône region, passing through vineyards with famous names, such as Châteauneuf-du-Pape, then into Provence with its lavender and sunflowers, ending up in Fréjus on the Mediterranean. We stayed in a well-known youth hostel there for 50 cents a night. As Klaus and I were leaving the hostel, the proprietress called us back and said, "*Non, non*! You must go back upstairs and sweep the floor. Here's the broom."

Guess which one of us did it? Yeah. A year or two later, we heard that the hostel was destroyed in a flood when the local dam broke and washed it away.

When we drove along la Côte d'Azur to Cannes, all I could say was "Wow!" We had heard about the star-studded film festival there, the spectacular Promenade de la Croisette and the enormous yachts in the Mediterranean. I fantasized, "Maybe someday I'll have a big yacht, maybe even a little one. Maybe a rowboat."

In Nice, we stopped for a seaside lunch at a café and discovered it was a topless beach. Yes, that was a first for me. It was shocking, but I tried to act cool. And I had to laugh when a young lady went to the showers on the boardwalk, put *on* her bathing suit top there, then took it off again to go back to the beach.

We passed through Monaco, then over into Italy and to Genoa. It was my first time in Italy, and I was tempted to sing "That's Amore" like Dean Martin. I was enchanted by everything from the salami to the incredible artwork. I couldn't speak a word of Italian, but I learned that by being expressive with my hands, I could manage.

We drove to Pisa, where Klaus and I took pictures of each other "holding up" the Leaning Tower. We loved telling the joke about how we heard that Hilton was buying the Leaning Tower and was going to call it the "Tiltin' Hilton, for people who aren't on the level." That gave us a big laugh.

I was thrilled to spend time in Florence, where we walked everywhere and were overwhelmed by the sights: Da Vinci, Raphael, Michelangelo's "David." (I knew I would never have muscles like that, especially if I kept eating the pasta!) We bought guidebooks and earnestly read up on all the museums and landmarks as if we were going to become tour guides.

We explored many villages along the way, but in Rome we

stayed about four days, taking in all the highlights: the Colosseum, the Forum, the Pantheon, the Vatican. On our second day in Rome, while driving toward the Vatican, I stopped for a traffic light. The car in back of me stopped for the light, but a third car traveling at high speed plowed into all of us. Luckily no one was hurt, and the damage to my car, mainly the right fender, was not extensive. It needed to be repaired, but there was no Peugeot dealer in Rome. I was referred to the Volkswagen dealer, who said he could fix the fender for about $100. But the next day he gave me a bill for $200, because he told me the insurance company would only pay half, so if we billed them $200, he would get his $100.

At the Trevi Fountain in Rome, I wanted to sing "Three Coins in the Fountain…" like Sinatra.

I spent hours in the office of the insurance company, and everybody there looked at me as if I were an idiot. Finally, the man came back and handed me $200. He called me a stupid American and told me I could have it done for less money and they were taking advantage of me. Nonetheless, he paid the entire bill. It wasn't my fault that I made a nice profit from my fender bender.

We ate stellar pizza and seafood in Naples, then our next major destination was to cut across to Brindisi on the eastern coast. Our plan was to take a ferry to Greece from there, but we learned the cost was prohibitive. We mulled over our options and decided to just drive all the way around, up the coast of Italy, into Yugoslavia and back down to Greece and to Athens. We were lucky to be able to buy gas coupons from GIs for 11 cents a gallon, so going this distance was not going to break the bank. Shortly thereafter we were waiting for a traffic light, when a Ferrari backed out of a driveway at full speed and—boom! The *same* fender was damaged. We couldn't believe our bad luck. The Italian driver said it was my fault because I was blocking his driveway. But he was eager to settle and gave me $100 for the damage. Again, we were glad no one was hurt, and the damage didn't affect the car's ability to drive, so we took it in stride, consulted our maps and stayed the course.

We had a great time driving up the eastern coast of Italy to Venice, where we spent a few days taking it all in before continuing to Trieste. One of the best places we stayed on the entire trip was the youth hostel in Trieste, in a villa with spectacular views of the sea and the Castle of Miramare.

When we reached Zagreb, Yugoslavia (now Croatia), the sights changed dramatically. Almost no one had a car. People were very poor but incredibly hospitable. A family we met invited Klaus and me to dinner and we were happy to accept their invitation. They wanted to give us their weekly ration of meat to treat us royally. They couldn't have been more kind and generous. We traveled into Belgrade (now part of Serbia). We stopped at the American Embassy because we found out the road south to Greece had been washed away and would not be repaired for about a week. At the embassy, they told me I could not leave the car on the street. They suggested I take my vehicle to a garage, where I could have the fender repaired. They said this would only cost a few dollars versus paying $20 a night to store the car in a public garage while we toured Greece. It seemed like a good solution. We had documents signed saying that we were leaving the car, and it was stamped in my passport that I would be returning in a few weeks to pick it up.

That evening we boarded the train for Athens, and when we got to the Greek border the usual customs police came aboard to check our passports. The officer first spoke to Klaus, and he gave him his French passport. He asked my friend if he was French. Klaus, who spoke fluent French, answered that he was German, but he had a French passport, as Saarland was annexed to France after World War II. The officer asked why he was studying medicine in Heidelberg. "Is there not a medical school in Saarland?" Klaus said yes there is, but he wanted to go to the school that his father had attended.

The officer seemed satisfied and then turned to me. He asked if I was French and I answered in French, "I am an American" as I gave him my American passport. He examined it closely. "You have a car?" I said, "Yes, it is in Belgrade because the roads were under water." He asked, "What do you do?" I said in French, "I am studying medicine in Heidelberg."

"Aren't you too old to study medicine?" he asked. I said no. "Why do you go to school in Heidelberg?" I told him I had a scholarship. "Do all Americans have automobiles?" I said no. He said, "I think you'd better come with me." Uh-oh. The officer took me off the train, which then pulled away with Klaus looking out the window, saying, "What is happening? What are you doing?"

The officer, who thought I might be a spy, put me under arrest and locked me up in the station house on the Yugoslavia side. Two others were there in jail with me: One was a woman whose car hit an oxcart with no damage except to her car. Still, the owner demanded $200 for "damage" to the cart. She finally settled for $50 and was released. The other person was a Swedish reporter whose visa had expired by one day. After many hours they let him go, too.

My charge was more serious, and yes, I was scared. They put me in a room that was riddled with bedbugs. It was impossible to sleep on the infested bed, so I slept on the desk. It was not a real prison; just a room locked up with bars on one door. I opened a door to see where it led and started to walk outside to stretch myself. A guard came running, pointing a gun at me and shouting, *"Halt! Halt! Halt!"* Of course, that scared me even more, as I hightailed it back into the building. And the food was terrible, mostly an insipid bean soup.

The arresting officer put me in a chair under a light and attempted some superficial interrogation. We spoke mostly in French and in German, as his English was not good. He wanted to know why I was in Europe and how I had money to buy a car. He asked a whole list of questions. Who did I work for? What kind of work experience did I have? Why did I decide to attend medical school in Germany? Why didn't I go to school in France since my French is better than my German? (Hmm, I thought they were both pretty bad!) He also wanted to know more about what was happening in the United States and what life was like there.

The next morning, Klaus went to the American consulate in Thessaloniki, Greece (which would have been the next stop on our itinerary), to try to get some help for me. Alas, no one spoke French or German. Luckily, Klaus had studied Greek for about nine years in school, but mostly composition, not conversation. So he wrote out the whole story of what had transpired in ancient Greek!

The consulate representative on duty was very sympathetic but said, "This is not official business. If you'll pay for the phone call, though, I'll call Belgrade and make them aware that you're being detained." Klaus said OK, even though he knew I had all our money with me, rolled up in a jar. Not knowing what else to do, he went to the train station every day to look for me.

On the fourth night, the officer who had arrested me relented and invited me to have a drink with him at a local pub. After the fifth glass of Slivovitz (plum brandy), he said, "I believe you are not a spy. I'm sorry, but I thought I might get a promotion if I captured a spy." He was devastated that his suspicions had been wrong. He also confessed that he was an engineer and not part of the Communist party. Then he asked me if I would perform an abortion on his girlfriend. I said, "I wouldn't know where to start."

The next day, Klaus was elated when he saw me step off the train at the station in Greece.

Pretty much unscathed from the episode (except maybe for a few tagalong bedbugs), we figured it would make a great story to tell our friends. We set off to hitchhike and were lucky when a truck picked us up and left us right in the center of Athens. We found a shabby hotel for $2 a night, including two meals, and thoroughly enjoyed visiting all the attractions, from the Acropolis to the Parthenon.

We still wanted to visit Turkey, too. We learned the cheapest way to go was to take an inland ferry, steerage class. It took us to the island of Chios, off the coast of Turkey nearest a town called Çesme, west of Izmir. When we arrived there the next morning, we found a man with an outboard motorboat who said, "Well, I can't go into Turkey but I can take you near there and signal for someone to pick you up." A young woman who was going through a divorce also came with us. I tried my best to charm her, but she wasn't interested. We got to about 100 yards from Turkey and a man with another motorboat came to retrieve us. We put the woman's big suitcases in the boat and rode with her to Izmir. We stayed there for a couple of days and explored nearby sites such as the Acropolis in Pergamon and the temples of Ephesus.

After a few days we took the train to Istanbul, which looked like it had been devastated. The whole center of town was badly damaged. I asked a local if it had been hit by bombs during the war. He said, "No, they knocked down the slums and they're rebuilding the city."

I met a young lady and managed to persuade her to go to dinner with me. Afterward, in the back seat of a cab, I tried to kiss her. The driver screeched to a stop and said, "Get out, get out! It's forbidden. You're not allowed to do that in Istanbul!" I didn't know. Despite that failure, we loved the Blue Mosque magic of Istanbul, which became one of my favorite destinations later (where all my big yacht fantasies came true)!

*I hated to sell my camera to pay my way back, but I'm glad
I preserved the memories in a photo album.*

At that point, we were out of money and it was time to end our epic journey. We decided to sell our cameras to finance our return trip. That enabled us to take the Orient Express from Istanbul back to Belgrade, which was very elegant and exciting. There we quickly fetched the Peugeot with no mishaps and had just enough money left for gasoline to get us to Venice. Luckily, in Venice we found some students who wanted to return to Germany and were willing to pay for the gas. We made it safely back to Heidelberg in April 1958 as planned. The German word *Erlebnis* came to mind as I thought, *What an experience!*

Getting back into "sit still and study hard" mode after that grand adventure wasn't easy. But I hadn't lost my resolve to become a pediatrician. While I was more competent in German after speaking with Klaus on the road for two months, I still needed help with the language if I was going to master the material enough to do well on my final exams. Doing my externship in the States that summer didn't help. So when I returned to Heidelberg in the fall of 1959, I knew I had to buckle down and get serious.

I searched for a German translator or language teacher who might help me think, speak and write more clearly and found the perfect one. Her name was Crystal Muhleissen. She was beautiful, charming, intelligent and German, majoring in English at the Institute for Translators. When I met her, I knew immediately that I wanted to do more than study with her. At first it was all business. She was a living dictionary. We would practice and practice: "What time is it?" "How are you?" "What do you do?" And slowly, slowly, she helped me become more fluent.

As I approached my final year of medical school, I was focused on my pediatrics research project, which delved into how much intravenous fluid to give to a baby. Inspired by something similar I had seen in the States, I had conceived a plastic wheel that clamped onto the IV line and served as a valve or dial to calibrate the flow. You could click one, two, three or four times to regulate the speed of the amount of fluid going into the child based on the baby's weight and the amount of time. This removed the guesswork and made the procedure more precise. (I ended up donating the idea to the university. It was definitely patentable, but I don't think they ever did anything with it.)

Crystal helped me, yes, *crystallize* my thoughts and get them down on paper. We also started dating. She invited me to spend the Christmas holidays in 1960 at her home in Frankfurt. Her father was not happy that she invited me, but he consented and allowed me to sleep on the porch only after she told him that we were becoming engaged. The next morning, we went to a store that was like a German version of Woolworth's and bought two inexpensive rings.

The engagement hadn't exactly been my idea, and it didn't seem real to me, but word got back to Heidelberg about us. When we returned after the holidays, our friends threw us a surprise engagement party. And I thought, *Maybe this is meant to be.*

In order to graduate from medical school, we had to take the final examination, which included 17 different subjects. We averaged two to three exams per week, so it took about two months to complete. The exams were mostly oral. I was in a group of four applicants, and for each oral exam, we followed the professor for two days. We examined patients, and the professor would ask questions: "If you have swelling under the neck, what could it be?" The first guy would name a few possibilities, and the professor would ask us, "Give me some more. How would you prove it? What test would you do? What if you did find this? And if you gave medicine and the medicine didn't work, would this tell you that your diagnosis is not right?" He pitted us against each other and would ask, "Do you agree with him or disagree with him?" His goal was to determine if we knew enough medicine to save a life or, if we didn't know enough, to refer it on to a specialist. These exams were very tough but practical, and by the end the professors would be able to tell if we knew something or were just bluffing. They wanted to feel that we were competent to go forth and practice medicine.

I did very well on my exams, receiving mostly A's, although I did get a B in surgery. The surgery professor's notes were not very good, so I had also studied notes from a professor at the University of Vienna, because they were outstanding and very thorough. The examining professor said he had to give me a B because he could tell I had studied notes from Vienna and he didn't agree with all of that doctor's methods.

When you graduate, you are a physician, which in German is *Arzt.* You do not earn the Doctor of Medicine title, though, until you go before a tribunal and present your research thesis. When we presented ourselves for this examination, we dutifully followed a hallowed tradition of wearing a tuxedo and carrying an umbrella.

Appropriately garbed in rented finery, I went before seven professors to present my thesis. Most of them were very kind and asked me about the work I was doing. One of the examiners, who was from East Germany, asked me in English, "Why were the Americans afraid of the Russians?" He said, "They should've gone right into Moscow and beat the dickens out of the Russians!" I didn't know what to answer, but I said, as diplomatically as possible, "I guess the Americans thought the timing was not right."

The professor in pediatrics asked me if I wrote my thesis myself. I said, "Honestly, no. I have a German girlfriend who helped me write it." He said it was one of the best papers he had ever read, and if she would be interested, he would love to hire her to work in his department.

While I had long doubted it would ever happen, I graduated from medical school in 1961—with honors. Crystal and I planned our future. We decided that I would return home to take the necessary state license exam and return for a small wedding ceremony in Germany, and then we would have a larger one in New Jersey together.

Before I headed home to the States, I sold the Peugeot to a woman who worked in the anatomy department, then spent some time walking around the unlikely city that had welcomed me and helped mold me into a doctor.

On a warm night before I said *auf Wiedersehen* to Germany (for a while), I walked toward Ludwig's castle, on the same route I had walked that first day I'd so naively arrived in 1955. To commemorate Louis XIV's burning of the castle, several times a year the city simulated the conflagration with flickering colored lights, flares and fireworks. I watched the spectacle in awe. It seemed a fitting send-off. I was standing next to a couple, and the man looked at his wife and said, "This is so special, it's an *Erlebnis*," a once-in-a-life-time experience. *Yes,* I thought. *I feel the same way—about all of it.*

CHAPTER 7

"Hi, Dr. Sparrow!"

*Wow, I did it! But with a snafu
in my residency, will I give up my dream
of helping children?*

I returned to New Jersey that summer of 1961 with an immense sense of relief that I had made my family proud—and proved the naysayers wrong. While I'd been in Germany, a lot had changed. Two new stars had been added to the farm's flag, for Alaska and Hawaii. We had a charismatic young president in the White House, the civil rights movement and the space race were heating up, and there was a new sexual openness reflected in hit songs like "Will You Still Love Me Tomorrow?" and "Itsy Bitsy Teenie Weenie Yellow Polka Dot Bikini." I was shocked at the first sight of my father, who was only in his 50s, thinking, *When did he become an old man?* It brought tears to my eyes.

I was happy to be home, optimistic about my future and ready to start my new life, but I still had one hurdle: I had applied for an internship at Orange Memorial Hospital, and I needed to pass the ACFMG exam, required by the Educational Commission for Foreign Medical Graduates, before I could start. It took me a few days to adjust to hearing, speaking and thinking in English again, but it was like riding a bike. And it confirmed I had learned my material well. I passed the exam. I was going to be a pediatrician!

To celebrate, my parents and my sister, Irene, and her husband, Abraham (known as "Bummie"), threw a grand graduation barbecue on the farm, with all the trimmings, and invited 75 family and friends. An article in the local newspaper reported on the party and added:

> *"Dr. Robins has just returned from Europe where he has completed over five years of medical studies at the University of Heidelberg, where he has graduated cum laude. At the present time, Dr. Robins will be interning at the Orange Memorial Hospital, Orange, N.J., where he will be completing his requirements, before he opens his own office of general practice in the vinicity [sic] of West Essex or Morris County."*

That was the plan, anyway. Meanwhile, I was thrilled to start my internship. I moved into a fourth-floor apartment for residents on the hospital property, and it was exciting to begin making decisions like a doctor. I was worried about my mother, though. At age 62, she was not well. With her diabetes, she had been under a cardiologist's care for years. One day not long after I'd started my internship, she didn't feel well and went to see her cardiologist in Montclair. He said he wanted to admit her to Orange Memorial right away, as she was at imminent risk of a heart attack. But instead of going directly to the hospital, she insisted my father first drive her the 10 miles home so she could take a shower. She said, "I want to smell nice if I'm going to the hospital." That was my mother—always thinking of others.

She was in the hospital for two days, and she started to feel better. I visited her as often as I could, despite the grueling hours required of an intern. I was happy when the doctor said, "She should be able to go home in a couple of days." That day she had a big smile on her face, and I thought she was going to be fine. That night I was on call. My German colleague and roommate, Hubert Lang, had finished a rotation in the States and we were throwing him a farewell party. He was still up late talking to friends and he knew I was exhausted. He said, "Go to bed. Get some sleep. I'll take calls for you."

An emergency call came in at midnight. A short time later Hubert woke me up to tell me, "I'm sorry. I just pronounced your mother." She'd had a massive coronary and passed away before anything could be done for her. It was devastating—a nightmare. I had missed the chance to be there with her at the end. I wasn't sure I'd ever be able to forgive myself for going to sleep that night.

My father had gone home after visiting hours, so we had to wake him and deliver the bad news. My mother's cardiologist came to the hospital at 2 AM to console us. Many of the interns and physicians paid their respects at my sister's house in the days that followed.

I called Crystal in Germany to tell her that my mother had passed away, and that in the Jewish faith we could not have a wedding for six months. I wanted her to come to the States, though, and be with me. We could have a civil ceremony for moralistic reasons, and later have a beautiful ceremony in Frankfurt. She would not come, but she said she would wait for me, and told me to come back for her when I was ready. (As it turned out, I never was ready.)

I felt abandoned by Crystal, overcome with grief about my mother and guilty for having been far away from my family for so long. If I'd been closer, maybe I could have helped my mother become healthier and avoid her heart attack. At the beautiful service for her, I heard stories from so many people about her acts of kindness and charity. I wanted to be like her. I knew how much it meant to her that I become a doctor, so I tried to stop feeling sorry for myself and focus on learning all I could during my internship.

My rotating internship included three months of internal medicine, three months of pediatrics, three months of OB-GYN and three months of surgery. I loved every moment. Each rotation seemed more exciting than the other.

Internal medicine was the most interesting. We saw all kinds of patients with some diseases I'd never heard of. But I was especially attentive when I rotated through pediatrics. I asked the most questions and observed closely to see which doctor I would most want to be like. I was a little disappointed that one of the pediatricians was too busy to spend more than a smidgeon of time with me. When I told him I was interested in doing a residency in pediatrics, he wasn't rude so much as indifferent. He just said, "Oh yeah, that's fine. The pediatric hospital is close by. You'll like it." And the head nurse in the ward could never remember my name. I told her to think of a flock of birds. The next day when I made rounds she waved at me with a big smile and said, "Hi, Dr. Sparrow!"

In OB-GYN we had many welfare patients and delivered a lot of babies. I did a bunch of them, about 20 or 30. Well, at least the nurses made us feel like we actually did the deliveries. The nurses knew everything and taught us more than the doctors did. I don't know what we would have done without them. They'd say, "Now, not so hard. Pull gently, turn it a little bit to the right, rotate it a little bit, tell her to press." It was such a great feeling to deliver a baby. During the three months there, I even had two mothers name their babies after me. I was thinking, *Maybe I should go into obstetrics.*

I delivered a baby to a 17-year-old girl who was not married. A year later, when I was working in the emergency room, I was called upon to deliver another baby to this same young woman. I said, "Mary, why don't you marry one of the fathers?" With big, bright eyes she looked at me and said, "Doctor, you don't want me to marry someone I don't love, do you?"

We had duty in the emergency room every fourth night. The chief surgical residents were unrelenting. They would sit in the ER and say, "Doc, find me a kidney, a gallbladder, a hernia—any kind of surgery that we can do tonight!"

I was thrilled to start my internship at Orange Memorial Hospital in 1961.

One night while on duty, I received a call from my sister that her daughter was running a fever of 104. She couldn't get in touch with her pediatrician and asked me to come over right away. The chief surgical resident said he would cover for me, so I jumped into my car and drove like an idiot toward her home, going about 80 miles an hour on country roads. When I was stopped by a police officer for speeding, he saw my hospital uniform and said, "I am not going to give you a ticket, but please drive more slowly." When I finally arrived, a few sponge baths did the trick. The baby's fever came down, and she was fine.

About two weeks later, when I was on duty in the ER, the same police officer came in with excruciating back pain. We determined that he was trying to pass kidney stones. Yes, we did give him some medication for the pain, and the surgical residents took over. But some of my colleagues joked that if he had given me a speeding ticket, he might still be waiting in the ER—in pain.

I must confess that surgery was the most difficult rotation. All we did was stand on our feet for hours and hold retractors. There was strong competition among the surgeons, and they all talked about each other. I asked the anesthesiologists how they survived with all the gossip and politics, and their message to me was, "Keep your mouth shut and do your work." One of the anesthesiologists said that is how he survived for 22 years there.

My feelings about surgery changed one stormy winter night, when I was the intern on duty. It was sheer ice out there, and people were streaming into the ER with cuts and wounds. The surgical resident said, with his distinctive Italian accent, "Eh, Robins-a, what's-a-madda with you? You don't know how to sew. You take too long! I teach you how to sew!"

He took me under his wing and taught me. I sutured for 20 hours straight on people who'd slipped or gotten drunk and fallen on the ice. And during those intense 20 hours I got better and better and thought, *You know what? I'm good at this!* It wasn't pediatrics, but I loved doing it.

Then a wealthy woman from South Orange came in with her mother, who had been in an automobile accident. They couldn't get a plastic surgeon to sew up her lip that night, so I sewed it up. I did such a fabulous job they bought me gifts and invited me to their home for dinner.

Later I said, jokingly, "Maybe I should be a plastic surgeon." There were two plastic surgeons on the staff of Orange Memorial, and they said, "You're Jewish. Forget it. You'll never get in."

About a month before I finished my internship in June 1962, I went to the well-known Babies' Hospital about five miles away in Newark and filled out an application to start my residency there in July. A few nights before I was to begin, I went to the hospital to meet some of the residents who were completing their training there. I was devastated when several of them told me not to come to this hospital, as it was losing its accreditation. It was probably too late to find another pediatric hospital for my residency. What was I going to do?

An alternative seed was planted a few days later. When I was on duty in the ER at Orange Memorial, Arlington Bensel Jr., MD, an attending dermatologist, would sometimes come in to have a cup of coffee and schmooze. He'd also been observing my work. I was surprised when he invited me to dinner. He and his wife, Mildred, a nurse, welcomed me into their magnificent (and expensive) home. After dinner he showed me a photograph of his yacht in Brielle, on the Jersey Shore. You know how I feel about yachts!

He said, "I have been watching you. I like the way you treat patients. If you would consider going into dermatology, I would like to offer you the opportunity to join me in my practice. You would be starting at about $60,000 a year, and after a few years you could become an equal partner."

I thought to myself, *What are you smoking?* I had been making about $50 a month. After seeing my parents barely get by all their lives, this was a salary beyond my imagination. I said, "Wow, that is incredible!" He told me about the advantages of dermatology: There are no emergencies. Your patients don't die. It's a "gentleman's specialty." I must confess he was quite convincing. I told him that although I was geared toward pediatrics, I would think about it.

For three nights I twisted and turned and could not sleep. My head was buzzing. I'd had a great professor in dermatology while I was in medical school in Germany. He was very personable. Despite that, the specialty, which at that time seemed to be mainly about acne and psoriasis, just didn't excite me. Dermatologists didn't do any surgery, either in Europe or in the States, and I was learning to love surgery. Plus, I would have to do additional training—and I would have to find a residency quickly.

I'd had a wonderful experience in pediatrics, and I felt guilty about giving up my wish—and my promise—to work with children. But after being poor for so long, I couldn't turn down this opportunity. On the third day, I called Dr. Bensel, thanked him for his offer and told him I would try to find a dermatology residency.

Then I had a moment of depression. Was I selling out? Would I like practicing dermatology? Would I regret giving up my chance to save the world with children? Would Dr. Strominger, my mentor in Tokyo, haunt me for the rest of my life? Time would tell.

It was nearly July. Almost all residency positions had been filled, so once again, I was behind the curve and scrambling. I went to the medical library, scoured the recent medical journals and found that there were two dermatology vacancies that had not been filled. One was at the University of Texas Medical Branch in Galveston, one of the best dermatology training programs in the country. I spoke to the chair of the department and told him about my military experience and that I spoke French, German, and some Spanish and Japanese. He said, "By God, we need you here!" He immediately sent me an acceptance letter.

I was elated, as this was a great opportunity at a great department. I went to see my father that night and told him that I would be leaving for Texas in 24 hours. I had never seen my father cry, but he was destroyed. He was having trouble coping with the loss of my mother, and now he would be alone. I'd been away at college, overseas in the army, then in Europe for medical school. He pleaded for me to find a residency closer to home. I told him I would try.

The other opening was at the Bronx VA Medical Center. I made an appointment to see Harry Shatin, MD, the department chair. After listening to me, he said, "I'm so sorry, but I do not take foreign medical graduates. I have many applicants who were outstanding in their studies, so why should I take you?"

I explained that I had been accepted at the University of Texas in Galveston, but since my mother had recently passed away, my father asked me to find a place closer to home to complete my training. "I would truly appreciate the opportunity to study with you here in the Bronx," I said. He looked at me and said, "Don't BS me. That program in Texas is one of the very best in the country and one of the hardest to get into. Why would they take you?" I told Dr. Shatin that I could show him my acceptance letter. He replied, "Show me that letter and you can start tomorrow." So I went and got it, delivered it and started at the Bronx VA the next day.

I was grateful that I had been able to snag a residency near my father, who needed me. I was also still close to my childhood best friend, Buddy Shenkin (who grew up in the Bronx not far from the VA), even though he'd been less than enthusiastic about me going to medical school. But I missed treating women and children during my time at the VA. I was one of four dermatology residents. Our instructor, who operated in a rather hands-off manner, would assign us topics. Then the four of us would work together to teach each other. I was still thinking about joining Dr. Bensel in his practice after completing my training, and I didn't want to be second rate. I wanted to be the best! I was conscientious and a pretty good student.

Now I really looked like a doctor!

However, I was sick of being poor, so I made time for a little moonlighting doing medical histories and physicals for $3 or $5 a pop. I asked my roommate, John Forline, who was one of the dermatology residents, if he wanted to join me. He said, "You're crazy. What are you doing that for?" I said, "I have to eat." John, who had gone to medical school at Duke University, was brilliant but not exactly ambitious. And he didn't have to worry about money like I did. He preferred to lie in his bunk and read all the time. We were making a small salary at the VA, but it was barely enough to live on without having to ask my family for money. The extra work brought in enough cash to put gas in the car and go on an occasional dinner date. I did meet quite a few nice young ladies in those days. I was tall (and cute, right?). I showed promise as a young doctor, and I could turn on the charm and tell a good joke or story. Still, I often seemed to run short of funds.

For example, I went out with the daughter of the founder of a large grocery chain. She wanted to go to Rapoport's on the Lower

East Side of Manhattan for the fantastic cheese blintzes. She ordered three drinks, and I realized I wasn't going to be able to pay the bill if I ate anything. So I just said, "Gee, I've got an upset stomach" and watched her eat her blintzes. Even so, when the bill came, I had to borrow 50 cents from her.

To keep my entrepreneurial "get rich quick" antennae tuned, in my spare time I formed a small investment group with Alan Simonson, a childhood pal, and a couple of his friends. We had a few meetings and came up with an idea. *Ben Casey,* a hospital drama on ABC starring Vince Edwards as the intense young surgeon, was dominating the ratings. We agreed we should create a line of "Ben Casey" stethoscopes! We could buy cheap stethoscopes in Japan, license the name and sell them for a good profit in the States. Since I could speak Japanese and knew my way around a stethoscope, I would be the "sweat equity." The three other guys put together about $1,000 to send me to Japan for a few days. Since I had a two-week vacation from the VA coming up, I added a few of my own shekels and thought, *Why don't I take this chance to go around the world?* I knew I could find inexpensive places to stay, and it would allow me to see countries I hadn't yet experienced. My partners agreed to the plan.

I flew to Tokyo, where I met a manufacturer who made stethoscopes and negotiated the $1.50 price down to 90 cents apiece. I ordered 10,000 of them. Then I went on to Hong Kong. My cousin Harold wanted to import plastic flowers, a decorating trend that was just starting to catch on. In Hong Kong I found a Chinese representative who introduced me to a manufacturer, and I spent a day ordering *faux fleurs.* When I was there the rep said to me, "You know, we make beautiful suits here in Hong Kong, and we can make them for one-tenth of what they cost in the States." I said, "OK, send me over a couple of men's suits, and I'll see if I can find you a rep or someone to import them."

After that, I hopped on a flight to Bangkok, Thailand, and spent

48 hours getting a quick overview of that exotic city. Next, I spent two days in India, where I saw the main tourist sites around New Delhi and took a quick side trip to visit the Taj Mahal. When I got off my Air France flight in Karachi, Pakistan, I walked out of the airport with my small suitcase and saw beggars, people who were maimed and filth and flies everywhere. I got back on the plane and the pretty hostesses said to me, "You don't believe in staying very long, do you?" When I landed in Tehran, Iran, I didn't have a visa, but they allowed me to stay for 48 hours. In those days before the Revolution, Tehran, with its wide boulevards and beautiful palm trees and flowers, felt like a prosperous oasis after the poverty and teeming masses in India and Pakistan. My final stop before returning home was Tel Aviv, my first visit to Israel. I'll never forget an Israeli girl, looking tough as nails in her Army uniform, who plopped down next to me and put her feet up on a chair. I don't remember if she was carrying a gun, but let's just say she was different from any of the girls I'd known in the States. I was intrigued. When I flew home on El Al Airlines, the flight attendant said, "We have coffee, but I can't give you any until I make more because I'm saving it for the captain. We really don't want him to fall asleep." I hoped she was joking. All in all, I'd say my first impressions of Israeli women were positive!

Back in New York, our investment group secured a license to use the Ben Casey name for 5 percent of sales. The stethoscopes sat in a warehouse while two of our partners fought over what company was going to have the exclusive rights to sell them. Then the company that was chosen fell apart. I found a local sales rep who assured us he had somebody to buy them. "I'll get your $10,000 back and everything after that, we'll divide," he said. Well, the group never got its money back, and let's just say it was not a successful transaction. It was an important lesson in understanding that you can't trust everybody, even if (*especially* if!) they promise you the world.

As for the plastic flowers I'd ordered for my cousin to import? He married his competitor's daughter and because of the merger, dropped the idea. Shortly thereafter, imported plastic flowers popped up like weeds in every house in America. We were just ahead of the trend. As for importing suits, I knew a man in the garment business. I went to him and said, "Look! I had some cashmere sports jackets made in Hong Kong, and they're beautiful. If you want to import suits from Hong Kong, they're dirt cheap, like $7 to $10 a suit." He said, "Nah, they'll never compete with the American market. They'll fall apart if it rains. They won't get the sizes right. The shipping will be prohibitive." He pooh-poohed the idea, and sure enough, that industry soon took off, too. (I still have one of those jackets, and it still looks great.)

Our ideas might have been ahead of their time. I also realized I couldn't do it all while trying to complete my residency. It had been an adventure, but really, I thought, *Who has time for this?* It was back to the grind for me.

I still found some time for fun, though. I was excited when I had the chance to attend a medical conference in Mexico. I loved to practice my Spanish. While there, I met a charming young lady who worked for Barnes & Noble in Mexico. When I got back to the VA hospital, she would call me there every day, as she had access to a T1 telephone line to the States. Every time, someone would page me on the hospital loudspeaker: "Dr. Robins! Dr. Robins! Your girlfriend is calling you from Mexico." Boy, did I get teased for that.

I met another young woman, a dietitian, who invited me to her hometown for one of the holidays. She lived in the posh neighborhood of Shaker Heights in Cleveland. We were not really in sync. She would stay up all night watching movies, and I would go to bed early.

One morning before she was up, I went with her father to get some bagels and the newspaper. When we passed a temple, he said, "I guess this is where you two will be getting married soon." I took the next plane back to New York. I was not ready for any major commitment beyond starting my medical practice.

During my second year at the Bronx VA in 1963, not long after the horrible news of the assassination of President Kennedy, I was invited to participate in a three-month fellowship on tropical dermatology in Central America. Sponsored by Louisiana State University in New Orleans, the fellowship was funded by the China Relief program, which had been created by Eleanor Roosevelt in the 1940s to help support the sick in China. After China became the Communist People's Republic, the funds were given to LSU, where they were then being used to improve the health of people in Central America.

I was one of four physicians in the program. We started in New Orleans for our orientation, then traveled to Panama, Honduras, Costa Rica, Guatemala, El Salvador and Mexico before returning to LSU for debriefing. During those three months, we saw many leprosy cases, exotic infections and rare dermatological conditions. We also enjoyed side trips to banana plantations, coffee *fincas* (estates) and of course provided the local people with the latest medical information. I took hundreds of photos, which a pharmaceutical company made available to dermatologists at no charge. I loved being able to combine my medical knowledge with a chance to see places I'd never been before.

I was thrilled that I had been able to feed my appetite for travel, but I had no grandiose ideas then about lecturing in other countries or doing anything more than joining Dr. Bensel as a partner. Or if he'd changed his mind, maybe I'd just open up a nice little practice in northern New Jersey where there was no dermatologist. I'd see patients and blend in with the community. I was just happy that I would be a physician and would be helping people. To me, that was the most important thing. But, if a little more moola than what I'd been scraping by on came with that satisfaction, well, I wouldn't turn it down!

The training at the VA was very good but unfortunately very limited in relation to children and women. Toward the end of my two-year program in 1964, I learned that I was able to transfer to another hospital. So I signed up for a third year of training at New York University Medical Center in New York City. I had a good feeling about it.

CHAPTER 8

Time to Specialize

*Can I compartmentalize my new
aspirations in medicine, money
and . . . marriage?*

The World's Fair was the hottest ticket in town (besides *Hello, Dolly!*) that summer of '64, with its optimistic, futuristic imaginings and 12-story Unisphere globe as its centerpiece in Flushing Meadows, Queens. It felt like a time of incredible innovation, with prototypes of picture phones, robots and flying cars like on *The Jetsons* cartoon. Anything seemed possible. I loved that I lived close by and could get there easily.

I packed up my belongings in the Bronx and moved about 10 miles south to First Avenue and 32nd Street in Manhattan. It felt like a different world, and I was thrilled to be continuing my dermatology education at NYU Medical Center, one of the top hospitals in the United States. While it had been an honor to work with veterans at the Bronx VA, it felt great to see women and children as patients again.

Happy as I was to be there, I also knew that until I started my medical practice, I was going to have to take part-time jobs to make ends meet. One of the residents who was leaving told me about a night executive job at Goldwater Hospital. Since 1939, Goldwater had provided care for patients with chronic conditions, and NYU had research units there. The hospital was on Welfare Island in the East River, renamed Roosevelt Island for FDR in 1971. The tramway connecting the island to Manhattan opened in 1976; there was no subway until 1989. So in those days I had to drive across the Queensboro Bridge and then take the Welfare Island Bridge from Queens.

I worked with a Dr. Horn, a Holocaust survivor and refugee from Austria. She liked me because I could speak German with her. It was a posh job. I didn't do calls. I didn't have to see patients. The medical staff did that. All I had to do was sleep there, get up in the morning and sign half a dozen or so death certificates.

I also jumped at the chance to make a little extra money when Murray Gruber, founder of pharmaceutical company Dermik Laboratories, asked me if I would lecture his salesmen (they were all men in those days) once or twice a month. In Europe, it was customary to use physicians as pharmaceutical sales reps to call on other physicians. In the States, we initially used pharmacists, but there was an inadequate supply of pharmacists to call on doctors, so pharma companies hired people with bachelor's degrees and trained them. Gruber was a chemist who developed medications for skin problems, and he wanted his sales team well versed in dermatology topics. I was happy to do it for the extra scratch, and I learned a lot from Murray, too. He was an innovator, and I remember he printed the name of his products on all four sides of the box they were stored in, so they would be visible no matter how they were placed on a shelf, helping to avoid mistakes. I thought that was clever!

His company did something else that was smart and ahead of its time. On one of my sessions at Dermik, the sales manager called me into his office and told me that a beautiful young blonde, who was very bright, charming and charismatic, had applied for a job. It was the early 1960s, and there were many kinds of gender bias then. Doctors often used their wives as secretaries or receptionists, and the thinking was, they might not be too keen to let a beautiful young saleswoman meet with the doctor. The sales manager asked me, "Do you think we could use her as a sales rep?" I thought she would be good at it. I said, "If you don't hire her, I would consider it when I go into practice." Dermik did hire the young woman, and she outsold the men two or three times over. Since then, many, many women have been hired as pharmaceutical sales reps. In fact, most of them today are women.

I also found a job working with Schering pharmaceutical company on some weekends and my days off. I would go to medical conferences in St. Louis, New Orleans or Los Angeles, sit in the company's "Doctor to Doctor" booth and tell attendees about Schering's dermatological products. One day the director of a booth representing beauty products came over to me. "Dr. Robins," she said, "can you help me? My baby has a rash in her ear. Do you think it could be psoriasis? Can you give me some medicine for it?" I said, "Children usually don't have psoriasis in the ear. It's much more likely to be seborrheic dermatitis or something else." I said, "I'll give you a cream you can put in the ear, twice a day. If it doesn't clear up in 48 hours, take her to see a doctor." She exclaimed, "Fifi will love you!" I said, "Who's Fifi?" "That's my baby." It was her dog.

Thankfully, most of my encounters in the booth addressed human patients. During my training at NYU I worked at a few of those conventions. I liked traveling and seeing new places, and the money helped get me through.

I wasn't dating much at that time, but one day, while waiting in line for coffee at the hospital cafeteria, I noticed a stunning

young woman with blond hair and blue eyes. I saw her a couple more times, and when I finally had a chance to say hello, I
learned that her name was Ingrid, she was an airline hostess for
TWA and volunteered at the hospital one day a week when she
wasn't flying. Born and raised in Germany, near Hamburg, she had
gotten her teaching degree in Canada before coming to the United
States. She was friendly and polite, spoke several languages and
was involved in sports. I was excited to speak German with her. I
was also instantly attracted, and I said, "Let's go out. How about
Saturday night?"

Unfortunately, I had forgotten about a conflict. I occasionally
played matchmaker by organizing parties for some of my bachelor
doctor friends to meet young ladies. I had arranged a party for that
Saturday night for a nurse I knew and five of her friends. I'd invited
five fellows, but I figured they could make do without me. Before I
left to meet Ingrid, my nurse friend called me in a panic. She said,
"Perry, you have to come over. Only one man showed up, and I have
five other girls besides myself."

I knew the right thing to do was to honor my first commitment. I called Ingrid and said, "I'm sorry. Unexpectedly I have to be
on duty tonight, so I have to cancel our date." I went to the party
to help even up the gender ratio. Another guy showed up, so we
were three men and six women, but even so, the party wasn't very
exciting.

Ingrid volunteered at the hospital on Thursdays, so the next
Thursday when she came in, I knew I was in trouble when I saw the
look in her eye. She said, "I know you were not being honest with
me, because I called the hospital. A dermatologist who was on duty
said you were off to go to a party." I felt bad. I wasn't trying to give
her the brush-off, and I should have been honest about it. So I asked
her to forgive me and go out with me that weekend. She said yes.

We had fun together, and the chemistry between us was hot,
hot, hot. But between her flying schedule and my working nights at

Goldwater, we were only able to see each other once or twice a week. The relationship was very spotty. I have to admit, during those first few months together, I didn't get to know her very well.

My childhood friend Buddy had married and was working as an engineer in northern New Jersey. He and his wife, Lou, invited Ingrid and me to have dinner with them. We drove to his home, and there we saw the most idyllic scene: a light snowfall, a white picket fence, and inside there was a fireplace, the dog, the baby, the food on the table. Jokingly, I said to Ingrid, "Let's get married." She said, also jokingly (I thought), "Are you serious?" I said, "Of course," with a big grin. Then it grew.

When Bud and Lou heard this, they went nuts, saying, "This is wonderful! We'll help you plan the wedding!" I thought, *Oh, my God! What have I done?* But I felt like I couldn't backtrack at that point. I said to myself, *OK, maybe I'll try it. If it doesn't work out, we can always get divorced.* We started planning the wedding and the honeymoon.

My family thought I was crazy to be marrying a shiksa—and a German one at that. Some of my friends asked me why I wanted to marry her, including a lawyer pal who pointed out that she didn't come from a wealthy or distinguished family. Well, neither did I! On her airline hostess salary, she was struggling financially even more than I was. She could barely make the payments on her Volkswagen. She wanted to get extra work but couldn't find anything. I felt sorry for her and wanted to help her.

Yes, I had some doubts, but I figured, *Well, all that glitters is not gold. She's good-natured, and she'll make a good wife.* I thought about the "three K's" slogan in Germany: *Kinder, Küche* and *Kirche*. Kinder is children, Küche is kitchen and Kirche is church. Of course, we weren't in sync on that third one, but I reckoned, *She'll be faithful and good. She'll provide a home, and it's not necessary to marry a wealthy girl.*

In the spring of '65, I was approaching the end of my training at NYU and didn't know where I would start my practice. I knew I had to figure it out soon, because as a foreign medical graduate, I was required to take a medical licensing exam in any state in which I wanted to practice. Maybe I could still join Dr. Bensel, whom I'd met during my time at Orange Memorial in New Jersey. Or maybe Ingrid and I could move somewhere else to start our life together, perhaps in California. My friend and former roommate at the Bronx VA, John Forline, said he would consider starting a dermatology practice with me in Los Angeles. I was open to any possibilities.

I could only take about two weeks off, so I did some research on when different states scheduled their exams. I then decided to do something incredibly stupid: I lined up three state licensing exams (Indiana, Montana and California) in one two-week trip. My modus operandi was, "Damn the torpedoes; full speed ahead!"

It nearly killed me. I didn't eat or sleep much. I was taking things to keep me awake, and then things to fall asleep. I'd stay up all night studying, always compensating for my dyslexia. I'd go and take the exam, then get on a plane. Get to the next place. Take another excruciatingly difficult exam for three days. Repeat. It was mentally and physically exhausting.

First up was Indiana, a state I knew nothing about. I could take it or leave it, but I dutifully took the test. On my way to Montana, I met a man on the plane who owned a car dealership. He said, "We want you to practice in Montana. I'll lend you a car. You can visit the other doctors, and I'll have you meet a friend at the bank." At the bank, his friend said, "Sign here and we'll give you a $100,000 loan to set up your practice." (That was a lot of money in 1965!) I met a pathologist, originally from New Jersey, who said, "You'll like it here. I know of a spread with about 2,000 acres. You could buy it for about $10 an acre." The people couldn't have been nicer. It was very tempting. I could have been a dude ranch dermatologist. The only problem was that Montana has only two seasons: winter and winter.

On to California, which was booming in the mid-1960s. Los Angeles didn't excite me very much, but a doctor there was wooing John Forline and me to take over his practice. He was outgoing and charming. He said, "I've never had a son, and it would have been a privilege to have a son like you. I'm going to give you my practice." I was thinking, *Wow, could I be any luckier?* Then he dropped the bomb. "Well, there's just one condition. You have to buy my office building on Wilshire Boulevard."

The price was around a million dollars, which was mind-boggling to a penny-pinching doctor in training making $100 a month. Instead of blurting out, "Are you out of your mind?" I said, "No, I think that's a much bigger bite then I would really want to undertake at this time."

I had a cousin of a cousin practicing in San Diego, so I headed south to visit him. He was an internist, and he had space in his basement office that he said he would be pleased to rent to me. I called on a well-known dermatologist in the area to find out how he felt about another dermatologist joining him in San Diego. He said, "Perry, I'd love to have you join us, but we have two other dermatologists, and we hardly have enough patients to fill our schedules."

I asked, "How long do you think it'd take before you need a third dermatologist?" He said, "Oh, you're talking *years*." Today there are more than 200 dermatologists in the San Diego area!

By the time I'd finished the two weeks, I was dazed—a nervous wreck, at times almost suicidal. Despite that, I passed all three states' licensing exams with a B average. At that point I figured it was "Westward ho!" for me.

When I returned to NYU Medical Center, I gave notice to Alfred

Kopf, MD, a professor of dermatology, and Rudolf L. Baer, MD, chairman of the Department of Dermatology, that I would be leaving at the end of the year.

Dr. Kopf told Stephen Gumport, MD, a renowned cancer surgeon who had been teaching surgery at the NYU School of Medicine since 1949, about my plans to leave. Truly a gentleman's gentleman, Dr. Gumport was a charmer who spoke softly, elegantly and eloquently. He said, "Perry, I need to go to the optician and pick up some glasses. Can you drive me there?" I said, "Sure, I'm free this afternoon. I'd be glad to take you."

After Dr. Gumport retrieved his glasses, we sat in the car in front of the optometrist's office for about two hours while he did his best to talk me out of leaving NYU. He said, "Perry, we need you. You're playing such an important role here. I want to assure you that you would be doing the smartest thing if you stayed on at NYU. They're offering you a great opportunity. You'll be helping people. You'll be a leader in the field. You know you can count on my support 100 percent. And I know you'll be so proud of what you accomplish."

He went on and on. He really cared about me, and it touched my heart. After two hours, I said, "Dr. Gumport, I will think carefully about all you said and will try to give it my best shot." That's what spurred my decision to stay. If it weren't for that two-hour conversation in the car, I'd probably be a millionaire in California. Steve Gumport remained a great friend and became a legend in tumor surgery. (He specialized in breast cancer and trained Matthew N. Harris, MD, and Daniel F. Roses, MD, two of today's leaders at NYU. I was sad when Dr. Gumport died in 1989.)

When I told Dr. Kopf that I'd be staying, he said, "We're excited to have you, and we're going to try to help you make it very successful." My first thought was, *I guess this means I have to take another licensing exam!*

Then something happened that changed the course of my life. While I had been busy with part-time jobs, getting engaged and taking exams, my friend and former roommate John Forline had remained an avid reader. He wanted to show me several articles he'd read about chemosurgery, a procedure developed by Frederic Mohs, MD, at the University of Wisconsin to treat certain skin cancers. John said, "You love working with your hands. You'd be a natural at it. Maybe you could specialize in this and become an authority on the technique. You could save lives! You should go to Madison and visit Dr. Mohs."

I was bowled over, intrigued and excited. I did love working with my hands. I loved the idea of curing cancers. I thought this was something that might be right for me, and John was totally the catalyst. In chemistry terms, he was like the platinum that changed my carbon monoxide into carbon dioxide (which, as every chemistry geek knows, is what happens in a car's catalytic converter).

Energized, I read up on Frederic Edward Mohs and learned all I could about his technique. While he'd been performing chemosurgery since 1939, it was still little-known, and there had been some resistance to the procedure from the medical community. Interest in it was starting to pick up, however. I immediately wrote to him, asking if I could come to Wisconsin and train with him to learn chemosurgery. Dr. Mohs was very accommodating and said I could stay as long as I felt necessary to learn the procedure. I flew to Chicago at my own expense and rented a car for a month. Early Monday morning, when I reported to his office, his assistant said, "Just follow Dr. Mohs, and If you have any questions, he will be pleased to answer them." She recommended that I buy his book on chemosurgery that was available by mail.

Dr. Mohs was a brilliant man but very quiet. He didn't talk much, and his answers to questions were short. He and his staff worked hard, starting at 7 o'clock in the morning and working through the early hours of the evening. He had enough cases that he only did chemo-surgery. During my weeks there, I was finally allowed to pick up a scalpel and cut a layer of tissue from a gangrenous toe. That was quite a thrill! But yes, I mostly had to learn by observing.

I was surprised that when we went out for lunch together, he never paid for anyone but himself. I guess having so many visitors, it wasn't necessary. The doctors who came to study chemosurgery with Dr. Mohs were mainly general surgeons; some were general practitioners. But none were dermatologists—until I showed up. Remember, dermatologists did not do surgery in those days. The department of dermatology was across the hall from Dr. Mohs' office, but there was not good chemistry between the chairman and Fred. As a result, there was never much interaction between the two departments. I was to be the first bridge!

HOW DID CHEMOSURGERY WORK?

In 1933, while 23-year-old research assistant Frederic Mohs was injecting different chemicals into cancerous rat tissues, he discovered that a zinc chloride solution could "fix" skin tissue and allow its

cells to be studied under a microscope. When he created a chemical paste made of zinc chloride and applied it to a cancerous lesion, the tissue would harden, so a surgeon could cut out, or excise, the tumor with no anesthesia and no bleeding. Then the tissue could be sliced and examined under a microscope to pinpoint the location of cancerous cells.

continued

After training as a surgeon, Dr. Mohs (above) began performing this chemosurgery (named after the zinc chloride paste) on human patients. It was a time-consuming process. After the paste was applied to a skin cancer lesion, it took many hours or until the next day to reach an adequate level of fixation. This was not fun for the patient, as the paste caused much discomfort (in other words, it hurt a lot).

Dr. Mohs would then remove the dressing and, using a scalpel, excise a saucer-shaped layer of the fixed tissue. (At this point, though, the patient didn't feel anything.) He would cut the removed tissue into sections and sketch a corresponding map. He would paint the adjoining edges of the sections with different dyes and also mark reference points on the surgical site.

While the patient waited, a technician would freeze the tissue sections, slice them horizontally and mount the slices on slides so Dr. Mohs could examine them under a microscope. If the underneath sections and edges showed no cancer cells, no further surgery was required. If any cancer cells remained, more surgery would be needed, but only in that precisely mapped area of the surgical site.

When that happened, Dr. Mohs would reapply zinc chloride paste to the appropriate area, cover it with a dressing and the whole procedure would be repeated until no more cancer cells remained in any tissue specimens.

Five to seven days after that, a scab called an eschar would separate from the fixed-tissue site, leaving healthy, healing tissue behind. The patient would return so Dr. Mohs could then close the wound with stitches.

This technique had many advantages over standard excision of a tumor, in which the surgeon removed the visible tumor plus a wide swatch of healthy tissue as a safety margin. But skin cancer may have "roots" that are not immediately visible to a surgeon. Doing the lab work in stages while the patient waited allowed all of the cancer to be removed while sparing healthy tissue. This made for smaller scars and a better cosmetic outcome.

The chemosurgery procedure was slow; it could take many days to complete a case. It was also painful. One patient came from Florida for a consultation and was told to lie down. Dr. Mohs applied the paste and bandage and told him to return the next morning. The gentleman said, "Dr. Mohs, my ice cream wagon is at the airport in Florida. I cannot come back tomorrow. I have to go back, otherwise I will lose all my ice cream and I may get fired. All I wanted was a consultation."

Observing and learning chemosurgery with Dr. Mohs was a revelation. The zinc chloride paste had been used through the years on thousands of patients. One day I asked Dr. Mohs if he had ever applied for FDA approval for the paste. He simply replied, "No." Chemosurgery might have been controversial to some, but I observed successful results. I thought it was exciting, something I could really enjoy. I felt like I had found my calling. I wanted to become an expert in the technique and maybe teach it to others. What a wonderful thing to be able to help people, and even save lives.

After about five weeks of training, I purchased a jar of zinc chloride paste and Dr. Mohs' textbook (he called it a "do-it-yourself kit"), which I took back to New York. When I returned to NYU, I met with Dr. Kopf, who was very supportive of the idea of starting a chemosurgery section at NYU. He gained the support of Dr. Baer, the chairman of the Department of Dermatology, and J.M. Converse, MD, chairman of the Department of Plastic Surgery. I received a grant to kick-start the effort, and I would be put on staff (on probation) to see if the program would succeed. I was very excited to get started.

CHAPTER 9

A Thicker Skin

Chemosurgery feels like my true calling;
why can't dermatologists be surgeons?

By bringing chemosurgery to New York, I knew I was about to embark on something exciting and new, but I had no idea of the obstacles—or rewards—that would lie ahead. Remember that in the mid-1960s, dermatologists did not do surgery, so this concept was likely to be controversial (to put it mildly). While I loved surgery and believed I had an aptitude for it, my training and skills were minimal. I knew I still had a lot to learn.

Dr. Kopf, today a professor emeritus of the Department of Dermatology at NYU School of Medicine and still a good friend, says with his typical calm understatement, "When you have a large skin cancer, it becomes a very substantial surgical procedure. It was understandable that some surgeons would be upset by having a dermatologist with almost no surgical background do this potentially large surgical procedure. We anticipated problems with the introduction of this into a medical center."

I did not anticipate, however, that I would have to face a gauntlet of naysayers. Quite a few of my colleagues believed that dermatologists should not be surgeons. That's how it had always been. They didn't even do skin biopsies in those days. I was surprised by the vehemence of their resistance. When I would walk to my office in the medical center, some of the dermatologists would make nasty remarks or even shake their fingers at me and say, "Shame, shame, shame! We're not surgeons; we're medical doctors. You shouldn't do this. You're going to give us a bad reputation!"

I was extremely fortunate that Al Kopf set up our new chemosurgery unit as a joint project with the Department of Dermatology and the Department of Plastic Surgery. That was a smart move that gave it legitimacy and proved essential to its success. The partnership gave me world-class training and a built-in support network. Appropriately, "Kopf" means "head" in German, and he was no dummkopf. Al Kopf remains my hero to this day, and I send him *ein Kuss auf den Kopf* ("a kiss on the head") for all he did for me.

During that year of the fellowship, I was always assigned a plastic surgeon to work with me. The first was Hugh Brown from Newcastle, England, who was in New York on a Fulbright scholarship to study with Dr. Bob Beasley, one of the top hand surgeons in the U.S. I learned that by British tradition, male surgeons are referred to as "Mister." So, Mr. Brown worked with me daily when we had patients to treat. This was a godsend. He taught me surgery, and I taught him dermatopathology, or how to analyze the prepared slides of a tumor under a microscope.

I would excise the fixed tissue tumor and prepare it for the technicians to make the microscope slides. When it was time to close the wound, Mr. Brown would do the reconstruction and suturing. After a while, he said, "Let me teach you how to do the closures." I learned fast, and I loved it.

The medical center powers that be allowed us to use one table in the surgical suite, another room adjacent that was 9 feet by 9 feet, and before the year was over, we had four people working in very cramped quarters at the end of the hall. There was also a small room I could use for consultations and to meet new patients. This arrangement was barely adequate, as there was no place to keep supplies, slides and patients' records or to do our billing. I wasn't complaining, though!

I was never one to let frustration or anger get the best of me, and I kept my resolve in the face of the protesters and doubting Thomases, too. Besides those opposed to dermatologists performing surgery, some of the physicians considered chemotherapy to be "black magic" and pointed out how painful the zinc chloride was to patients. I would say, "I hope that in a couple of years I can show you more results of the successes we have, and you'll be less doubting." That was the best way to handle it. But I did get tired of hearing the comments again and again, and I'd have to take detours to get to my office to avoid seeing those doctors. Some attempts were even made to have me removed from the NYU faculty and expelled from the American Academy of Dermatology (AAD). Luckily, neither happened.

Meanwhile, I had a little wedding to attend to. Our wedding invitations were printed, addressed and ready to be mailed. On a rainy afternoon in front of a mailbox at 33rd Street and Park Avenue, I sat in the car for two hours. Should I do it? Should I *not* do it? I confess that I had deep reservations about getting married. But I'm nothing if not a man of my word—sometimes to a fault. Finally, I shook my head and said to myself yet again, "Well, if it doesn't work out, you can always get a divorce" and placed the invitations gently into the mailbox.

The day of our wedding in November 1965, I was supposed to dress at my sister's house, which was a couple of miles from our farm. I had picked up my rented tuxedo the day before, but when I looked closely, I realized I only had the jacket. I was standing there with half a tuxedo like a schmuck, thinking, *I'm going to my wedding and I don't have my trousers.* My family never used profanity, and I was raised that way. But I said, "Damn it, that's a sign." Not a good one. When I drove over to Irene and Bummie's house, though, there they were: The pants were hanging on the doorknob.

Our wedding was a modest affair. Ingrid had converted (at least for one day) so we could have a kosher celebration at Short Hills Caterers in Millburn, New Jersey. Many of my family and NYU colleagues attended, as did Buddy Shenkin, John Forline and other friends. Unfortunately, we couldn't afford to bring Ingrid's Catholic family from Germany to attend. In fact, we couldn't pay for our big day until we cashed the checks we received as wedding gifts!

We spent our wedding night at an airport hotel, then went on to a resort in Aruba. We were lying around the pool, and I realized we didn't have much to talk about. I was thinking, *You know, Perry, I think you should have waited.* We just had very different interests, and I was eager and anxious to get back to New York and get my medical practice started. It was not a great beginning, but I wanted to make it work.

My father had started seeing a longtime family friend after my mother died. They decided to marry, and my father moved into her home. That left the house where I'd grown up on the farm in Morris County, New Jersey, empty, and my father said Ingrid and I could use it. When we returned from our honeymoon, we moved into the farmhouse. It was a good way to save money, but the long commute into New York City every day was brutal for me. Because of construction on a new highway and a new shopping center along the route, the trip that was usually an hour took two hours each way. That made for *long* days, especially as "The Chipmunk Song (Christmas Don't Be Late)" was the most popular tune on the radio that holiday season. My Christian friends: Can any of you explain that to me? Ingrid continued to fly for TWA and was away a lot. We both had jobs to do, and we focused on that.

As 1965 drew to a close, I received my New York license to practice medicine, which left me feeling official—and confident in my choice to specialize in chemosurgery for skin cancers. The harassment from a few of my colleagues did not abate, however. Nonetheless, the potential value of the procedure was all too clear to me, and I was convinced that with some additional training, dermatologists could become experts in it. After all, we were the physicians best trained to recognize skin cancers, so we should also be the best at removing them. And chemosurgery seemed to guarantee the most successful outcomes. Fortunately, a few other physicians agreed with me.

I was grateful I had support from leaders in their fields, including the chairmen of both departments, and fellow dermatologist George Popkin, also known as Gorgeous George, since he was so good-looking he could have been a movie star. He served at NYU for more than 50 years, and he helped support my efforts in many ways. The plastic surgeons Hugh Brown and Phillip Casson were also always there for me. They would say, "Ignore it. It's always like that. They pooh-poohed Louis Pasteur at first, too." I was even more grateful that after so many years of training while counting every penny, I was finally making a little money. Not a lot, but enough to make me feel like I was making progress.

When Hugh Brown rotated back to England, other plastic surgeons from the department at NYU were assigned to help train me, but several refused to do so. Luckily, Phil Casson was friendly toward dermatology and enthusiastic about the potential of chemosurgery. He was well trained in his native Australia, in England as a fellow of the Royal College of Surgeons and in the States at Sloan Kettering and at NYU. He taught me how to do beautiful repairs. I also worked with Daniel C. Baker, MD, who is still a prominent plastic surgeon in New York City and professor at NYU.

After that, some of the other plastic surgeons in the department clamored to help me. They loved having a chance to do the repairs after the chemosurgeries were finished. The residents used to come to my office and beg for cases: "When are you going to have another nose case for us?" "We want to do a scalp flap!" "Call me. Let me know!" I felt like the most popular kid on the block, and I made good friends with many of the plastic surgeons. Once I started doing my own closures, I didn't charge patients for the first year until I was fully confident of my artistry.

As I gained confidence as a practicing surgeon, I wanted to start spreading the gospel. At a meeting in Munich, Germany, five other Mohs surgeons and I gathered at a dinner hosted by Dr. Mohs. We agreed to form a chemosurgery society, and we called it the American College of Chemosurgery. We had our first gathering in 1967 in the Palmer House's Wabash Room in Chicago, during the annual meeting of the American Academy of Dermatology. (We continued to meet there for years.) Only about 20 of us attended that first meeting—we were essentially the only physicians practicing the technique in the country. We established a constitution and selected our first officers, with Frederic Mohs as president. I became secretary and treasurer. Our regulations were almost nonexistent at first, and the dues were $10 a year. It was a start.

In our early years, some of the people who were admitted to the society had minimal training—sometimes as short as a day to a week of observation on the technique with Dr. Mohs. He felt strongly that any physician who wanted to do chemosurgery should have the opportunity. I worried that some of the doctors going through this revolving door were not being adequately trained, and I argued hard for tighter requirements. The society was later renamed the American College of Mohs Surgery, and now has about 1,400 rigorously fellowship-trained Mohs surgeons as members.

Dr. Mohs was a great spokesman for the society, but he antagonized surgeons by saying repeatedly that all skin cancers should be treated by chemosurgery, which made surgeons angry. Even though we thought it was true, it was still incorrect to say so because other methods also frequently produced good results. I preferred to say that if they had not been previously successful in eradicating skin cancers, chemosurgery offered a chance for a cure.

While I was busy getting my practice off the ground, I was concerned about a colleague from medical school who was having trouble starting his own. He had been making a living singing opera and radio commercials before attending medical school in Heidelberg. His dream was to become a physician. When he returned to the States after graduation, however, he was having serious financial problems. He never had time to study for the qualifying exam to practice medicine because he had to work so much to provide for his family and pay the bills. He told me, "I'm so much in debt that I'm almost thinking of killing myself. I have enough life insurance that my wife would be able to pay expenses for a few years and carry on."

I was horrified and told him not to even think about that. He said, "I wish I could get a job where I could study part time and that would help bring in some money to put food on the table." I had a brainstorm. I knew someone in the mail-order business who had a warehouse downtown. I asked him, "Can you do me a favor? You have a place where this friend of mine could study at night. We'll call him the night watchman. We'll have a desk with a phone and no television or radio. He can study, and I'll pay his salary, but you cannot tell him that I'm doing this."

He said, "I don't need a night watchman. I don't have that much merchandise there. But if it helps, I'll go along with it." I called my in-debt friend the next day and said, "You lucked out, because I know someone who needs a night watchman. Just make sure no one steals or enters the property. He's willing to pay you a decent salary, and it will give you an opportunity to study." He said, "I can't believe it! It's a godsend. I don't know how to thank your friend for this opportunity."

I gave my friend the money to pay his "night watchman," and

he gave him a check every two weeks. After about three months, he took the medical exam and passed with flying colors. He said, "Without your friend I never would have passed. I owe him my life." I thought to myself, "*I'm your friend.*" But I never said a word.

I was invited to lecture at some of the leading dermatological institutes in the States. At my first presentation before a group of about 90 doctors, I was a little too "off the cuff" and used expressions like, "It was so painful, the patient wanted to escape. But we captured him." After the conference, Dr. Kopf reprimanded me and bluntly said it was the worst talk he'd ever heard. He insisted I rehearse any future presentations. I took it to heart and never forgot that lesson.

Once, I was lecturing before a group of plastic surgeons in New York, demonstrating the advantages of the chemosurgery technique. I talked about how we remove the tumor layer by layer until we can trace the cancer out to its extensions, or roots. After the talk was over, during the question and answer phase, a plastic surgeon got up and said he'd never heard such hogwash in all his life. He said that plastic surgeons were very competent and knew how to remove all the cancer cells the first time around. He said there was no need to go back again and again for tiny, successive layers of tissue.

After his comments, there was light applause from the audience, and the moderator, who was a friend of Phil Casson's, said, "Would you like me to answer him?" I kept my cool and said, "No, he verbally attacked me. I will answer him." I said, "Sir, I want to thank you for your comments. I appreciate them. I just hope that I'm invited back in a few years with more evidence to prove how effective this method is, and at that time, there will be nobody in the audience who will agree with you."

I remember one occasion after a lecture at Emory College in Atlanta, I was given a cup with the words "visiting professor" engraved on it. I was so proud of that! It was the first time I had ever been called a professor, and I was so glad that chemosurgery was starting to be accepted. When I began to teach, I insisted to all my trainees that when they talked about cancer, regardless of the type, they must be 100 percent serious. It is cancer, and we respect it.

As I acquired experience, I attended more medical conferences and presented many cases at the meetings. Unfortunately, the cases I chose were all big. As a result, the dermatologists referring patients to us felt it was inappropriate to send a small skin cancer case, or one that had never been treated before—the type that would have been much more easily curable. Most of the cases that I treated then were extensive ones, or even horrendous ones—huge cancers that had been treated five, eight or 10 times without stopping the cancer before being referred to us. Nonetheless, we were persistent, and often successful.

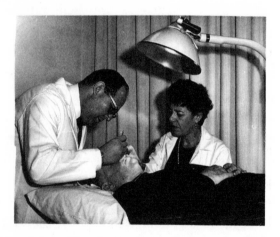

I didn't need gloves while performing chemosurgery (here with medical assistant Leona Mandell), as there was no bleeding.

We had some very tough cases, though, and some of the patients, frankly, were just inoperable. For example, one was an 85-year-old woman who had a lesion on her scalp. It was so foul smelling that her coworkers insisted that she see a physician. She had been covering it with a wig. I proceeded to apply the zinc chloride paste to the lesion, but we found out the next day that the tumor I was planning to treat had destroyed the bone and penetrated the brain tissue. She remained in the hospital for two weeks and died.

In my first year using chemosurgery, I treated 70 patients, and each year that number increased slowly. I found that the technique could also work well in other locations besides the head and face. For example, a few patients were referred to me with skin cancers on their fingers that were scheduled for amputation, and I was able to save the digit. Some also were referred to me with cancers on the penis, and we saved those from amputation as well.

Dr. Kopf taught me so many things that helped me to be a better doctor and surgeon. First, he insisted we keep impeccable records on punch cards to be computerized (I always knew how many surgeries I'd done). Second, he recognized the value of the technique and felt that doctors practicing it should be well trained. I did, too, even though Dr. Mohs was opposed to such formal training. In 1967 I was thrilled to be named assistant professor of dermatology at NYU Medical Center, and in 1968, Dr. Kopf helped me establish the first one-year fellowship training program in dermatologic surgery at NYU.

"Without Perry, I'm not sure the field of dermatologic surgery would exist today," Dr. Kopf said in 2017. "Mohs surgery would have grown anyway, but plastic surgery is the most likely field it would have found as its resting place."

"Fred Mohs himself, at that time, had not gained much professional acceptance," said Phil Casson in 2004 (sadly, he passed away in 2006). "Thanks to Perry, there was acceptance for the Mohs technique, which had not existed before, and then he also brought it *prestige*. His biggest contribution, in my opinion, was his establishment of the fellowship program."

We taught the full complement of skills required to perform the technique successfully, including head, neck and ocular surgery; medical and surgical oncology; gross anatomy; dermatopathology;

wound care; and plastic and reconstructive surgery. Dermatologists began coming from around the country and from other countries such as Germany and Portugal to train with me, which helped disseminate the technique to Europe and elsewhere.

HAUNTED?

Although Dr. Strominger, my mentor while I was in the Army in Tokyo, had threatened to haunt me for the rest of my life if I didn't become a pediatrician, I never felt it. In fact, quite the contrary. I think he was happy that I went into skin cancer surgery and helped so many people. I often thought about looking him up, but I never did, and he died in 1983. I met doctors through the years who were at Barnes Jewish Hospital in St. Louis, and they remembered him. They always said he was a great teacher. There's still an endowed professorship in his name at St. Louis Children's Hospital. I loved being a skin cancer surgeon so much. I love knowing that if I hadn't cut out those cancers, people would have died. I loved saving lives. That's an achievement that is second to none. Therefore, I never felt bad that I chose not to go into pediatrics after all.

A dermatologist from the south of France named Robert Baran came to NYU to learn more about American dermatology. He spoke almost no English. My skills in French, despite quite a few visits to France, remained only adequate. Always eager to improve, though, I invited Dr. Baran to my office and we hung out together. He improved my French more than I improved his English. Soon we bonded and became good friends—which we are to this day. He would often call and say, "Perry, when are you going to come to France?" I'd say, "I'll come this summer." "Perry, when are you coming to France?" I'd reply, "I'll come this fall," et cetera. He'd say,

"Perry, my goodness, what is wrong with you? I asked you so many times, and you don't come."

"There's one way to make sure I come," I said. "We're going to start a meeting in France, and therefore I have to come, *non*?" I called it the International Chemosurgery Group. He arranged to have the meeting at a five-star hotel near his home in southern France in Saint-Paul-de-Vence. There were only about 12 or 13 people there, since so few doctors were doing chemosurgery at that time. We had fun and a lot of laughs, though, including when one of the doctors who came to my villa wasn't looking where he was going and walked right into the pool. Later, to help the organization grow, we decided to call it the International Society for Dermatologic Surgery (ISDS).

As for my home life, I was almost too busy to think about it, although I knew it wasn't what I had hoped. I was working all the time, or traveling, and Ingrid was often flying for TWA, too. It was a much more glamorous era for travel, that's for sure. Thanks to Ingrid's flight benefits, I would travel with her when I could—first class when the seats were available. She was such a good-natured person, but we were just totally different. I loved practicing my languages, but she didn't want to speak German with me. She said, "No, you don't need German anymore. I want to improve my English." Her parents were both in Germany, and her mother was a beautiful, wonderful person. I liked to be able to speak to them in their native language. When Ingrid was flying overseas and would have a two-day layover in Frankfurt or Paris or Milan, sometimes I would cancel my Friday patients and join her.

When I was invited to speak at Heidelberg University School of Medicine in the Department of Dermatology, I did need to polish up my German. Ingrid came with me, although she didn't attend my lecture. I was thrilled to be able to give something back to the place that had given me so much. I said, "It is such an honor to be invited back to lecture where I was a student. I sat in these same seats, listened to the same lectures—and slept through some of them." That got a laugh. I shared with them how I became a pioneer and was changing the way people thought about dermatology by bringing skin cancer surgery into the specialty. I ended by saying, "I hope each of you can achieve something important in your life, remember where you came from and also have the honor of giving back." I was touched when the students gave me the traditional German academic version of enthusiastic applause by knocking or pounding on the tables. It was a thunderous sound I'll never forget.

Since we had some vacation days, Ingrid and I were planning to travel from Heidelberg to France to visit Robert Baran. The weather was cold, rainy and miserable, though, so I suggested a slight detour. I said, "Let's go to the land of milk and honey." We got on a TWA flight to Tel Aviv, stayed in Israel for three days and then headed to Cannes, France. We went to Robert's home, but he wasn't there, so we stopped at a restaurant where I'd eaten with him before. After we were seated, the manager hurried over and said, "Excuse me, do you have news from the States?" "No," I said. "What has happened?" She said, "You're Dr. Baran's friend, *oui*? They've been looking for you for several days. Please call home." I found a pay phone and learned that while Ingrid and I were relaxing in Israel, my father had died.

The long flight home was grim. Ingrid was kind, but her German stoicism was not exactly comforting. I flashed back to the horror of my mother's unexpected death and not being with her when it happened. Similarly, I felt guilty for not being there for my father when he needed me most.

I learned that my father's entire life savings amounted to $10,000, and I knew how hard he'd worked and sacrificed to save that. I hoped I could do better. My father had adored Irene's young daughter, Fern, and called her the apple of his eye. He often promised to buy her a car when she was older. After my father's death,

Irene wanted to give Fern one-third of the $10,000 and split the other two-thirds between the two of us. I felt that our father's savings were meant to be split 50-50 between Irene and me. I was still struggling financially, and that money was important to help my practice and my family grow. She finally agreed, but then we didn't speak to each other for a couple of years.

Looking sharp with my father (above), when I was about 13.

That was a sad, tough time for me, with criticism coming at me on the work front as well as the home front. I tried to keep my sense of perspective and did what I could to keep the peace. Ingrid and I attended some counseling sessions together. The therapist said, "When you have kids, it'll help bring the family together, because you'll share a responsibility." In the spring of 1969, as "You've Made Me So Very Happy" by Blood, Sweat & Tears played constantly on the radio, I learned that I was going to be a father.

CHAPTER 10

Smiley Face

*Staying positive as I juggle my roles
as a father, husband, surgeon, professor,
mentor, innovator, investor and citizen
of the world.*

Ingrid decided to stop flying for TWA, at least for a while. We also decided to look for a place in New York City to be closer to NYU Medical Center, where Ingrid would deliver the baby, and to shorten my daily commute from the farm. We found a three-bedroom, three-bath apartment in Washington Square Village, a complex often used for NYU faculty housing. The rent was $212 a month.

On the evening of July 20, 1969, Ingrid and I watched TV in amazement as astronaut Neil Armstrong, in grainy black-and-white, climbed down the ladder of the lunar module and stepped onto the surface of the moon. Apollo 11 seemed like a miracle. I was embracing my expanding role as a professor and lecturer, although to my younger self that would have seemed about as unlikely as a walk on the moon. I gave a talk on chemosurgery at Geisinger Medical Center in Danville, Pennsylvania, and a young dermatology resident there became interested in learning the procedure from me. In the fall of '69, Henry W. "Bud" Menn, MD, became my first chemosurgery trainee in our yearlong program. (He went on to become the first chemosurgeon at the University of Miami.)

The Beatles' *Abbey Road* was the number one album in America that fall, even though the band was actually falling apart. As Ingrid's pregnancy progressed, I hoped a baby would allow our little family to "come together," as the first song on that album is titled. On October 9, John Lennon turned 29—and our baby boy was born. We named him Lawrence Edward (the "L" is a tribute to my father, Lewis, and the "E" honors my mother, Esther).

He was an extraordinarily beautiful baby. With his golden blond hair and sweet smile, people would stop us and say he should do modeling. Everyone fussed over him and pampered him. It was exciting to be a father, and when everyone raves about your child, how can you not be proud? Most of the nurturing, however, fell to Ingrid. With my traveling, lecturing, organizing meetings, seeing patients, performing surgeries and training other doctors, I wasn't there much for diaper changes, feeding or reading bedtime stories. We hired an au pair that we loved but were disappointed when she decided to return to her native Germany.

I had accepted an invitation to lecture at the Medical Center of the University of Munich at the end of 1969, so Ingrid and I decided to take the baby and spend the holidays in Germany. I had recently met a distributor for the Swiss skiwear line Bogner, and he said he could get me new boots and skis at wholesale prices. How could I resist such a bargain? I had done a little skiing and Ingrid was an expert, so we decided to visit our former au pair, meet her husband and hit the slopes near Oberammergau in Bavaria.

The snowy peaks were stunning, there was a holiday spirit in the air and I was excited to try out my new equipment. The au pair's husband and I were on the tow line for the idiots' hill when I realized my new boots and ski bindings had not been adjusted properly. When one ski fell off, I let go of the line and tried to gain my balance on one ski to retrieve it. Instead, I slid sideways on the icy slope, fell and fractured my tibia.

At the local hospital, a doctor put a cast on my leg, said I would heal in two to three months and told me to follow up with a physician back home. I decided the show must go on, so I traveled clumsily on crutches to my lecture in Munich.

Günter Burg was the resident on duty at the University of Munich that evening, assigned to handle the slide projector for the lecture. He remembers: "It was Christmastime, and there weren't many of us sitting in the auditorium. In walked this big American, with a cast on his leg from a ski accident, to teach us about chemosurgery. I was expecting to be bored, but instead, I was intrigued."

The chairman of the Department of Dermatology decided to send this young resident to train with me for six months in 1970. "One year later, chemosurgery was started in Munich and soon spread all over Europe, thanks to Dr. Robins' active mentorship, guidance and promotion," says Dr. Burg. He went on to become chairman of the Department of Dermatology at University School of Medicine in Zurich, Switzerland, and we've remained good friends.

Ingrid and I were missing our former TWA fringe benefits. She and her friend Joanne, who had worked for American Airlines, decided to start a travel agency called Professional Travel in Cherry Hill, New Jersey. I invested a few shekels to get the thing started, since it came with a lot of travel benefits. Joanne's husband, Jim, was a great chap and became one of my best friends. He was so charming, we would go on a cruise together and within a few hours he would know everyone on the ship.

Jim was a heavy smoker, and he had a nagging cough. I told him many times he should get it checked, but he always had an excuse, saying it was just a lingering cold or an allergy. When he was diagnosed with advanced lung cancer and died, we were all devastated. Joanne didn't want to see me anymore because I reminded her too much of her husband and all the wonderful times together. It hurt. We sold the travel agency and, to my great sadness, stopped seeing each other.

Since I'd always done a little moonlighting, had a passion for the airline industry and missed those free travel benefits, I wrote to several airlines telling them that I would like to be their medical officer. I talked with the Irish airline, Aer Lingus, but they wanted someone with more experience in internal medicine. Then I met with the people from El Al, but their flight coupons were too limited. I liked Lufthansa, where I'd be able to practice my German. While it would pay me only $10 for a patient visit, it offered good flight benefits, so I took the gig.

It was fun for a while, but several things happened that started to sour me on it. Some of the patients required a lot of paperwork and inconvenient hospital visits—at $10 a pop. When Ingrid and I signed up to go on a safari in Kenya, we planned our flight using my Lufthansa benefits. The flight was wide open, as they say in the business. But when we arrived at Kennedy Airport, there was a woman from Alaska Airlines with five kids and higher priority benefits than we had, and some others, too. Suddenly only one seat was left. So we paid full fare for a flight to Frankfurt, then caught another flight to Rome, and then yet another flight on Zambia Airlines to Nairobi. We missed the first day of the tour, and Lufthansa would not reimburse me for the unexpected expense.

I went to a meeting in Hamburg, where I met the medical director for Lufthansa and learned how to give patients prescription pills when they cross the international date line, calculating the time differences and dosages. He often bragged about how Germans are the best drivers in the world. I said, "They're crazy. They all think they've got little Messerschmitts flying down the highway." He said, "No, no, when you drive fast, you have to be careful." Unfortunately, a few months later, his daughter, who also worked for Lufthansa, and her fiancé were speeding down the highway, missed a turn and were both tragically killed.

I decided I'd had enough and quit the Lufthansa job. My practice was getting busier anyway. And my invitations to speak on chemosurgery now usually included airfare. I wondered if I could start asking for business class on international flights. Hey, I'm not a petite guy; I needed as much legroom as I could get!

An alternative way of performing chemosurgery began to emerge late in 1970, and it would change the course of dermatologic surgery—and my life.

When we treated skin cancer around the eyes, we couldn't use the zinc chloride paste to fix the tissue because its caustic nature would damage the cornea and cause blindness. Dr. Mohs had shown me how to use a local anesthetic to numb the area and then excise a layer of tissue in the same manner as if the paste had been used. He had been using this technique around the eyes for years. Meanwhile, at the University of California, San Francisco, Ted Tromovitch, MD, a professor of dermatology, and his colleague Samuel Stegman, MD, were experimenting with using this "fresh tissue" technique on other areas of the body besides the eyes. Dr. Tromovitch presented more than 100 of these cases at the December 1970 Chemosurgery Society Meeting in Chicago, and it caused quite a stir.

When I asked Dr. Tromovitch what had motivated him to study this, he told me that he had visited two physician brothers in northern California who worked together doing chemosurgery. On a typical Monday one brother would apply the paste to the cancer site, and on Tuesday he would remove the first layer of tissue. If it was still positive with more cancer cells and needed another layer excised, he would reapply the paste and leave the lesion "map" for his brother to continue the surgery on Wednesday. The second brother would excise the fixed tissue, and if it was still positive (by then usually in a very small area), he decided to just numb the site and then take the additional tissue without applying the paste. It worked well, and it was less painful and much faster. But he kept it to himself because he assumed his brother would have objected.

Dr. Tromovitch's study results were good, and there were clear advantages to doing the surgery this way. Still, I was skeptical at first, saying, "This is heresy. How can you call yourself a chemo-surgeon if there's no chemical fixative?" He simply replied, "Try it; you'll like it." I decided to look into it.

E. William Rosenberg, MD, chairman of the Department of Der-matology at the University of Tennessee, had seen one of my presenta-tions on chemosurgery and thought it made sense for dermatologists to learn how to perform this treatment. He suggested that one of his residents, Rex A. Amonette, MD, apply for my fellowship.

"Dr. Rosenberg knew that I had better hands than most of the other residents. I'd done some surgery when I was in the Air Force," Dr. Amonette says. "He said, 'Rex, there's this new thing coming out that seems really popular and important. You might want to look into it.' I flew to New York in January 1971 to interview with Perry, and I knew right away that I wanted to work with him."

The soft-spoken, genteel Southern gentleman and I hit it off right away, and I accepted him as my second American chemo-surgery fellow. He and his wife, Johnnie, and their two little girls moved to New York that summer.

"Our year in New York was a great experience," Dr. Amonette says. "Dr. Robins was so kind. He set us up in an apartment across the street from where he lived, looking downtown to where the World Trade Center's twin towers were under construction. We went to work together every day. We loved New York from the start. It was a great honor for me to get to know Perry and to learn from him."

I taught Rex chemosurgery, but we also did some cases together using the fresh tissue technique around the eye. We began to study the effectiveness of the new method, comparing it with the fixed tissue technique, something I would continue for several years.

When Dr. Amonette completed his training, he took his skills back to Memphis and started a movement to do chemosurgery there. "It was like starting all over," he says. "No one was excited about this, or even knew about it. I had to do some persuading."

It was comforting to have someone else know what I'd been going through. Rex was a pioneer for chemosurgery in the South, and he faced some pretty harsh resistance to the technique.

Dr. Amonette describes what it was like at that time: "I was giving a lecture about the surgery and I noticed a man in the back of the room pacing, clearly agitated. I thought, *This one is going to be trouble.* I had already picked him out as a surgeon who felt I was infringing on his territory. When I finished my slides and lecture, I saw a roll from the buffet flying toward my head. I ducked, and it didn't hit me.

"Then the surgeon in the back yelled, 'That's the craziest thing I have ever heard of in my life!' I kept my composure and said, 'Well, sir, what if in your removal you don't get all of the tumor out?' He said, 'I'll take the patient back to the operating room and cut it out again.' I said, 'Well, how many times would you do that before you stop?' He said, 'Eight, ten times, whatever it takes.'

"In those days skin cancer patients were often treated many times like that, sometimes going under general anesthesia. I had explained that you didn't have to do that with chemosurgery. At the end of the procedure, with the lab work done on-site while the patient waited, you knew that you had gotten all the cancer cells. I looked at the audience, with many surgeons sitting there, and when I looked into their eyes, I knew I had won the battle. I started getting referrals quickly after that," Dr. Amonette says.

Meanwhile, I'd been working on a little restaurant project with a few of my *copains français.* On a visit to Cannes, I had met Robert Baran's cousin Pierre Levy when he and several friends had greeted me at a restaurant wearing neckties with their swim trunks, cheering, *"Vive l'Américain!"* It was hilarious. Pierre had been working in dry goods for the fashion industry, but *prêt-à-porter* ready-to-wear clothing was killing the business, and he wanted to try a new venture.

His English was very good, as he had served as a translator for American troops stationed in Paris during World War II, and he liked us Yanks. He had observed the proliferation of fast-food chains in the U.S. in the 1960s and decided to come to the States and talk to McDonald's about creating a franchise in Paris. I know. *Quelle horreur* for those who love French cuisine. Nevertheless, he asked me, along with Robert Baran and another French dermatologist, if we'd consider investing in this project. I'd managed to save a few shekels, so I said yes.

The McDonald's people told Pierre, "We would like to give you Paris, but you'd also have to take over all of France." That was going to be expensive. Pierre said, "No, we don't want all of France. We don't have that much money. We just want to open one in Paris." They said, "Sorry, that's impossible."

Pierre stayed with me for a couple of weeks in New York and hired a consultant who worked with other fast-food companies. They came up with the idea of an American Wild West–themed joint in the heart of Paris, and it was going to be called "Frenchie's Saloon." *Pourquoi pas?*

Next came the difficult task of finding the right spot for it. In Paris, it's hard to find affordable space because so many buildings are under long-term leases of 99 years. You have to shell out "key money" to the lease owner, and you can imagine that in the heart of Paris the cost would be prohibitive. Pierre was clever, though. He negotiated a low price for half of two buildings and then got a permit to combine them. At 123 Champs-Élysées near the Arc de Triomphe, it was a great location and a great deal. A beer company lent us $100,000 with an agreement that we carry its brands, and that helped us get started. It took about six months to acquire all the necessary permits before the saloon opened in the spring of 1972—with a literal *bang*.

Old West-style "gunfights" were staged outside of Frenchie's, but the actors spoke French!

"Main Street" was always mobbed, in the heart of Paris.

The servers wore cowboy outfits and carried real pistols in their belts (we had the firing pins removed). "Gunfights" were enacted out front, complete with a stagecoach. Many guests came in costume, and everyone had a blast. We served water like any American restaurant, but the French customers often said, "*Monsieur,* you are crazy. We do not want to rust our pipes! We don't want water; we want wine!"

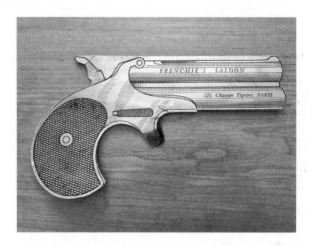

The cocktail menus shaped like a derringer were so fun to play with, everyone stole them. Priced in French francs, a local beer was about 70 cents, a dry martini $1.60 and a bottle of Moët et Chandon Brut Imperial Champagne was $10. We served "pioneer cuisine" with a French twist, such as a steakburger with Roquefort. A Texas newspaper reported:

PASSEZ-VOUS LE KETCHUP!

Texans visiting Paris may be surprised to find Southwestern style cooking in a new restaurant on the Champs-Élysées. They'll feel right at home in "Frenchie's Saloon," because the decorations consist of travel posters furnished by the Texas Highway Department. Turnabout is fair play, we suppose, and if there's a Maxim's in Houston, why not a barbecue stand on the Champs-Élysées?

The formula felt right for the times. Customers loved it, and the restaurant started to do well. We began to negotiate with the through-way authority to open restaurants on the highways outside Paris. Pierre thought he would be able to raise money from other investors, because we were making a profit in less than a year, which is unheard of in the restaurant business.

We thought we were in like Flynn. But on the night of September 28, 1972, a fire rapidly spread through the seven-story building next to Frenchie's. Occupied by Nazis during World War II, that building then housed the headquarters of the Publicis ad agency as well as the famous night spot Le Drugstore, with its bar, restaurant, pharmacy and cinema. Hundreds of people were evacuated, and one was killed. The building was completely destroyed.

Rumors circulated that the fire had been a terrorist attack. On the *CBS Evening News,* Walter Cronkite reported that Le Drugstore was a Jewish-owned business and that Black September Palestinian terrorists had claimed responsibility for the blaze. Later, however, investigators determined that the fire had started in garbage cans in the basement and the claims had been prank calls. (We weren't so sure.)

After the fire, people said, "Oh, now Frenchie's has no competition. You're going to be an instant success!" Because of the destruction and investigation, though, that side of the Champs-Élysées was blocked off for a long time. The only way to get into Frenchie's was to go in through the back door and, of course, nobody did.

We ended up selling the space to investors who put in a steakhouse that's still there. So, I lost a couple of shekels on it—but not much. It was my first big deal, and of course I was disappointed. If it weren't for that fire, we might have been a big operator of restaurants up and down the French highways.

I didn't let it get me down, especially since just a few weeks earlier, on August 8, 1972, Ingrid and I had a beautiful baby girl. I was scheduled to appear on a TV news program that morning to talk about sun protection and skin cancer, so once I knew Ingrid and the baby were fine, I left the hospital to head to the studio. On the air, the hosts shared the news, saying, "Oh, you just had a daughter. What's her name?" Without thinking, I blurted out, "Elizabeth Rachel Robins." It just sounded regal to me. When I returned to the hospital afterward, Ingrid said, "Well, I'm glad I now know the name of our daughter." *Oops.* We hadn't discussed it first. Ingrid said she hoped I hadn't named her after my former Danish girlfriend of the same name, but I hadn't. The "E" was to honor my mother, Esther, and I had always thought Elizabeth was a beautiful name.

Baby Elizabeth was very quiet and sweet, and caused no problems at all. Lawrence, not so much. Now almost 3 and more beautiful than ever, he was used to being the center of attention, pampered by absolutely everybody. His world probably felt like it was crumbling when his little sister came along to steal some of his thunder. He became angry and jealous and would even try to hit her. We had to watch him like a hawk. Most of that responsibility fell on Ingrid, as I was so busy at work, and also lecturing and traveling. We were a little worried about Lawrence. Luckily, we had found another good au pair to help out.

In my practice, it was starting to become clear to me that the fresh tissue technique was probably the way to go. That first year it was introduced, I did about a third of my cases using this new technique, and two-thirds with the chemical fixative. The next year, it was half and half, and the next year I was using the fresh tissue procedure two-thirds of the time. Although I'd been skeptical at first, my study showed that the two ways of doing the surgery were equally effective. The newer technique had many advantages, including less pain, you could finish many cases in one day and you could begin repair and reconstruction the same day. Starting in 1974, I used the fresh tissue technique in all my cases.

Dr. Amonette recalls: "Even after I was in Memphis for a few years, I was still doing the fixed tissue technique because we didn't think fresh tissue was the way to go. But by golly, we were mistaken about that." Soon he was exclusively using the new technique, too.

WHATCHAMACALLIT?

At first, the two methods of surgery were called **chemosurgery fixed tissue** technique and **chemosurgery fresh tissue** technique. But it seemed absurd to keep using "chemosurgery" as part of the title when we were no longer using the chemical fixative. In 1974, dermatologist Daniel Jones, MD, coined the term "micrographic surgery" to highlight the procedure's use of the microscope and the drawing of tissue maps. Eventually the name was officially changed to **Mohs micrographic surgery,** but for brevity's sake, many just call it **Mohs surgery.**

Of course, Dr. Mohs started it all, but Dr. Tromovitch and Dr. Stegman, who both died in 1990, deserve credit for being the fathers of this great improvement to the procedure. Some people think I deserve the credit for its growth. "Robins surgery" has a nice ring to it, don't you think? I'm kidding, of course. But it is true that an estimated 40 percent of the dermatologists performing Mohs surgery today were trained by me or one of my students. I truly feel I have been one of the greatest proponents of Mohs surgery, and perhaps most responsible for its success.

As always, I remain grateful to Dr. Alfred Kopf, who paved the way. He says, "Perry is recognized today for his persistence in introducing this remarkable procedure in our department at NYU but also subsequently for his spreading its use worldwide. I'm proud that I played a role in that."

If I thought I was busy before, when word got out about the fresh tissue technique curing nonmelanoma skin cancers, my practice didn't just boom; it exploded. When I went to the American Academy of Dermatology meetings, I'd go up an escalator and there would be people waiting in line at the top to talk to me. Doctors wanted to learn the technique. Residents wanted to be trained in it. Everybody was dying for a new idea, a new concept and new skills. We had visitors come to NYU from all over the world to see what we were doing.

People assumed I was a rich doctor, but I didn't feel like one. I had been struggling for years to build a specialty and a practice, and I never seemed to be able to get ahead. Ingrid and I had lived frugally in the first years of our marriage, first living on the farm, then in the NYU apartment in Greenwich Village. We were both so busy we didn't have time for many extravagant evenings or shopping expeditions. We used flight benefits for as much of our travel as possible.

I had been scrimping and saving since I was a boy, always dreaming of a better life than my parents had. I loved practicing medicine, getting to know my patients and treating skin cancers. That was rewarding beyond belief. But by the mid-1970s, well into my 40s, I was getting tired of living hand to mouth. I was longing for some of the fancy trappings I'd always imagined. Ingrid and I had two young children and fantasies of owning a beautiful house in the suburbs for them to grow up in. I had always been interested in real estate, like my father and his brothers had been before the Great Depression squashed their dreams. Ingrid loved looking at houses, too. Maybe it was time to just mortgage ourselves to the hilt and go for it. That's the Great American Dream, right?

CHAPTER 11

Acquiring the Trappings

I've always longed for wealth and security;
will buying the perfect home, boat or plane
give me the perfect life?

I knew it when I saw it: a sprawling white elephant of an English Tudor in Rye, New York, north of Manhattan in Westchester County. Ridiculously huge and showy with more bedrooms and bathrooms than I could count, it was my childhood Great Gatsby fantasy come to life. On Long Island Sound near the Connecticut border, the 10,000-square-foot fieldstone manse was set on 10 acres with beautiful trees, an arboretum and a large pool and cabana.

Priced at $250,000, the house was more than we could afford, and certainly more than we needed. But I loved it and wanted to create a wonderful new life there.

During that frenetic time in the mid-1970s, as Karen Carpenter warbled about being on "Top of the World," when you couldn't avoid the Captain and Tennille optimistically hoping that "Love Will Keep Us Together," I felt driven to create the perfect life I'd always dreamed of. In addition to my usual work and travel during those years, I plunged in and bought the big house, moved to the suburbs, took flying and sailing lessons, acquired planes and boats, dabbled in plane and boat side businesses, and even started up and ran a medical journal.

How did I do all this, and *why*? I'm not sure. Being a child of the Depression and watching my parents struggle for every dime as I grew up had influenced me, of course. My folks had big dreams, but they couldn't make them happen. I had seen my father give up, retreat and not even try. I had been a passive child, but somewhere along the way, I'd learned by doing. I'd become a man of action! I wanted to see and do it all, and I kept pushing to achieve success. I wasn't going to stop now, but I knew it would take some extremely creative accounting.

I qualified for a mortgage of $100,000, scraped together what cash I could and then negotiated terms with the owner to pay off the balance. I guess I confidently projected "rich doctor in the making," because the owner accepted my plan.

I sold off two lots on the site to help pay for the house and some needed renovations, and I put a lot of sweat equity into it, too. I used all those "good with my hands" skills to fix up the upstairs bedrooms, the attic, the laundry room, the finished basement. Of course, the place became a money pit, and one expense begat another. Where I would have been happy with simple comfort, Ingrid went for elegance and commissioned an expensive interior designer from Bloomingdale's. We didn't agree on anything that came into the house. What did I need with a fancy chandelier when there wasn't a comfortable chair where I could sit and read the paper?

I asked a gardener to put in a couple of rose bushes around the pool. Then I saw him unloading rose bushes and more rose bushes from his truck—he'd bought about 100. I said, "Are you crazy? I only wanted three or four!" He said, "Mister, this place is fabulous. Three or four rose bushes wouldn't do anything. You need 100! You can afford it." I said, "Yeah, right."

The long driveway had a beautiful old wrought iron railing along one side. I went to the local high school to recruit some kids to help scrape the rust off it, and a couple of them came over on their bicycles after classes. I had offered to pay a wage of 50 cents an hour. When they arrived, they looked at the house and said, "We think we should get more money. This is a very expensive house." Everybody wanted a piece of me! And yes, I had to renegotiate with the high school "labor union."

The residence was just half a block from the water, with access to a nearby dock where I hoped I could make my yachting dreams come true. The kids loved the grounds and the big house. We had two beautiful but rather undisciplined dogs. Gigi was a gorgeous white standard poodle that the previous owner of the house had given us. Gigi loved to jump into the pool and swim whenever she felt like it, but she also suffered from wanderlust and would occasionally escape for new adventures. A work colleague of Ingrid's gave us King, a Doberman pinscher. King got along fine with Gigi but not the neighbors' dogs, so we eventually had to find him a new family. I wanted us all to live happily ever after, but to be honest, I'm not sure our place in Rye ever really felt like home.

Ingrid loved to fly, and she wanted to take flying lessons. I encouraged her to do it. We lived close to the airport in Westchester, so she started flight training there and acquired her pilot's license. She was a natural.

I liked flying with Ingrid, and we thought about leasing a plane for our own use. Friends strongly suggested that I take some basic "pinch hitter" flight training in case the pilot ever became incapacitated. But instead of doing that I said, "Why don't I just get a license, too?" Of course, I couldn't take a big chunk of time off from work to do it right, so I did a little bit of flight training in New Orleans, a bit at Teterboro in New Jersey. I took a few lessons in Westchester, and a few more in Vero Beach, Florida. I learned the basics: how to take off, turn and land. But I was not a stellar pilot by any means.

I hadn't let fear stop me from much in life, but I had an epiphany while I was doing my first solo flight from St. Augustine to Fort Myers, Florida. I was flying at 10,000 feet over Orlando by myself and suddenly thought, *What the hell am I doing up here? I must be out of my mind! If I need a pilot, I can always hire one.*

But I wanted to pass the exam and so talked myself into doing another solo flight, from Westchester Airport to Hartford, Connecticut, then to Bridgeport and back to Westchester. I felt like I knew the highways by heart, so I said, "Oh I don't need to watch the compass; I'll just follow the highway." I touched down in Hartford to get my logbook signed, as required. As I was approaching Bridgeport for the second part, the controller said, "Flap your wings when you're five miles out." I flapped my wings and he said, "We don't see you. Flap your wings again." I flapped again. "We still don't see you. How many runways do you see?" I said, "I see two." And they said, "You're not in Bridgeport; we only have one runway." My overconfidence had sent me off course to New Haven, which has two runways. *Oops.*

I said I was sorry, then headed south to Bridgeport, where I landed safely. The instructor wrote in my logbook, "He needs more training." That was humbling. After I earned my ticket (my license, that is), I never flew alone again. I figured the life I'd save would probably be my own. After that, I would take off and land the plane, but I always had a pilot with me.

We acquired a Piper Turbo Arrow III in Vero Beach, Florida, where the factory is located, after a salesman convinced me it would pay for itself as a tax write-off. It was a nice little single-engine, and Ingrid and I took a few trips together in it. We flew up to Nova Scotia and landed at Kejimkujik National Park one weekend. We learned that fuel was sold only on weekdays, and I needed to get back on Sunday. We had half a tank, and a storm was brewing in the area.

Always an optimist, I said, "Well, we can probably go around the storm and still make it back on half a tank." But Ingrid was emphatic, and I'll give her credit for that. She said, "Absolutely not. You need a full tank of fuel. Weather can change in a second, and it can add hundreds of miles to a trip." We waited until Monday morning, got fueled up and returned safely. I wasn't even late for work.

We never used the plane for business; it wasn't cost-effective. When I traveled to give lectures, the host would usually send me a commercial plane ticket. Once, however, after lecturing at the beautiful Sunriver Resort near Bend, Oregon, I had to take a private puddle jumper to get back to Portland to catch my flight home. I enjoyed it, but the pilot wouldn't let me fly it. I said, "I could do the takeoff." He just said, "No, no, no, no."

We traded in the Piper for a Cessna 172. Ingrid gave lessons on that one. Eventually we upgraded to a Beechcraft Baron twin-engine that seated six, which seemed like a good deal. But after a couple of years, we sold it. We were having marital problems and we just didn't use it enough.

After buying the Baron, above, I even bought and sold used aircraft for a while, but that business never really got off the ground.

Since I seldom just dabble in anything but tend to go full throttle, I let the man who sold me the Baron convince me to go into business with him, buying and selling used aircraft. When that didn't go so well, it morphed into a real estate subdivision deal in New Jersey (where we named one of the streets Robins Lane). I was always dreaming about my next big deal—the one that would really pay off.

As Mohs surgery started to catch on, I wanted to ensure that more dermatologists in other parts of the world could learn how to do it. In 1974, as the resignation of President Nixon grabbed all the headlines, I closed my practice for almost five weeks and flew to Sydney, Australia, which has very high rates of skin cancer, to train doctors there. It had taken me six months of paperwork to get a temporary license, and I was only the fourth American to do so. But it was worth it. I didn't want to claim Mohs surgery as just my thing, or an American technique. I wanted to share it with everybody.

When I arrived, about 10 newsmen crowded around me. They said, "Dr. Robins, we hear you have a technique that has a 99 percent cure rate for cancer." I said, "Yes, for skin cancer that has never been treated before, that is true." They said, "Since Australians have the highest rate of skin cancer, don't you think you should have been here earlier to make it available? Do you think the doctors were negligent for not bringing you here?" I thought fast, and answered, diplomatically, "No, quite the contrary. They were prudent and astute because they waited for the evidence to be unequivocal that this technique did achieve what it claims, and then they brought me here."

My visit garnered a lot of local press, and the Australian dermatologists were very open to the Mohs technique. Most of the Australian plastic surgeons, on the other hand, wouldn't have anything to do with me. Fortunately, there was one plastic surgeon who had trained at NYU and practiced about 30 miles away. He was familiar with the technique and appreciative to be able to do the closures after I removed the tumors (at that time I wasn't doing all my own closures yet).

My Australian hosts couldn't have been nicer. Every night they had a different party or event for me to participate in, including going to the opera, taking a harbor cruise and enjoying many great meals. I learned that Aussies sure can drink and party. They kept me up late at night, and then I had to get up at 6 the next morning to get over to the hospital to do the surgery. On the weekends I did a little sightseeing, and my new mates showed me different parts of the country, from seaside resorts to blowholes that shot water nearly 200 feet into the air—and, of course, kangaroos galore.

When it was time to head back to the States, my hosts threw a farewell celebration for me. I had a late afternoon flight, and the revelers were feeling no pain. We had a hard time finding anyone sober enough to drive me to the airport, and I barely made my flight. In fact, the airline had given away my preferred aisle seat, so I had to squeeze my big, tired body into a cramped middle seat for the long trip home.

I cherish the boomerang from my grateful Australian friends.

I did 39 pro bono surgeries on that visit, many of which had been treated unsuccessfully before, and that started a Mohs surgery movement in Australia. The facility where I did the surgeries is now called The Skin Hospital and is affiliated with the Skin & Cancer Foundation of Australia. They now have several Mohs surgeons on staff. A few years later, I received an aboriginal boomerang from the foundation, with a plaque that reads: "To Perry Robins, the father of Australian Dermatosurgery, from your friends and grateful disciples." It's one of my prized possessions.

SUN WORSHIP IN THE 1970s

In the mid-1970s, tanning was at its fever pitch. Ads proclaimed that you could "turn on your tan" with baby oil. A dark-tanning oil or lotion would give you "the tan people notice," "a better tan" or "a faster tan." It was a status symbol of leisure, wealth and the ability to travel to tropical getaways on spring break or during the holidays. A tan was sexy.

There was also a deeply held belief that sun exposure was necessary, beneficial and healthy. I fought that notion in every TV appearance and article I could. For example, in a July 1973 article in *The New York Times* titled "The Suntan Question: Is the Ritual Worth It?" I said, "This belief is absurd."

We didn't have sunscreens with SPF yet, but I urged for moderation in the sun and use of "creams and lotions that block the ultraviolet rays," which cosmetic companies were starting to produce. The article ended with this prognostication:

While there is no thought that pallor will ever again be a requisite for beauty, there is hope that suntans, as they become ever more common, will eventually lose whatever status is attached to them. "I think it is possible that 20 years from now a person will perhaps say, 'How do you manage to keep out of the sun?'," said Dr. Robins. It was evident that the thought pleased him.

I had always liked boats, ever since the day in 1945 when Buddy Shenkin tipped over the rowboat I was paddling on Lake Hiawatha, New Jersey, and we became best friends. During my epic road trip with Klaus Giese in 1958, I gawked in envy at the enormous yachts moored in the Mediterranean. In 1962, when Dr. Bensel invited me to his home, a photo of his yacht on the Jersey shore helped persuade me to become a dermatologist.

In 1970, on a trip to Annapolis, Maryland, I decided to take several days of sailing lessons and fell in love with the sport. The lessons were on small, stripped-down 20- or 22-foot sailboats. At the end of each season, I learned, the school sold the boats and would get new ones the following season. I inquired about buying one of the boats, but they were already spoken for by people who had taken the course earlier. The seed had been planted, though.

A few years later I took more lessons at a sailing school on City Island in the Bronx. I got to know the instructors and mentioned that I was often in Europe. We did a little entrepreneurial brainstorming, as they had a place on the island where they could sell boats and had lots of experience. I always liked any idea that involved me traveling to find a great bargain product, bringing it back to the States and selling it at a big profit. Just because I hadn't succeeded yet didn't mean I wouldn't this time!

I lined up a vacation where I could visit some sailboat shows. In Hamburg, Germany, I spotted a beautiful 36-foot sloop that was a bargain at $10,000. But I didn't feel comfortable going from a little 22-footer to that, so I passed on it. For my partners I ordered a 42-foot boat, made in Hamburg by a professor who taught marine engineering, to serve as a show boat. In a Paris expo I discovered some beautiful Puma 24-foot sailboats from Spain, which were a steal at around $3,000. We decided to order four of those as samples and hoped to sell many more.

Alas, when the German boat arrived, it was a dog. I mean, really bad. Even though the designer was a marine engineer, he'd never built boats before. The interior was awkward and not user-friendly, and we had to sell it at a loss.

When the four Spanish boats were in transit over the Atlantic, the dollar became devalued, so I knew we were going to have to raise the price to make a profit on those. Meanwhile, my partners were fighting with each other and saying they both wanted out of the deal. I said, "Wait a minute. Let's meet in the lawyer's office in the Pan Am Building; I'm sure we can work it out." I got there at 6 PM. After 7, the lawyer looked at me and said, "Perry, I think you own a sailboat company." *What?* I had paid about $12,000 for the four Pumas, which seemed astronomical. I couldn't afford to do this on my own!

A patient of mine told me he had a boatyard on City Island and that I could rent some space and store the boats there. Several boat shows were coming up, so I hired a fellow to run the company and show the boats. I even had my sister, Irene, working at one of the shows. We had sorted out our differences and were close again, but she didn't know her port from her starboard! Nevertheless, we took orders for 20 boats from the four shows. I was thrilled.

We flew to Barcelona to meet with the boat manufacturer. I was excited and said, "My gosh, we've got 20 orders just from these boat shows. I would expect to sell many more." I ordered 100 boats, 10 a month for 10 months. We set up a little office back at City Island and did some advertising and promotion. And then we waited. And waited.

Ingrid had returned to work at TWA, so I was able to fly free to Barcelona to go to the factory and see what the heck was going on. "Where are our boats?" I'd ask. I didn't speak much Spanish, but my French was good enough to learn that they were selling boats out the back door for the full list price, so our discount wholesale order was never going to be a high priority.

Only a handful of the boats were ever delivered, and the transactions were not exactly smooth sailing. One boat went to a dealer in Boston, who sold it to three or four people and gave us a bum check. We sued him, and the judge said, "If I put him in jail, he can't pay you back, so let him work and pay you back $50 or $100 a month." The guy made two payments and then that stopped, and we were never able to recoup.

Another of the boats went to a dealer in Canada, and the trailer broke down in no-man's land. I got the call while I was in the middle of surgery. I had to hire an international transport company to pick it up, and it cost a fortune to take it to the dealer.

On trips to Italy I had become friends with Luigi Rusciani, MD, who served as the Pope's dermatologist. When I was there for a meeting, I told him about my misadventures in the sailing world, and he said, "Hey, Perry, you want a real sailboat? I know of a beautiful one, a Grand Soleil, very affordable." I drove to the factory in Ferrara, about halfway between Florence and Venice. I recalled the first time I had been to Ferrara with Klaus Giese on our epic trip in 1958. It was where I first heard the song "Volare" and remember saying that I thought it would be a big hit. When I saw the magnificent 48-foot sloop that Luigi had recommended—all gorgeous teak, mahogany and soft Italian leather—I thought *Volare* ("to fly") would the perfect name for it.

I loved the sailboat business, especially on the rare occasions when I made a profit!

Joe Healy, a partner in one of my real estate ventures (more on those later), said, "Perry, I'll partner with you and maybe we can get the distributorship to sell these boats in the States." So we ordered one boat, and the company said they had one with a dealer in Annapolis who wanted to get out of the sailboat business. (Maybe that should have been a warning sign to me.) Anyway, they agreed to sell it to us at a remarkably reduced price.

We performed the naming ceremony and christened the *Volare* with Champagne. We sailed it up from Annapolis to New York and then found a spot for it in Stamford, Connecticut. We moved the boat company's office up there, too. While we never did sell any boats, we loved sailing the *Volare*. She was a beauty. (Joe and I alternated weekend access to it.)

One weekend I invited my trainee Carl to meet me at the dock in Stamford to go sailing for the day. He brought his wife and a baby who was only a few months old. I wasn't expecting that, but I said, "OK, there's a very light breeze, we shouldn't have any problems and I can handle the boat myself."

Carl didn't have any experience, so I did all the work while he sat with his wife and baby. I released the lines, steered us out of the harbor into the sound and raised the sails. We were doing fine. All of a sudden, a squall came up. One of the sheets came loose, and the sail was flapping in the breeze. The boat started swaying right and left, and I could have used a hand. But I didn't think we were in much danger. The wife became hysterical, screaming, "We're gonna die! We're gonna die!!" I tried to stay calm and said, "OK, Carl, come here, hold the wheel and keep the compass at 30 degrees." He had never done it before, and he couldn't keep it steady but would overreact instead of nudging it a bit to bring it back. Finally, I said, "OK, this is terrible." It was time to abort. I immediately dropped the sails and motored us back to port.

Hey, storms happen, and I learned my lesson. If I had fallen overboard, my inexperienced passengers would not have been able to pick me up. I swore I would never go out in that big boat again unless I had a good hand with me. And no babies!

The thrill was gone. After that, it seemed like every time I wanted to use the boat, it was Joe's weekend. And because his construction company wasn't making money, I was making all the payments on the *Volare*. So after about three years, we sold the boat.

My dreams of getting rich off beautiful sailboats had dissipated like a breeze on a hot summer day. It was hard for me to admit I couldn't do it all. I had a million other responsibilities, so I closed down the sailboat company for good.

CHAPTER 12

Building a Foundation

My mother embodied the Jewish proverb
"charity is the spice of life." Giving back
may be the missing ingredient I need.

From the time I began practicing in the mid '60s, I had been longing to create a charitable organization called The Skin Cancer Foundation. My first effort was in 1966, when I needed to raise money to train other doctors in the chemosurgery technique. I wasn't allowed to call it The Skin Cancer Foundation then, because it might cause confusion with the Skin & Cancer Unit at NYU Medical Center.

Instead, I named it the Chemosurgery Research Fund. We organized a couple of fundraising parties at Rockefeller Center, in a restaurant near the ice-skating rink and Promenade (where I wondered if the tree purchased from my family's farm in the 1940s was still growing). We charged a whopping $40 a person at those fundraising parties—far less than the $75 paid for that one tree 20 years earlier! Even at that bargain price, sadly, the Chemosurgery

Research Fund didn't excite anyone, and it only lasted a year. I had to pay for some of my fellowship trainees out of my own pocket.

I wanted to do more to raise awareness about skin cancer, but maybe my idea was still a little ahead of its time. I would try again in the late 1970s, but first, I got myself into a different nonprofit endeavor.

In 1970, some physicians who were doing hair transplants, dermabrasion and other cosmetic procedures had formed an organization called the American Society of Dermatologic Surgery. I hadn't joined at first, since I was focusing entirely on Mohs surgery and the organization wasn't interested in it then. But when George Popkin told me the ASDS wanted to encourage more dermatologists to learn basic dermatologic surgery, he asked me to help. I couldn't say no to Gorgeous George.

I had seen the bad quality mimeographed newsletter the organization had produced. So at a small breakfast meeting in 1974 with a few of the ASDS founders, I impulsively opened my big mouth and said, "What we need to enhance this society is a medical journal." Our budding specialty needed credibility and authority. The attendees there said, "OK, you should do it."

Oy. I immediately started backpedaling, saying, "Why me? I'm the youngest of the group, with the least experience in surgery. And I don't know anything about publishing." I heard some muttering, "Just like everyone else—all talk, talk, talk and no action." Well, you know me. I agreed to see if I could find a company to do it.

I was incredibly busy, so I asked a patient of mine who was having trouble paying her bill if she would like to do some work for me. I asked her to call on a couple of publishers to see if they would be interested in doing a journal on dermatologic surgery. After a week or two, she came back and said, "They laughed at me. They said, 'Why would anyone want to do a journal like that? No one knows anything about dermatologic surgery. It's too new.' "

"OK, forget about it," I said. "You don't owe me anything for the surgery." Later, when I saw her at a Christmas party, she said something that really struck home. She said I was a hypocrite because I believed in this journal but didn't want to put in the work to create it. She was right.

I decided to launch the publication myself and call it *The Journal of Dermatologic Surgery*. Unfortunately, when the officers of the ASDS learned about it, some were vehemently opposed to it. A delegation of three doctors came to my office and said, "You don't know anything about publishing, you're going to fail and it's going to give the specialty a bad reputation. We beg you not to do it." They were adamant about not supporting me in this venture.

I was discouraged. Despite my initial reluctance to take on yet another project, I believed strongly in doing the journal because I knew if it worked, it would enhance the specialty and give it a voice. It would be an opportunity for physicians to learn and to share their experiences. After all, I had been trying for months to publish in other journals, but the dermatology ones refused to publish articles on chemosurgery. And the plastic surgery journals refused to publish anything on dermatology. I spoke to George Popkin that night. While he had decided not to practice chemosurgery himself, he was a wholehearted supporter of it. He said, "Perry, never mind what they said. If you believe in this project, I will support you 100 percent." Because everybody loved George, the naysayers backed down a little, and I kept going.

My idea was to do four issues the first year and ask a different pharmaceutical company to sponsor each one. During a big industry meeting, I went to a party for a drug company and said to an executive, "I'd like to know if we can get you to support this new journal." He said, "We don't talk to reps here. You can come to our booth at the meeting and talk to me. This is for dermatologists." I said, "I am a dermatologist." He turned around and asked two residents and said, "Do you know Dr. Robins?" and they said, "No, we've never heard of him." So he said, "I'm going to have to ask you to leave." A woman who was a dermatologist in New Orleans overheard the exchange, walked over and said, "What? You don't know Dr. Robins? He's one of the most famous dermatologists in the world. I referred my aunt to him, and he saved her life. He's the best. You should be glad you have a chance to even talk to him!"

The pharmaceutical company ended up saying yes to sponsoring the first issue. The second and third companies I approached said, "Maybe," and then the fourth company said, "We don't want to be fourth. Why don't you put ads for all of us in each issue and that way everybody will be happy." I was ecstatic. It was a start.

I set up the journal as a 501(c)(3) tax-exempt nonprofit organization, and I asked all my friends to write articles. I named myself the editor, because why not? Some called me the biggest egotist in the world, but I was just trying to do it right. The first issue, which debuted in April 1975, included an article by George Popkin on excision of basal cell carcinomas and one on biopsy techniques for malignant melanomas by Steve Gumport, the renowned cancer surgeon who had talked me out of leaving NYU. Ted Tromovitch and Sam Stegman, my West Coast "rivals," both wrote articles for the second issue in June of '75. A few issues later, my French dermatologist friend, Robert Baran, wrote about nail biopsies and went on to become the world's leading authority on nails, writing many books on the subject. I once asked him how he could write so much on something so tiny, and he said, "Because you have 20 of them!"

We wanted our articles to be accessible on the Index Medicus database, a curated subset of Medline, which was known for covering only the best quality journals. When our content back to Volume 1, Number 1, was approved for Index Medicus, people said that was unheard of and asked how we were able to get such a new journal approved. "What was the secret? Did you have to bribe someone?" Well, its president was one of my patients. He said, "Perry, there are two things they're going to check: spelling and references. If you check every reference page on every manuscript, and every spelling, I can help you get approved." We did just that, and sure enough, we got approval.

I was proud to show off our inaugural issue of the journal to an NYU librarian.

We produced four issues the first year, five the second and six the third. For many years, the ASDS refused to support the journal with articles or subscriptions. I sent it for free to 6,000 dermatologists and plastic surgeons, then to 6,000 general surgeons, and we solicited paid subscriptions and got a few. I did get the support of some foreign subscribers, which helped the International Society of Dermatologic Surgery grow and thrive. I made George Popkin my co-editor, and we also used guest editors and consultants to pitch in. The journal definitely helped to establish our credibility.

A few years later, the first society to approve the journal as an official organ was the International Society for Dermatologic Surgery. When Fred Mohs saw that ISDS was onboard, he agreed that the American College of Chemosurgery would be, too. And finally, after some board changes at the ASDS, we got them to make the journal its official organ as well. Still, the publication lost money for many years.

When the science publishing company Elsevier was interested in buying the journal, I had to pay some debts to convert it from a non-profit to a for-profit company, but in 1990 I got back all the money that I had lost, plus some interest. I was tickled pink. The editor-in-chief at that time was C. William Hanke, MD, known as Bill.

THE MAGNIFICENT FINESSE

How I Helped Free the *Journal* from Elsevier and Set the Course for the Future.
By C. William Hanke, MD

I was thrilled to meet Perry in the early 1980s when I was a newly minted Mohs surgeon, after training at the Cleveland Clinic. Everyone knew who Perry

was! I also got to know George Popkin, then editor-in-chief of *The Journal of Dermatologic Surgery,* who appointed me as a contributing editor in 1983. I wrote a series of articles on various aspects of Mohs surgery, which brought me a little attention. In the spring of 1985, George and Perry pulled me aside at the American

College of Chemosurgery Annual Meeting and asked me to be the new editor-in-chief of the journal. This was a huge surprise, and to have these two icons of dermatologic surgery show such confidence in me was a great honor.

That fall, I flew to New York and spent several days at the journal office with George, meeting the staff and learning the ropes. There were nine full-time employees at the time. I traveled to the New York office four times a year, and meeting with Perry was always the highlight—a really big deal for a young surgeon who had been raised in Wisconsin and Iowa.

Perry had invested a lot of personal time and capital in the journal. In 1990, Elsevier Science Publishers made an offer, and Perry sold his interest. I was still the editor-in-chief, but the office was downsized by Elsevier, and things were not the same after that. I turned the editor-in-chief position over to Perry Robins–trained Mohs surgeon Len Dzubow, MD, in 1991.

Since the ASDS was the largest of the sponsoring organizations for the journal, I felt strongly that it should ultimately own the publication. A plan began to form in my head. When I took over as ASDS president in 1995, I decided to try to make that happen. With the support of the ASDS Board, I asked the presidents of the American College of Mohs Surgery (John Skouge) and the International Society for Dermatologic Surgery (Sheldon Pollack) to help. In a series of forceful letters signed by all three presidents, we told Elsevier that the three sponsoring organizations would withdraw membership and financial support for the publication unless it was sold to ASDS. Otherwise, we would start a new journal that we would own. We made it clear that the journal would collapse without our editorial and financial support. Elsevier begrudgingly agreed to sell it to ASDS for $300,000 in royalties, which amounted to their profits for three years. In other words, it cost ASDS essentially nothing.

Twenty years after its founding, the journal became an asset for ASDS, as a resource for the future of dermatologic surgery. Perry

continued

felt this was one of the biggest coups he had ever seen. He called it "the magnificent finesse." It cemented our friendship, which remains strong to this day. The journal continues to thrive, too. (The photo of Perry and me, previous page, was in 2011 at the ISDS 32nd Annual Congress in Heidelberg, Germany, with the view from the famous castle.)

Once the *Journal* was up and running, I began thinking again about creating a Skin Cancer Foundation. The "Age of Aquarius, Let the Sunshine In" '70s were literally a golden age for tanning. Swimsuits were tiny, and sporting a dark tan was considered sexy, fashionable and a sign of affluence. Popular TV shows like *Charlie's Angels* and *The Love Boat* celebrated the "fun in the sun" lifestyle. Remember the famous Farrah Fawcett poster with her in the red swimsuit? She was the tanned, sexy, girl next door who helped people believe that getting lots of sun was healthy, too.

Most people didn't know anything about skin cancer then. They didn't know that most skin cancers are caused by ultraviolet radiation from the sun. When UV light hits your unprotected skin, damage to the DNA in your skin cells starts within minutes. Your immune system repairs some of the damage, but not all of it. Over time, that damage can cause mutations that lead to skin cancer.

Doctors didn't do skin screenings in those days, and most patients weren't diagnosed until there was something big and dangerous on their skin. When my patients learned they had skin cancer, they would be shocked and sometimes furious. They would berate me and say, "Why didn't anyone tell me that the sun isn't good for me? I was using reflectors, baby oil, iodine."

I had to do something about this awareness gap. I had never forgotten the selfless acts my mother performed whenever she learned of someone in need. I recalled the stories people told at her funeral of acts of kindness that she never mentioned to anyone. I wanted to follow in her footsteps, give something back and make a difference.

I approached the American Cancer Society and the American Academy of Dermatology, to see if they would work with me to create the foundation. They were not interested. Almost no one was interested in educating people about skin cancer then, except some of my closest friends, including Al Kopf, Phil Casson, George Popkin, Rex Amonette and some others, who supported my idea from day 1.

We had no funds, however. We didn't even have our 501(c)(3) status. So I lent the Foundation about $30,000 or $40,000 of my own money to get it started. I hired a young woman as a part-time employee for the Foundation and found her a cubicle in the small office we had on 32nd Street and Park Avenue for *The Journal of Dermatologic Surgery* staff. I knew a doctor whose wife worked at a law firm, and she said she would get us our 501(c)(3) for $10,000. I said that was ridiculous; we couldn't afford it. Then a patient who was a lawyer said he'd do it for less than $1,000—basically the filing fees. That was great, except that it took many months to get it done. Finally, in September 1978, we were granted our nonprofit status.

The underqualified young woman who had been working part-time left, and I hired a young man to be our first (although still part-time) executive director. Some of my grateful patients had asked what they could do to help, so I recruited some of them as cofounders of the Foundation. I joke about my fantasy fundraising strategy at that time: Holding a scalpel over the patient and saying, "What's it going to be: a donation or a scar?" Of course, I wouldn't do that, but I thought about it!

I put together an advisory board of doctors who would help the Foundation gain credibility, as well as a couple of grateful patients who were financially savvy. In 1979, we organized a founders' meeting at Windows on the World in the Twin Towers at the World Trade Center in downtown Manhattan to talk about how we would raise money, and the Foundation was officially under way. Ted Tromovitch came all the way from California to lend his support.

During the dinner, I cringed when I heard our new executive director mispronouncing the word "melanoma," telling people we would be educating the public about *"megalanoma."* Afterward, I had a little talk with him. I lent him a textbook on skin cancers and asked him to study up, saying, "And for crying out loud, learn to pronounce the words correctly. It's melanoma, not *megalanoma!"*

The next day, I got a rather frantic phone call from him, saying, "Dr. Robins, however you pronounce it, I've got one of these things on me. Can you take a look?" When he came to my medical office, I asked, "How did you come to the conclusion that you have a melanoma?" He responded, "I opened the book you gave me, and on the very first page was a photograph of a thing that I have on my chest." He showed it to me, and I said, "Yes, we have to remove that." Sure enough, a biopsy found it to be a melanoma. The good news: I excised the cancer, which very likely saved his life. The bad news: We soon parted ways.

I was naive to think that I only needed a part-time employee, since I knew nothing about how to run a foundation—the legalities or otherwise. But before I came to my senses, we had two events, one of which could have gotten us into serious trouble.

One of our first fundraisers was an Easter egg hunt in Central Park. A couple of pharmaceutical companies supported it. We placed little toys and prizes in plastic eggs, a few celebrities attended, the kids had a blast and we at least raised awareness about the Foundation, if not much money.

The other event, in October 1980, was yet another lesson in the pitfalls of absentee management. It was an elegant Monte Carlo night, complete with a casino for gambling. I don't think we had a license for it. People were writing big checks to the Foundation and were given chips for gambling. They'd play just a few dollars, eat the free food and then turn in the chips for cash. Yes, we were giving people back their donations—in cash. Hello! Let's just say we didn't make much money that night, and we were lucky we weren't arrested for being ignorant of gambling laws in New York City. You live and learn, right? I still have the elegant poster for that event hanging in my New York apartment, a reminder of the folly of believing I could do it all, and do it well, without some experienced help.

Then, in 1981, I did what I should have done in the first place: I hired a real executive director who had plenty of nonprofit experience. Her name was Mitzi Moulds, and for the next 26 years, she would lead the Foundation forward. She changed everything. I was grateful because I needed all the help I could get then, as my family life was crumbling.

CHAPTER 13

We've Got Trouble

*I thought I could have it all, but
juggling too much can backfire big time,
especially in my family life.*

Lawrence was smart and extremely creative, but he was also difficult at times. He would not listen. Ingrid and I took him to a psychiatrist when he was quite young, but he told the doctor, "It's not me who needs a psychiatrist; it's my parents!" He said we were just wasting our money to pay for psychotherapy, saying, "All we do is play games." We sent Lawrence to boarding school when he was 12, hoping it would help.

It's obvious in hindsight that Lawrence felt abandoned. While I am regretful about that, I can't change the choices I made at that time. I was working so hard to create not just the financial security that my parents never had, but also something meaningful that would make a difference in the world. It took me a long time to learn that I couldn't do everything I wanted to accomplish and do it well. I'm afraid that my parenting suffered, with Elizabeth as well as

Lawrence. My frequent absences and the problems in my marriage were hard on both of the children.

Lawrence is very open in talking about it now, which is probably healthy (at least for him). He remembers that time:

> *"I was a very immature 12-year-old. My parents were loving, but they didn't talk to me that much or teach me about things. My father was hard-working, and I never thought my parents weren't good people—I just didn't feel loved. And when you feel a lack of love, you don't build self-confidence.*
>
> *"Because my father wasn't around a lot, I was more tied to my mom. And when he was around, my parents were usually fighting. I took some of my frustrations out on my sister. I know I wasn't good to her. But rather than teaching Elizabeth and me how to build camaraderie between us, our parents just decided to separate us.*
>
> *"They didn't even tell me I was going to boarding school. I had no understanding of what was happening in my life, and it was traumatic for me. For example, I showed up to my new school, where we were required to wear a jacket and tie. I had never tied a tie in my life, so I had a clip-on tie. Who knew that kids would beat you up for that? I felt like I didn't know anything. I was one of the youngest people in the school, and a prime target for bullying.*
>
> *"I had to escape. I found the only room with a door that would lock, which was the piano room, so kids couldn't get at me in there. I would lock myself in and experiment with the piano and other instruments, and I started to learn music as a way to communicate with people. That helped a lot, but I still ended up getting kicked out of every boarding school I went to (there were quite a few!), and they usually would not take me back no matter how much my parents offered to pay.*
>
> *"I was not considered a good student. I didn't get any A's, but I didn't get any F's, either. It's not because I wasn't smart; it was because, once I learned to come out of my shell, I had a weird ability*

to motivate people to get rowdy. We'd listen to Led Zeppelin and the Beatles, the kids would smoke pot and it seemed like the best thing in the world. That's how I survived in boarding school."

Lawrence as a teenager.

I dreaded getting calls about Lawrence. I'll never forget the day the headmaster at a school in Massachusetts called and said, "You'd better come up and get your son out of here. He's disruptive." I had a little puddle-jumper plane, and I called the pilot that I often flew with and said, "Let's go up to pacify the headmaster." I flew the plane up and handled the landing. I made a donation to the school, and they said, "OK, we'll give him another chance." Money talks.

When we returned to the small airstrip, I said, "I'll take the plane up for the takeoff." It was pitch-dark by then, and it had been a stressful day. I started to bank left, when the pilot yelled, "Are you crazy?!" He grabbed the wheel and banked hard right. If he hadn't done that, we would have crashed right into a mountain. Once we were out of danger, he said, "You forgot what the field looked like.

It was in a valley between two mountains." I said, "Well, you just saved my life." He said, "I saved mine, too!"

We tried a more disciplinary type of facility, but Lawrence soon called me and said, "Get me out of here! My roommate is here because he murdered his mother." We tried several schools until we finally found a public high school he liked.

When Lawrence went off to boarding school, Elizabeth decided that she wanted to go to one, too. "Ever since I can remember, my parents put me on skis. I always felt an affinity for the outdoors, the mountains and wintertime. So when I went to school in Lake Placid, New York, I got more and more into skiing." Elizabeth seemed to like it there. She was athletic and a bit of a daredevil, so this was the perfect setting for her. She also inherited her parents' love of flying: "On my eighth birthday, my mother took me up flying around the Statue of Liberty. I loved it right away, and it made me want to get my pilot's license." During school breaks, she and Lawrence bonded over their mutual interests. "We used to water-ski when we were little," Elizabeth recalls. "Then the movie *Jaws* came out, and I stopped water-skiing. But Lawrence and I are both adventurous. We went skydiving together once. I've done hang-gliding, paragliding, parasailing, you name it."

I couldn't believe Elizabeth and Lawrence wanted to jump out of a plane together, but they did it!

I'm sure it was hard on her to see that her mother and I couldn't get along, though. I felt like no matter what I did, whatever went wrong was my fault. We finally decided it would be better for everyone if Ingrid and I separated.

The early and mid-1980s were a tumultuous time in my life, and not just because of family problems. Getting people to take The Skin Cancer Foundation seriously was more difficult than I thought it would be. Having a presence at the annual meeting of the American Academy of Dermatology (AAD) would be a milestone. It had an enormous exhibit hall of fancy booths sponsored by beauty, pharmaceutical and medical companies, and thousands of physician attendees flocked there for information and free samples. In 1982 I had paid for a booth at the meeting, set it up and was ready to show off our brochures and publications about preventing and detecting skin cancer. One of our goals was to encourage people to use sunscreens rather than "deep tanning" oils and lotions. I was proud of the Foundation's role in this pioneering effort.

The first sunscreen was developed by Austrian chemist Franz Greiter. He often climbed mountains along the Austrian-Swiss border, and on one of his trips he became extremely sunburned. Knowing that high altitude makes exposed skin more vulnerable to damage from the sun's ultraviolet radiation, Greiter decided to develop a product that would help protect the skin of mountaineers. He called his company Piz Buin, for the highest mountain in the Silvretta range of the Alps.

One of his goals was to advise people on how much sun protection they needed. He collaborated with Harvard photobiologist Madhukar Pathak, PhD, to develop the sun protection factor system, or SPF. I became involved when there was a dispute over whether to use the sun as a criterion for this system, or a solar simulator, a machine invented in 1967 that produces a wavelength of the ultraviolet B (UVB) rays of the sun and can be used for human testing indoors. It was decided that in the U.S., we would use the solar simulator as the standard test for verifying a product's SPF value. This testing method is still used today.

The SPF number on a label tells you how long the sun's UV radiation would take to redden your skin when using the product (as directed), compared with the amount of time *without* sunscreen. So if your unprotected skin would burn after 30 minutes in the sun, if you used an SPF of 4, you could be out in the sun four times 30 minutes, or two hours, but you would still get burned. The first U.S. sunscreens with an SPF number appeared in 1978. They were often low at first, such as SPF 2 or 4.

In 1981 the Foundation formed a Photobiology Committee of professional volunteer experts to verify test results on sun protection products. It was chaired by Dr. Pathak. These physicians helped us establish SPF 15 as the minimum standard for adequate sun protection. We recommended that people apply sunscreens a half hour before going out into the sun to allow the product to penetrate the outer layer of the skin, and to reapply it every two hours. (Higher SPF numbers came along later, as scientists learned more, and the Foundation divided the sunscreen Seal into two categories, with a minimum SPF of 15 for "daily use" and 30 for "active," more extended sun exposure.) Products that passed the committee's standards earned The Skin Cancer Foundation Seal of Recommendation. Corrections were often needed to fulfill our stringent requirements, and some products did not pass the test. Today, approximately 100 brands, representing more than 1,800 products, including sunscreens, clothing, hats, sunglasses, umbrellas, awnings and window film, carry the Foundation's Seal of Recommendation.

We were very fortunate at The Skin Cancer Foundation to receive a $100,000 grant from the sunscreen division of Schering-Plough, a company that had been a leader in the sun protection market, to promote the use of SPF sunscreens.

So, you can imagine how excited I was to raise awareness about all of this with our first-time presence at the big AAD meeting. But before I could greet any visitors in the booth, someone tried to destroy it. Coleman Jacobson, MD, was president of the Dermatology Foundation, a nonprofit organization that supports research in various areas of dermatology. He approached me in the booth with a couple of other dermatologists and said, "You're trying to get money from the doctors here. You're trying to take money from the people we're also soliciting, and it's not right."

I said, "No, I'm getting my money from my appreciative patients." (That's where all the initial support for the Foundation came from.) Then Dr. Jacobson dramatically swept the materials and brochures off the table and pushed over the booth, saying, "We don't want you here. Why don't you leave? You should leave right now!"

It seems astonishing now that we couldn't all get along. After all, we had complementary goals, and skin cancer was only a small part of what the Dermatology Foundation focused on. Dr. Jacobson was a respected dermatologist and officer of numerous professional associations. We even had a family connection, as his wife was the daughter of my mother's best friend. I grew up with her, for heaven's sake! I didn't give up, though. I stood my ground, reassembled the booth, tidied up my materials and extolled The Skin Cancer Foundation to anyone who would listen.

Other people at the annual meeting thought The Skin Cancer Foundation was distracting from the goals of the AAD. I could have gotten discouraged, but we fought back by just doing the best work we could to help physicians and the public learn more about prevention, detection and treatment of skin cancer.

I'm happy to report that I did make peace with Dr. Jacobson later. I even flew to his Dallas office to meet and make some suggestions on how to raise money for the Dermatology Foundation.

It took a few years for the American Academy of Dermatology and The Skin Cancer Foundation to reach a reconciliation. But in

1995, my friend and former trainee Rex Amonette, MD, became the first Mohs surgeon to be elected president of the AAD. And the organization bestowed many awards on the Foundation after that, including one to me many years later "for a lifetime of dedication and distinguished service." Of course, none of that would have happened if I'd taken "no" for an answer in that first little booth!

A NEAR MISS

I had always wanted to own part of an airline, so I was intrigued when one of my patients asked me, "Dr. Robins, how would you like to invest in an airline? We're starting a regional carrier in South Florida called Air Sunshine. We need $75,000 by the end of the day." I really wanted in on this deal, but I was upset that he hadn't asked me sooner. How could I come up with that kind of money in one day? I certainly didn't have it in the bank. I called my stockbroker, who said we could probably do it, but it would take a few days to sell some stocks and get a check to clear.

I called the patient and asked if the investors could extend the deadline, but he said he had someone else who could help them meet their goal that day. "But don't feel bad," he said, "Maybe there will be another opportunity soon."

I was depressed for years about this, feeling like I had failed badly and missed a great investment opportunity. I loved planes and the whole business of flying. What made it worse was watching the small company's growth, and when Air Sunshine was bought out by Air Florida at five times the stock value, my would-be $75,000 investment would have been worth $375,000 in a matter of months.

Sometimes you win, sometimes you lose. Then tragically, on January 13, 1982, in icy conditions, Air Florida's Flight 90, a 737 bound for Fort Lauderdale, crashed into a bridge in Washington, D.C., then into the Potomac, killing 78 people. That led the company to declare

continued

bankruptcy and subsequently put the airline out of business in 1984. As horrific as the crash was, I figured it saved me the $375,000 that I would have lost if I'd invested in the start-up. The moral when it comes to investing is: There are no sure things, and sometimes you luck out when you miss out.

In 1981, doctors in New York and San Francisco started seeing cases of homosexual men with Kaposi's sarcoma—a rare and often fatal cancer that starts as purple or red lesions on the skin. Alvin E. Friedman-Kien, MD, a dermatologist at NYU Medical Center, was one of the early investigators who linked this cancer to what soon became known as acquired immune deficiency syndrome, or AIDS. A July 1981 article about it in *The New York Times* said, "The cause of the outbreak is unknown, and there is as yet no evidence of contagion." It's a reminder of how little we understood this disease then.

We treated many patients with AIDS at NYU, and once we understood its cause from the HIV virus, how it suppresses the immune system and how it is transmitted, we were extremely cautious. When we did Mohs surgery for a skin cancer on an AIDS patient, we used double gloves and made sure everyone was focused and concentrating fully. We didn't want any action in the OR that could cause a scalpel to slip and cut someone or lead to an accidental needle stick. I remember one patient with an enormous lesion that was nearly inoperable, but we treated it. There was fear, too, and some doctors didn't want to treat AIDS patients, but they would be reprimanded or reported. Soon we saw fewer and fewer Mohs patients with AIDS because, frankly, most of them died in those early years before treatments were developed. It was a very sad time. In fact, Sam Stegman, MD, who had been so instrumental in popularizing the fresh tissue technique of Mohs surgery, and who had supported my efforts and written articles for the *Journal*, died of AIDS in San Francisco in 1990.

My dear friend from my VA days, John Forline, the human catalyst who had first led me to Dr. Mohs, was a general dermatologist in New Jersey and had become a great supporter of Mohs surgery. He often sent patients from his two offices to see me. I remember one day he told me his wife was having a lump in her breast checked out. He called me later, relieved, to say, "Thank God, it was benign." Unfortunately, it was misdiagnosed, and just six months later, she died of breast cancer. That was tragic. Their daughter was about the same age as Lawrence, and when she was 14, John took her on a cruise up the Nile. On a felucca sailboat tour of Lake Nasser, a storm came up, they capsized and they both drowned. I couldn't believe such a beautiful family was gone—just like that. I was devastated.

I became the center of an unwanted controversy around Christmastime in 1982. Nancy Reagan, then the first lady, had been diagnosed with a basal cell carcinoma. *The New York Times* reported, "A small growth that was removed from above Nancy Reagan's upper lip was diagnosed as skin cancer, but it was 'adequately excised and no further treatment is required,' the White House announced." A plastic surgeon performed the excision and repair.

The next day I was asked to be on television by Dr. Frank Field, a meteorologist who also reported on science and health topics, to talk about skin cancer and the various ways it can be treated. After the interview aired, a reporter approached me and asked if I would have done the same procedure as Mrs. Reagan's plastic surgeon. Of course, I replied that I would have performed Mohs surgery, which would have assured that we eradicated all the cancerous tissue with the smallest scar possible.

Well, the following day, newspapers across the country interpreted my comment as criticism of the first lady's treatment. For example, the front page of the *Asbury Park Press* contained a very long article with the headline "Mrs. Reagan and Chemosurgery," including this: "A plastic surgeon removed a common form of skin cancer above Mrs. Reagan's upper lip recently, sparking objections from a leading skin specialist, Dr. Perry Robins, head of the chemosurgery unit at NYU Medical School. Robins argued that Mrs. Reagan should have undergone chemosurgery, a method he helped develop."

That's not exactly what I said. The article continued: "Chemosurgery has a 99 percent cure rate and is considered less destructive than office surgery because it can target cancerous areas with precision. But area skin specialists say it is an 'overkill' to use the procedure for the most common types of skin malignancy."

After this incident, I received letters saying that I should be expelled from the American Academy of Dermatology, as well as NYU Medical Center. To correct the miscommunication, I wrote a nice letter to Nancy Reagan telling her that there are many techniques for treating skin cancers, and that I do a different procedure that was equally effective. She was very polite and acknowledged that my comments were not an insult to the doctor or her standard of care. However, I was still quite surprised to find out that the story appeared in more than 1,000 newspapers, and perhaps more. The Associated Press said, "The controversy over what procedure should have been used for First Lady Nancy Reagan's skin cancer continues." Ironically, a skin cancer so close to the lip on anyone would most likely be referred to a Mohs surgeon today, especially if it were a first lady!

A Swiss medical student named Michael was doing a six-month fellowship with a noted dermatopathologist (a physician who examines skin tissue removed during a biopsy or excision under a microscope), whose office was near mine at NYU Medical Center. Michael would frequently come to my office to visit, and he said he was very interested in learning Mohs surgery. His documents showed he had studied medicine in Switzerland and had also trained for a short time in New England. I agreed to have him work with me as a fellow, and after he completed his training in dermatopathology in 1982, Michael studied the Mohs technique with me for a year.

I liked him. He always had a smile on his face, and I could practice my German and French with him. He was highly skilled, and he seemed much brighter than most students. When we started producing a series of videotapes on dermatologic surgery, he agreed to do the one on anatomy. He rattled off all the correct parts of the anatomy and the information needed, without once checking his notes. I was impressed.

I invited him to come to Europe for a meeting of the International Society for Dermatologic Surgery, and as we were leaving for the airport, he said, "Oh my gosh, I left my passport at home. I have to go back to get it." When he arrived in Europe a day later, he said, "I'm so sorry I left my passport and was delayed." This didn't arouse any suspicions at the time, but it should have.

As Michael was not an official fellow in my program, there was no stipend for him. Occasionally, he would ask to borrow money to get by. He said that his mother and father had died and left an estate from which he was going to receive hundreds of thousands of dollars. Because of that, I was supportive and lent him $10,000. When he needed more, I provided it. Then one day the police came to my office and threatened to arrest him for passing a bad check to buy his girlfriend a mink coat. Seeing police officers made everyone in my office nervous—and curious. "What's going on?" they asked. So immediately I wrote a check for $10,000 to cover my student's indiscretion. By the time he'd completed his fellowship, Michael owed me about $70,000. He signed a document promising to repay the money. Then he disappeared.

Later, I received a phone call from his sister, who lived in Berlin.

She told me that Michael wasn't Swiss; he was German. His passport was German, too, so that explained why he "forgot" it on our trip to Europe. Clearly, he didn't want to travel with others who might see that it wasn't Swiss, so he made excuses and traveled by himself on a later flight. He had gone to medical school in Germany and did graduate, but he didn't take all the necessary exams. The papers he had used to get his fellowships were fraudulent. His sister also told me that their father and mother were still alive, and there had never been an estate in Switzerland. It was all fabricated.

I ran into him once at a boat show in Newport. He denied everything and promised to make amends and repay me. Of course, I never got the money back, but I did get a letter from him, scrawled on an envelope:

Dear Perry,

I've spent another day and night trying to get in touch with you. It seems so easy just to call you, but in reality it is extremely hard for me to do. I wanted so much to talk to you before I go to prison. Not that I'm complaining about the prospect of being incarcerated for a while. I earned it. I was hoping that my mother has gotten in touch with you and paid you some of the money I owe you. She could simply deduct it from my inheritance. I saw you on Nightline with Ted Koppel the other day. It felt good seeing your face and hearing your voice. See you sometime.

Michael

I never heard from him again.

A woman who worked at The Skin Cancer Foundation did not like our executive director, Mitzi Moulds. Somehow the two irritated each other. As a result, this woman tried to get three NYU dermatologists who knew me well to start a new foundation to compete with us. They sent a letter to many doctors, saying, "We're starting a foundation and we'd like your support."

When Mitzi learned that another organization might infringe on our turf, she was adamantly against it, disappointed and offended. I said, "Mitzi, I don't own the Foundation. My goal is to save lives. And the more people and organizations that help me fight this battle, the better. I'd be appreciative and supportive of it. I don't consider them adversaries. I consider them helping our mission by making more people aware of the dangers of the sun."

But the doctors who received the solicitation responded very negatively, saying, "What's wrong with you? You already have a foundation! Why are you trying to start another one?" Well, I think they wanted to get rid of Mitzi—and also me! But they backed off and never did start it. Mitzi continued to oversee The Skin Cancer Foundation for many more years.

Mitzi and I organized a fundraising reception for the Foundation in the home of a dermatologist in Palm Beach, Florida, and invited some patients as well as wealthy potential donors. When I arrived and looked around the doctor's home, I couldn't believe the paintings he had collected: Picasso, Chagall, Modigliani, Miró and other artists from around the world. They were unbelievable. I was agog and blurted out, "How did you acquire these paintings? Did you inherit a fortune?" He said, "No, just made good investments."

I said, "You're so lucky. These are incredible. How can you afford to insure them?" He said, "I manage."

Toward the end of the evening, a woman came up to me and asked, "How do you like these paintings?" in her French accent. I said, "I love them. They're great! But I'd be afraid to leave these unguarded." She had had a few drinks, and confided, "My husband, he painted all of them." Her husband was David Stein, a talented painter famous for forging the works of brilliant artists. Earlier in his life he would knock out paintings in the style of the greats. It was easy for him. Then he'd create certificates of authenticity and pose as a representative of an auction house to sell the paintings at special "presale prices." That led to him serving prison time in France when Chagall pressed charges against him.

He was still painting, but often it was commissions for wealthy collectors who owned the originals. They would put the priceless original in a safe and hang the Stein copy. No one could tell the difference.

I was fascinated by his story and became friendly with Stein, who moved to New York. Both he and his wife became my patients. He did all the paintings for a restaurant on 33rd Street and Park Avenue. They didn't pay him cash, but they gave him credit of several thousands of dollars to eat at the restaurant. It was near The Skin Cancer Foundation office, so I helped him use up some of that credit.

I asked him to create about 20 paintings, without including the names or "signatures" of the artists he was copying, and we would have a fun fundraising auction of them to benefit The Skin Cancer Foundation. "No problem!" he said. I asked my nephew to bid up the prices just a bit to encourage people to open their wallets. "If worse comes to worst, we'll buy them and take them back ourselves," I said. Well, the putz got carried away and outbid almost everybody, so we had to buy half the paintings back. It was not a successful fundraiser. I still have some of those paintings in storage somewhere, but I've lost track of them. Stein died in 1999.

I had treated an interesting Italian businessman several times, and we'd become friendly. Before Ingrid and I separated, he told me about his 3,000-acre ranch near St. Augustine, Florida, and invited us to visit him. He even had an airstrip, so Ingrid and I could fly our plane there.

She piloted our little puddle-jumper down past Jacksonville and toward the ranch. When we flew over the "landing strip," though, what we saw was nothing but a cow pasture with a wind sock. We decided we'd land at the local airport in St. Augustine a few miles away.

We rented a car and drove down to visit the man. When we arrived at his home, his assistant apologized and said he had been suddenly called to Italy for some important matters and wouldn't return for several days. She offered to host us for lunch, but we decided to just make the best of it and explore the area.

We checked into a hotel a couple of miles from the ranch, on the ocean. After lunch, we took a walk along the beach and saw a sign that said, "Lots for sale."

One of the things Ingrid and I had in common was an interest in real estate. We both loved looking at properties. I'd been fascinated ever since 1944, when my father bought our farm in New Jersey. It was the best investment he ever made. I thought of him and wondered what he would think of these gorgeous lots. Some of them were just 110 feet from the ocean, and they backed up into the Intracoastal Waterway. It had an old A1A road providing access to the property. We agreed they were incredible lots, with stunning views in all directions. We stopped at the real estate office, and it didn't take me long to decide to buy 10 oceanfront lots at $50,000 each.

The senior real estate agent was out to lunch while the salesgirl in the office took care of us. When he returned and learned he'd missed out on the commission of a $500,000 sale, he said it was the most expensive lunch date of his life.

I was ecstatic. After speaking to the real estate agent, I decided to put some condo buildings and townhouses on the property, with a pool between them. I was sure it would be phenomenal. We had an architect draw up plans, and I persuaded a few friends to invest in the development, including my accountant. I went to three or four banks and was discouraged when they wouldn't loan us the money, saying there was a flood of condos on the market because of high interest rates, and people weren't buying. Someone suggested we sell them as single family lots, and we'd make a mint. He gave me the name of two builders he had worked with, who he said were very successful— going like gangbusters. I went to visit them, was impressed with the busy crew they showed me they were working with and decided to become a silent partner in a joint venture to build homes on the lots.

It was a disaster. The homes were horrible thanks to bad engineering and shoddy construction. In the master bedroom you couldn't even see the water. How stupid can you be? We were fortunate we were able to sell some of the homes at cost.

As for the Italian patient of mine, who had first led me to that part of Florida, he had family problems, and someone reported him to the U.S. and Italian authorities for evading taxes. One time after a visit to my office, he stayed in the waiting room until everybody had left. I asked him, "What's wrong?" He said, "I have a flight to Paris, and I thought I'd rather sit here than at the airport." He went to Paris and I heard a day or two later that he had killed himself. I was probably one of the last to see him alive. He must have been feeling hopeless and depressed, but I had no idea.

Apparently before he went to Paris, he learned that his wife was having an affair, and he turned over all his stocks and property to his handyman. His wife contested that, saying he wasn't in his right mind. The lawyers flew up to New York to talk to me and asked me to testify, but they ended up settling out of court.

I still loved the idea of being a real estate developer in my (nonexistent) spare time. A few years later, after Ingrid and I had separated, the builders I had worked with before talked me into investing in another "opportunity": a 110-acre parcel on Route 1 in St. Augustine on which we could put up homes, townhouses, shopping centers and office buildings. It was selling for $2.5 million.

They said they knew a bank that would give us a construction loan, but we had to put down 10 percent to buy the land. They asked me to put down $250,000 for just 24 or 48 hours—very short term. I met the loan officer and he said, "I'll give you your money back the next day, just bring the paper in and you can cash out." I had some cash from the sale of the *Journal,* so I figured, *Why not? It looks like a good investment, and it's only for 24 to 48 hours.* So we signed the deal. The next day I went to the bank, cheerful and smiling and waving the paper in my hand. I said, "I'd like to see the finance officer." A manager came over and said, "I'm sorry to tell you, Dr. Robins, that we fired him today." When I asked if someone else could help with the loan, he said no; they would not be making the loan. There I was, stuck with a note I had to pay off in the next two years for $2 million, which was unimaginable to me.

I went to a couple of banks and they laughed at me. They said no way in hell. "That's why that guy got fired. He was making bad loans to people like you." Where was I going to get the money to make the payments? I took out a mortgage. I sold my stocks. I sold everything I had.

Every two or three weeks, I would travel to St. Augustine to meet potential buyers. But the problem was, in order to develop the land for the homes, a road needed to be built, which would cost about $500,000. After a year, nothing had happened. Because of the flood of condos on the market, the company was going belly-up. We dissolved the partnership. I took back the land and kept trying to sell it. We had what was called a PUD, planned urban development, with 120 acres. We had a 10-acre commercial shopping center site on the highway. On the side, we had space for 420 single-family lots—small ones, a quarter of an acre. And we had a piece of land for 120 townhouses.

I had a chap working for me because I had also acquired a small office building, and he called me and said, "We have some people here who want to buy an acre of our outparcel for $500,000 cash."

"That's phenomenal!" I said. "Who are they?" He said, "They're not telling me." I wondered, "Is it Mafia money? Drug money? You can't just sell it to someone anonymously for cash." He said, "No, they'll give us a check. But they don't want to tell who it is until the closing." It sounded bizarre, but I said I'd meet with them. We planned the closing and we went to the lawyer's office. I was very nervous, wondering, "Who are these people? What's the big secret?" I said, "Now can you tell me who this is before I sign?" He said, "Yes. It's the Mayo Clinic." They had opened a hospital in Jacksonville in 1986 and needed some satellite offices.

I was ecstatic. I had been expecting Mafia drug money and instead got the Mayo Clinic! I could use the $500,000 to put in the necessary roads. Finally, I was able to sell some lots, and I started to get some of my money back. We built about 250 homes, half of what we had hoped. About five years later, we ended up suing the builder because he was being unreasonable in what he was offering for the lots. We had to get out of the contract, which was vague and very poorly written. There were also some problems with getting flood insurance.

The project, with all its ups and downs, continues to this day. I realized it needed someone's full attention if it was ever going to work. Eventually, I turned over the whole thing to my daughter, Elizabeth. She spent two or three years there, working on the development full time, and she did very well with it.

But back in those days, the project was wearing me down. Ingrid and I had been separated for a while, and after all the unexpected and difficult things that had happened in the 1980s, a divorce seemed inevitable. It felt like a failure to me, but it was never going to work between us, and it was time to admit defeat.

I do want to say, though, that Ingrid was an excellent mother.

She doted on the children and would do anything to make their life richer, better and more fulfilling. Because she was from Germany, she made sure Elizabeth learned German and spent time with her grandmother and grandfather in Hamburg. Lawrence didn't have the patience or the inclination to learn German, but fortunately his grandparents spoke enough English to communicate. The kids were able to learn firsthand about part of their heritage.

When I told Ingrid that I was leaving, she was devastated. She still had a soft spot for me, despite our problems. She knew that I was more of a "doer" than she was. I built things from scratch, I made things happen, and she was proud of that. We had an amicable settlement and joint custody of the children, who were both in their teens, and we committed to making that work.

To free up some money, I sold off two lots on the long entrance road to the property in Rye. I sold off one lot for $30,000, and with the other I went in with the builder and built a spec house. When we decided to divorce, I moved Ingrid into the spec house. But that did not work, because the kids had difficulty accepting that they couldn't go onto the property of the big house where they had grown up, and it was not theirs anymore. Ingrid wanted to get out of there and move on with her life. She loved Greenwich, Connecticut, so I bought a lot for her in Greenwich, built a house for her and she moved there.

When Ingrid moved to Greenwich, I sold the big house in Rye for about what I paid for it, even though I had put a lot of improvements into it. But it didn't matter; I just had to sell it. We all had to move on. *The Journal of Dermatologic Surgery* had a studio apartment in the city, and I moved into that. I sold some property and made a one-time settlement for the divorce, which was final in 1988. It was worth it. I had a clean slate and a chance to start over.

After the divorce, my daughter was a little more loyal toward her mother than to me, and she bonded more with her mother. She had always loved flying with Ingrid, so Elizabeth went to flight school, soloed and got her private pilot's license on her 16th birthday in 1988. "I was too young to drive myself to the airport," she says, "but I was able to get in a plane and fly the plane myself! When you're younger you don't have the fear. I might have more fear now, but I thought landing was a lot of fun and really enjoyed it." Although Elizabeth liked her boarding school, she didn't have good luck with roommates and eventually wanted to return to Rye. She blossomed in a prep school there, getting good grades and excelling in extra-curricular activities.

Lawrence attended public high school in Greenwich for 11th and 12th grades, where he created a drug education program for students. He became one of the most popular kids in his school of 2,000 students because he had his own rock 'n' roll radio show on WGCH Radio. He loved music—and even built a recording studio in the basement at home. I imagine it felt like an oasis to him at that time.

"My mother is a very good person," Lawrence says, "But she didn't know how to communicate her angst about her relationship with my father. And she never dated anyone after the divorce. She was so beautiful and so many people wanted her, but she just couldn't get over it. Whatever her issues were, they were so far ingrained that she wasn't able to separate from it. She was holding on to a lot of negativity about my dad when I was living in Greenwich. Because of that, it drove a wedge between my father and me, which we didn't repair until after I graduated from high school and moved to the city."

Of course, I love both of my kids. They love me too, but the divorce was hard on them. And it took years for us to develop a closer relationship.

CHAPTER 14

Skin in the Game

*For every failure, there is a success:
The Foundation's message about the
dangers of skin cancer starts to pay off;
can we change the world?*

The 1980s were not just about struggles, losses and endings for me. There were positive changes, too. For one thing, after some fizzles, fits and starts, I learned how to be effective at raising money for a good cause. I created a solid nest egg that sustained The Skin Cancer Foundation and allowed it to grow. And about half of that came from my patients.

We brought together a magic mix of celebrities, corporate leaders, journalists, physicians and people I had treated for skin cancer, organized elegant events and lavishly recognized them for their contributions. For example, in May 1982 we arranged an Awards Banquet at the Plaza Hotel on Central Park. We honored Dr. Frank Field, the popular meteorologist and NBC's health and science editor, who was a pioneer in covering health topics on radio and TV.

He had invited me to speak as a guest on his show many times, and we became friends. He did a lot to help raise awareness about skin cancer. We also recognized Greek shipping magnate Stavros Niarchos for a generous contribution, which allowed us to create an ambitious new melanoma education program. Tom Brokaw, then anchor of the *NBC Nightly News*, was the guest speaker.

We lined up an impressive Banquet Committee for the event, which included such titans as William M. Batten, chairman of the New York Stock Exchange, Rawleigh Warner Jr., chairman of Mobil Oil Corporation, Walter B. Wriston, chairman of Citibank and others. We also had an honorary board of celebrities, some of whom had been my patients, to help attract more people who might be moved to open their wallets. They included comedian Danny Kaye as honorary chairman, along with Lauren Bacall, Dick Cavett, Jack Paar, Harold Prince, Princess Lee Radziwill and Tom Selleck.

Leonard Goldberg, MD, who came from South Africa to train with me at NYU in 1979 and 1980, remembers that time:

> *"One of the highlights of my year with Perry was meeting some of the rich and famous people he had treated through the years. Danny Kaye was one of them. He came to Perry with a recurrent basal cell carcinoma on his nose, which Perry operated on with great success. I was privileged to go to Danny's hotel room at the Pierre Hotel to change the dressing on his wound. In return, he would sing to me some of my favorite songs from my childhood. One of the songs I loved that my father used to sing to me was the one about 'the little white duck, sittin' in the water, the little white duck, doing what he oughter.' Danny had recorded it in the 1950s, so he sang it for me. My parents were far away in South Africa, so he and Perry were like father figures to me—both so generous."*

Kaye was devoted to raising money for Unicef and did hilarious performances for children in many countries on behalf of that charity. He also performed at symphony benefit concerts. Still, once he experienced his own skin cancer episode, he made time for our fledgling charity to help raise its profile. He even welcomed me into his home in Los Angeles when I was there on business, with a spectacular dinner he had cooked himself. Sadly, he died just a few years later in 1987 at age 74.

Danny Kaye unabashedly displayed the bandage on his nose at a Skin Cancer Foundation event.

With the support of Al Kopf at NYU, we began to create more educational materials for the public and for physicians. The Foundation launched *The Melanoma Letter* in 1983 to provide doctors with medically reviewed clinical articles on the latest research. Dr. Kopf served as its first editor-in-chief. That year we also produced the debut of our annual magazine, *The Skin Cancer Foundation Journal,* followed by *Sun & Skin News,* a quarterly consumer newsletter (which is now a blog).

In 1985, Dr. Kopf and two other dermatologists at NYU, Robert Friedman, MD, and Darrell Rigel, MD, created a simple, easy-to-remember acronym to help people recognize the warning signs of melanoma by the "ABCDs." It taught people to notice if a mole had worrisome characteristics including (A) for asymmetry, (B) for an irregular border, (C) for color variation and (D) for diameter larger than ¼ inch. (An E was added later, for any mole that is evolving, or changing.) The Skin Cancer Foundation created a brochure and a nationwide melanoma awareness campaign based on this. We reached out to many journalists for help. We hosted our first Media Day, during which we invited health reporters to come and hear from experts talking about the latest research on skin cancer.

The New York Times writer Jane Brody was one of the first to do an article about the importance of early detection of melanoma, quoting me and including pictures of lesions. That article brought a lot of people into dermatologists' offices, including mine, saying, "I have something like that on my body." I received many letters thanking me for the information, because it made people recognize what they had on their body might be a warning sign of a serious disease.

At the Foundation, we created a poster about early detection of melanoma, called "Can You Spot a Killer?" We sold the posters to dermatologists to put up in their offices. One day we got a crumpled check in the mail for $10,000. Mitzi Moulds said, "Shall we deposit it? It's all wrinkled, and it has no return address or anything." I said, "All they can do is charge us $5 on a bounced check, so deposit it." It cleared the bank. Later, at a meeting in San Francisco, I met a dermatologist who solved the mystery when he told me he had the poster, which pictured skin cancer lesions, on his office wall. A patient saw it and told the doctor, "I have one of those." Sure enough, the man did have a melanoma. The doctor told him, "If you hadn't seen that poster, and had the lesion removed, you could have died in just a few months." The grateful patient sent us the crumpled, but very useful and appreciated, check.

"Skin cancers were less likely to be detected at their earliest stage when our public education programs began," Mitzi recalls. "People often didn't see doctors until their skin cancers were far advanced. As a result, disfigurement and the loss of an eye, ear or nose was a recognized risk of the extreme surgeries then required for treatment. Late detection was the cause of the many deaths from melanoma."

We were starting to make a difference, but we knew we still had a long way to go. We knew that the majority of people were not using sunscreens. And with more prosperity, more people were getting more sun. When my father worked, if he got two weeks of vacation, he was lucky. Now people would often get three weeks or a month, and they could jet off to the Caribbean, Florida or other sunny spots. People were spending more time in the sun than ever before. But the Foundation made great inroads with helping people become more aware of the dangers of sun exposure and how it can unquestionably lead to skin cancer. Without that, there would be many more deaths, especially from melanoma, than there are today. We take credit for that.

A person who helped to inspire me in my fundraising efforts in those days was Howard A. Rusk, MD, known as the father of rehabilitation medicine. He founded the Rusk Institute of Rehabilitation Medicine at NYU in 1948. He was ahead of his time, believing in the principle that physical medicine and rehabilitation shouldn't focus solely on illness or disability but should involve the whole person—physically, emotionally and socially. He lived near me and we often walked together down First Avenue to NYU in the mornings, as we both liked to get to the office early. One day I asked him, "You're responsible for building your medical specialty, and you have been incredibly successful in raising money for it. What is the secret?" His answer was simple: "You ask and you ask again, and then you still ask again. If you don't ask, you don't get it."

That's deceptively simple, of course. You can't just ask people to give money. If you do, they might be annoyed by it, or even slightly hostile. So instead, you say, "Do you have a foundation?" If you have a private foundation, then you must give money away; you can't keep it! So you ask if they have a foundation or know someone who has a foundation and would consider supporting such a deserving cause that's going to save lives and help many people avoid disfigurement. I would say, "This is such a worthwhile project, I can't tell you how sincerely I believe in this. You'd be helping so many people. You must have such a good conscience if you want to support this." Much of the time, it worked.

One of my grateful patients, businessman Joseph G. Gaumont, may not have been a celebrity, but he made all the difference in the world when he decided to give $1 million to the Foundation. We named a fellowship after him. Maritza I. Perez, MD, was one of the recipients of The Skin Cancer Foundation's Joseph G. Gaumont Fellowship in Dermatologic Surgery and began training with me at NYU in 1994. She went on to coauthor a book with me, titled *Understanding Melanoma: What You Need to Know,* now in its fifth edition.

Then Gaumont's close friend, H. Thomas Langbert, decided to donate $500,000. Those two contributions and some others from patients really laid the foundation for our foundation, allowing us to move forward and do even more. I couldn't have done it without them.

I wanted our message to spread around the globe and invite international participation, too. I had good friends in many countries who supported that vision, such as Luigi Rusciani, MD, in Italy, who started a skin cancer foundation, a journal and a society there. Cleire Paniago-Pereira, MD, did something similar in Brazil. So did my friends in Mexico. And it grew from there.

Our first World Congress on Cancers of the Skin, which The Skin Cancer Foundation cosponsors with organizations from the host nation, took place in New York City in 1983, and has traveled to various locales every two years since then, from Berlin to Sydney. At the World Congress meetings, doctors from all over share the most recent information on skin cancer. These meetings not only bring together doctors from the international community but also alert the host country's local media, who help spread the message about skin cancer and The Skin Cancer Foundation. They've been tremendously successful. Our 18th World Congress will take place in Buenos Aires, Argentina, in June 2020.

We also formed an International Alliance Against Cancers of the Skin, to make skin cancer education a priority around the world. The Alliance produces materials in many languages and cosponsors national and international conferences for the medical profession and the public. Today we have member physicians in 34 countries.

Another Reagan skin cancer caused a stir in October 1985, and this time it cropped up on the president. Ronald Reagan was diagnosed with a basal cell carcinoma on his nose and, unlike the first lady three years earlier, he had Mohs surgery. Not many details came out at the time, but we learned later that surgeons performed the procedure on the president at the White House and did the lab work at a private dermatologist's office nearby. Only a single layer of skin had to be removed to make sure there was a cancer-free margin beyond the president's tumor. Surgeons closed Reagan's wound with sutures and applied a small bandage, and he returned to his White House quarters after the procedure.

The terrorist hijacking of the cruise ship *Achille Lauro* required the president to go on national television the next morning to comment on the incident. In the White House briefing room, he reported that the four Palestinian hijackers on an Egyptian plane had been captured with the help of U.S. Navy F-14 fighter jets, but reporters were equally interested in the bandage on Reagan's nose. He spoke briefly about the basal cell carcinoma and joked with reporters that the doctors told him, "My nose is clean."

"When that story broke," Mitzi Moulds recalls, "Dr. Robins appeared on television to discuss the warning signs and the importance of early detection and effective treatment. It was one of our first big opportunities to bring national and international attention to the disease." It certainly was a highlight of The Skin Cancer Foundation's early public awareness efforts.

In 1987, surgeons performed Mohs surgery on another basal cell carcinoma on the president's nose. I had gotten a call about flying to Bethesda, Maryland, to be part of this surgical team, but I didn't get the message in time. I was disappointed to miss the opportunity to perform the procedure on a sitting president. Still, it was another chance to raise awareness, with the help of *The New York Times*:

> "Commenting in advance of the operation, Dr. Perry Robins, president of The Skin Cancer Foundation in New York, said: 'The chance of it coming back in the same spot is very small. The prognosis is excellent.' The procedure used on Mr. Reagan, Mohs' technique, after the surgeon who invented it, is the most precise form of treatment for skin cancer, with a cure rate that exceeds 99 percent."

After his surgery, Reagan told the press that his bandage was a "billboard" that said, "Stay out of the sun." That gave a nice boost to our message about the importance of sun protection!

In 1985 Deborah Sarnoff, MD, came to train with me. We bonded immediately. She was so appreciative to be there, and she did extracurricular work writing articles and assisting in other ways. Not only did we develop a teacher-student relationship, we also became good friends. She has been one of my biggest supporters and is one of the brightest doctors I ever trained. Dr. Sarnoff recalls what she learned that year:

"When I was doing my residency in dermatology at NYU, I heard about this procedure called Mohs surgery. People said it was good for removing skin cancers, especially cancers on critical areas of the face, and that it spared tissue and minimized the amount of skin that you have to sacrifice. I was intrigued and went to observe Perry Robins in action and, I swear, it was love at first sight.

"First of all, it was the famous Perry Robins. I teased him later and said, 'If you had been an astronaut, that's what I would want to be. If you were a butcher, that's what I would want to be. If you were in OB-GYN, I would have switched my specialty to that.' He's that enthusiastic and supportive. He's like a big teddy bear who embraces everyone, builds them up, makes them feel like a million bucks. In my medical school class of 150 at George Washington in D.C., only 30 of us were women. And they did everything they could, in my opinion, to discourage women from going into surgery. But Dr. Robins was totally supportive of women being surgeons, which was a breath of fresh air to me.

"From the first moment, I was thinking, Mohs has it all. You're using your hands, you're using your head, you're using your heart. You're making people feel better and curing them. This is the best thing since sliced bread. Then I knew that's all I wanted to do and all I wanted to be."

"I loved it, and I wanted to be like him. He was a wonderful mentor. He had the gift of gab but also a magic touch with patients like I had never seen before, not in any of the surgeons at George Washington, and not even in the people mentoring me in the NYU clinics in residency. He knew how to treat the patient, not just the disease. He was a genius at that. That is something you can't measure in a written test. He could immediately read the patient. We would

have a consult and within three seconds he could glance down at the information that they gave and he'd immediately find some common ground. He would ask, 'Where did you grow up?' If the person said New Jersey, he was on it with his Jersey stories. If he asked, 'Where do you work?' he knew something about it. If the patient owned a boat, he owned a boat, too. If they flew a plane, he flew a plane, too. He could always find the common ground and make patients—and their families—feel relaxed immediately.

"Of course, his patients had cancer and so they were scared. They'd ask, 'Dr. Robins, am I going to lose my nose?' He had a good answer for everything and was never smug. He would touch the patients, look at them, let them vent. He would listen and very quickly cut to the chase and tell them not to worry and everything was going to be fine. They would look at this doctor almost as if he were a god. He would do the consult first and then he would schedule the Mohs surgery. Nobody ever said no to him. There was a conversion rate of 100 percent. You can't teach that; it's a gift.

"Perry was a trailblazer in dermatologic surgery. He fostered relationships with plastic surgeons, who usually would have been considered enemies back then. He was a friend, not a foe. He believed that, 'If we play well together in the sandbox, then all of the surgical specialties can band together, form friendships and learn from each other.' That idea was so ahead of its time. There were turf battles with the plastic surgeons, like my husband, in those days. He was told he would have to pay mandatory surcharges to his professional organizations to fight the derms. And those of us who were dermatologists had to pay up to fight the plastic surgeons. Perry always saw beyond that—way beyond that.

"I learned about life as well as medicine from Perry. One of his themes was to use other people's money to accomplish things whenever possible. He taught me that. He taught me about real estate when I knew nothing about it. He made me be bold and take out a mortgage,

pay it back, then take out the next mortgage—I learned not to be afraid, but to go for it. I learned about running a business from watching him do it. He taught me how to be my own boss. He would say, 'Don't work for anyone if you can help it. Keep that control.' He taught me if you want things done, you ask a busy person because a busy person will get it done. He taught me how to juggle. I can take on a lot of tasks and wear a lot of hats, because I watched this man do it.

"He taught me to do more than just practice and be in my office. He said, 'Grab the brass ring and travel. There is so much fun in international teaching and the friendships you make with international people. You'll learn trade secrets that will make you a better doctor. You'll learn about other cultures. You'll always have a friend; wherever you travel you'll have someone to stay with. They'll open their homes to you.' That was an amazing gift that later came true. Today I am the president of the International Society of Dermatologic Surgery. It's a beautiful thing to have friendships with people all around the world, and that's a gift I got from him. (Below: Bill Hanke, Perry and I were delighted in 2007 when we discovered our Seal of Recommendation displayed at a farmacia in Italy.)

"Every day of my life, there is a moment or a pause in the day where I'm thinking, How do I deal with this difficult problem or

situation? WWPD, or What Would Perry Do? I remember how he would cross his arms, flare his nostrils, listen and let people vent—and just quietly fix it. Then I try to do the same."

CHAPTER 15

My Patients, My People

*Whether rich and famous or of humble
background, my friends and patients
enhance my life in so many ways.*

I loved doing Mohs surgery for skin cancer. I never got involved much in the cosmetic aspects of dermatology, even when laser treatments came out. I was friends with Leon Goldman, MD, who developed laser surgery starting in the 1960s and was founding president of the American Society for Laser Medicine & Surgery, and Phil Bailin, MD, who studied under Dr. Goldman at the University of Cincinnati and went on to became chairman of the Department of Dermatology at the Cleveland Clinic. Phil eventually talked me into buying a CO_2 laser. But to me, it was just too time-consuming. And why should I be second-best in something, when I was already the leader in Mohs surgery? I was always booked up and had 100 or 150 patients waiting for surgery. So, I decided not to pursue the cosmetic side of the business. I wouldn't be the richest man in medicine—but I was happy!

Most people don't know that if you've been diagnosed with a nonmelanoma skin cancer, you have better than even odds of getting another within a decade. And if you've been diagnosed with more than one, you have higher than a 60 percent chance of being a repeat customer within just two years. Because of that, I bonded with a lot of my patients and saw many of them year after year. I'd get to know their stories, their family members, their hobbies, where they went on vacations. I'd keep notes about those things in their charts, so I could ask about them on the next visit. They were often touched and surprised that I remembered.

Because Mohs surgery is done in stages while the patient waits, it can take several hours. Patients like to talk, and I would learn all kinds of fascinating details about their lives. After surgery, I would always call the patients that night to check on them. They appreciated that, although occasionally I'd get a response like, "Why call me? Call his girlfriend. He hasn't been here for months!"

I would give patients my phone number after a surgery, too, although they seldom called. On the rare occasions when they did, I often checked on them in person to make sure they were OK. I remember a call at 1 AM. I had removed a large lesion on a man's lower face and lips and had sutured it closed. Large surgeries can be disfiguring, especially at first until they heal. This patient was very worried about that. When he got home, he told his wife that he was afraid she would find him repulsive and not sexy anymore. To prove him wrong, they had enthusiastic sex. It wasn't the smartest thing to do after such a surgery, and he popped his sutures and was hemorrhaging a bit. I told him I'd meet him at the ER and fix him up.

I saw quite a few patients who were influential in business, finance, art, architecture and entertainment. I generally don't talk about the ones who are still alive, like the extremely successful male pop star with the beautiful voice and very fair skin (who was smooching with his girlfriend in the waiting room). But I do remember being rattled by a call from someone else whose work I admired: Lauren Bacall. I operated on her in 1981 while she was starring in *Woman of the Year* on Broadway. You know how "the show must go on," so she didn't want to miss a performance. That night I got a call that she was hemorrhaging. I was nearby when I was paged and immediately grabbed my bag and ran to the Palace Theatre, where I was escorted backstage. She had two drops of blood on the bandage. I changed the bandage, and she finished the show. She went on to win the Tony Award that year for Best Lead Actress in a musical.

Arthur Godfrey, the once wildly popular radio and TV entertainer, had the nickname The Old Redhead, which meant, of course, that he was genetically at risk for skin cancer. He was an aviation buff and had flown many aircraft in the Air Force Reserve. Pilots who spend a lot of time at high altitude are bombarded with UV radiation from the sun, which can lead to skin cancer. Although he had quit smoking years earlier, he was fighting emphysema after lung cancer, and now skin cancer, too. He was retired, but the other patients fawned over him. I recall someone even cut off his necktie in my waiting room.

SAVED FROM AMPUTATION

Quite a few patients were referred to me with skin cancer on a finger or toe that had resisted treatment and was scheduled for amputation. Some were also referred to me with cancer on the penis, where a doctor had determined that amputation was the only viable option left. One of my talented fellows, Maritza Perez, MD, remembers seeing a case like that when she started training with me:

"I was already an assistant professor of dermatology at Yale," Dr. Perez says, "but I decided it would be worth 'demoting' myself to do a fellowship with Perry. It was the best experience of my life! I started my fellowship in September 1993. On one of my first days, I was excited

continued

when he said, 'Oh we have a great case today. We have a verrucous carcinoma of the penis' [also known as a Buschke-Löwenstein tumor].

"I said, 'Oh my God, am I going to have to amputate the member?' That would be devastating to the man. But we did not amputate the member; we saved it. We did three stages of Mohs. I introduced myself to urology 101 dermatology, and I'm not afraid of verrucous carcinomas anymore. I was very happy I had been selected as a fellow."

Yes, and on a follow-up visit, the patient said he'd never enjoyed sex more than since his operation. We had another case where someone was scheduled to have the thumb of his dominant hand amputated. The thumb is very important, responsible for 60 percent of the function of the hand. You can't do buttons without a thumb. I didn't promise I could save it, but we'd make every effort to eradicate the cancer and save the thumb. In that case, as well as many others, we were able to save the valuable digit.

My chief nurse at the time, Iris Flick, recalls working closely with many of our famous patients. She especially bonded with Dominick Dunne, who wrote so prolifically about crime and was a victim himself when his daughter, Dominique, was murdered in 1982. It's hard to imagine how anyone carries on after something like that. Iris says:

"Yes, Dominick Dunne and I became soul mates through his relationship with Perry. Some celebrity patients did not want to be seen, but Dominick loved to be seen. He'd say, 'Keep the door open!' I wanted my husband to meet him because he was such a dear friend and influence in my life, so Perry took us all out to dinner one night, and we had a wonderful time.

"I loved working with Perry. He would never say, 'She's just a nurse.' He always treated me with the utmost respect, which made the patients feel confident. If he wasn't there, they knew they were safe in my hands.

"I wanted to learn, and I would attend his lectures. Perry also trained so many residents and fellows at NYU. I listened to what he was saying to them, so I learned with them. I became so adept at dermatology that he would say in front of the patients, 'Iris, what do you think this is?' That is a big thing for a surgeon like him to do. It was very respectful and loving.

"Our office had a flow. Everything was always for the good of the patient. It never seemed cumbersome; it was always fun. There was always a smile on my face. I sang; he told jokes. We were a great team."

Sometimes grateful and wealthy patients would try to offer me a gift of appreciation. I would try to gently steer them toward making a donation to The Skin Cancer Foundation instead. But some would persist, and a few of the promised gifts seemed over the top, even a bit alarming.

For example, I had done a surgery on David Marx. He and his brother, Louis, had created the toy company responsible for Big Wheels, which were in almost every driveway in the 1970s and '80s (remember Rock 'Em Sock 'Em Robots?). I had gotten to know Marx and his wife, and had visited them at their home in South Jersey. She called me that night after the surgery, saying they were concerned because the wound was bleeding copiously. They were staying in a suite in the Waldorf Towers.

I said, "OK, I'll grab my bag and be right over. Just put pressure on the wound." I went over to the Waldorf Astoria hotel. They said, "You have to go to the back side, because the Waldorf Towers are private apartments and have nothing to do with the hotel." I was frantically rushing to get to where they were. I finally found the correct entrance and elevator. I dashed in and was running to their apartment. When I got there, his wife said, "I'm so worried. Is he going to die?" I said, "Absolutely not, but I'm glad you called me, because I'm here to help if you have any concerns." When I got to

David, I saw that he had just a few drops of blood on the bandage, and he was most definitely going to live. I changed the dressing. He held my hand and said, "Doc, you're wonderful. I really want to express my appreciation. I'm going to do something for you. I'm going to give you my Rolls-Royce."

I tried to show a little humility and said, "No, that's very thoughtful of you, but I'm just doing my job. It's my responsibility, and I'm here to help you." How could I accept a Rolls-Royce? About a week later, Marx came to the office for his follow-up appointment, carrying a paper bag. He opened the bag, and I expected him to take out a chauffeur's hat or a set of keys. Instead, he pulled out a little radio designed in the shape of a car and said, "We sold a million of these to Radio Shack. Here's your Rolls-Royce!"

Another time, Sonny Werblin and his wife, Leah, were in my waiting room. He had been very successful as an entertainment executive and was an owner of the New York Jets and chairman of Madison Square Garden. He was also my patient. His wife said she wanted to do something very special for me. She said, "We're going up to Saratoga for the races this weekend. We have a couple of horses running, and I'm going to give you a pair of thoroughbreds." I said, "Wow, that's very generous of you," thinking maybe she meant an interest in the horses and certainly not the *actual* horses! But I was wrong on both counts: She sent me two bookends that were sculptures of horses' heads. They were very nice, and I was relieved.

I had another patient with a connection to thoroughbreds. Charlie Payson, a very successful lawyer and businessman, and his first wife, Joan Whitney, were wealthy art collectors and philanthropists. They had a beautiful Gatsby-style house in Sands Point, Long Island. After her death in 1975, he inherited her ownership of the New York Mets, even though he wasn't even a big fan of the team.

In 1977 he married an editor at *Sports Illustrated*, who had written an article about him. She was formerly married to the son of a patient of mine. Together, they created a thoroughbred horse racing training center in Florida. When Charlie Payson was diagnosed with skin cancer, he was referred to me. His much-younger wife came with him for the consultation. He needed surgery, but, as usual, I was completely booked solid for the next two or three weeks. She pleaded with me to fit him in sooner. "We don't want to wait," she said. "Is there any way you can do it right away?"

I said, "I really don't have a choice." My secretary would be furious if I pulled rank and tried to bring in someone who had money over the poor schnook who had been waiting for weeks. Why should he be bumped? She begged and said, "I'll never forget it if you can arrange something and squeeze him in."

I usually did not accommodate such requests. However, I had a regular Wednesday morning meeting at NYU, and I thought the chairman might excuse me this one time, on the assumption that the Paysons would make a generous donation to The Skin Cancer Foundation. So, I gave in and made the appointment right away. The surgery went well.

When I never heard from her afterward, I wrote her a note with a holiday card. I said, "You know, we really didn't meet our quota for the Foundation this year, and if there's any way you can help us, we'd be most grateful." I put in quotation marks, "I'll never forget you for doing this," similar to what she had said to me when she asked me to rearrange my schedule for Charlie's surgery. Her response? She sent a check for $100.

Charlie Payson died in 1985 and left almost all of his hefty fortune to his second wife, much to the chagrin of his kids and grandkids with his first wife. They sued. Their lawyers alleged that Payson wasn't in his right mind when he changed his will. His wife claimed otherwise. Her lawyer came and interviewed me about his state of mind, because I was the last doctor to see him alive. I told them the story about the $100. They never used me as a witness, and unfortunately, his kids lost the case.

RUNNING INTO PATIENTS EVERYWHERE!

I ran into patients in other countries all the time. I mean *all the time*. Here are just a few examples: Once I was getting off a bus at the Hotel Grand Bretagne in Athens. Another man stepped off the same bus, looked at me and said, "Dr. Robins! It's so nice seeing you." Then there was the time I was on a ferry going from Vancouver to Victoria, and there was a patient. I was in line at the Vatican, waiting to go into the Sistine Chapel, and the man in back of me said, "Dr. Robins, can you take a look at this spot on my nose?" After a conference in the Black Forest in Germany, I was telling my friends, "Wherever I go, I run into patients." They said, "No, it's just a coincidence." Then as we were leaving the famous Brenners Park-Hotel in Baden Baden, a woman came over to me and grabbed my arm. "Dr. Robins! What are you doing here? I'm glad to see you! I'm supposed to see you next week, so I'll save you a visit. Can you look at my mole here?" My colleagues couldn't believe it. They said I must have known the whole time that she was there, but I had no idea.

As a dermatologist, I know I shouldn't judge a book by its cover, but sometimes human nature takes over. A new patient came in one day looking disheveled, with dirty nails and dirty clothes. He had rhinophyma, which is like W.C. Fields' nose, with a big, bubbly thing at the end. It's easy to treat; you basically just shave it off.

I had a trainee at that time, so I said, "Do you mind if I have my assistant help you?" He said no. So I let my fellow do the shaving and the trimming. We pared down the nose to an acceptable shape. I thanked him, and I told the nurse to charge him half the usual amount because my fellow helped do the surgery and the patient didn't look like he could afford to pay much at all.

I was still living in Rye then and went home by train. That evening I got a call that my patient was in Greenwich Hospital and was bleeding. They just wanted me to know that. The doctor there took care of him. I said, "Well, tell him to wait for me and I'll come up and see him." I was surprised that he was in Greenwich Hospital because it is a very upscale area. When I arrived there, he was already bandaged up and doing fine. He said, "Can I give you a lift home?" I said, "No, I'll take a taxi." He said, "No, I'll give you a lift. I have my chauffeur outside." I'm thinking, *Yeah, right; you have your chauffeur outside.* Sure enough, he did. We got in his limousine and drove to Rye. I asked him, "What do you do?" He replied, "I build airports around the world." You can't tell a book by its cover.

You can't always judge a book by what it says, either. After I performed surgery on a lawyer, he told me he was going into the witness protection program. "I have to disappear," he said. "You're not going to see me for a long time. Please tell me what I should do and what I'll need for my care after the surgery, as I'm sure they won't have a dermatologist there." I wrote out everything and gave him some supplies to last a year, should he need it. I said, "Well, I'm glad I'm able to help you. Thank you for supporting this government system." Two days later I read in the paper that he was going to prison for swindling. He got 10 years.

Speaking of criminals, I had the odd experience of treating two widows whose husbands had been murdered, out in the open, in pretty high-profile cases. One was the wife of Donald Aronow, who manufactured sleek, *very* fast speedboats and sold them to wealthy celebrities and heads of state around the world. He also made headlines for having ties to drug smuggling and the Mafia. He was gunned down in 1987 in Thunderboat Row in Miami. That was the street where he built those needle-nosed cigarette boats that could outrun military or government patrol boats. You can imagine there might be quite a demand for such things!

I asked my patient how they met, and she said she was a model and used to sit on the boats during the boat shows to entice the customers to buy. So many models, by the way, were often pressured to get tanned for photo shoots. Many of them used tanning beds and would lie baking in the sun, and like her, many got skin cancer at a relatively young age. They still do.

Aronow's murder was a sensational crime that went unsolved for about a decade until a career criminal confessed. There was even a book about it called *Blue Thunder: How the Mafia Owned and Finally Murdered Cigarette Boat King Donald Aronow,* by Thomas Burdick and Charlene Mitchell.

The second widow was from the Chicago area. She had been married to a man who owned a plumbing company. His accountant had been with this company for many years and apparently caused problems by being argumentative or disruptive. I believe he was asked to retire and was given a nice pension, but he was unhappy about leaving. He often contacted the company and said he wanted to come back to work. The owners said no but eventually two of them agreed to meet him at a restaurant, hoping they could put an end to it. They sat down at a table and the former employee came in. He pulled out a gun and shot both of them dead. At least, that's how she told it. As I said, patients loved to talk.

Patients also came from all over the world to see me. A countess in Germany referred a patient to me who needed surgery for a large melanoma on her leg. I didn't know it at the time, but she was from one of the wealthiest families in Turkey. She flew in on the Concorde and was in my office the next day. I excised the tumor and closed the wound, treating her as I would have treated any nice patient. Melanomas can leave very large scars, but on this one I got a phenomenal result. Later, she and her husband invited me to visit them in Turkey. It was a wonderful experience, and we became close friends and saw each other often. To this day, you almost can't see her scar.

On another occasion, while I was on the island of Mykonos, one of my Greek friends took me to a restaurant at the Santa Marina resort, on a hill overlooking the harbor. During our dinner, my friend called over the owner of the resort, Elias Papageorgiou, to introduce me. He said, "Can you take a look at Mr. P's ear? He has a dark spot there." Papageorgiou said, "I understand you're a specialist. Tell me, what do you think?" I asked, "What did the Greek doctors tell you?" He replied, "They said, 'It's a birthmark. Don't worry about it; you'll live to be 100.'"

Despite that, I didn't like the looks of it, so I said we should do a biopsy. The next day was Sunday and nothing was open, but through connections we found an orthopedic surgeon who agreed to open his office for us so I could perform the biopsy. No surprise to me, it turned out to be malignant melanoma. Three weeks later, Papageorgiou came to New York and I performed surgery to remove the tumor. I was so glad we caught that one. We became friends after that. My daughter went to a wedding of a Greek friend on Mykonos at that hotel, and he refused to charge her a penny. Sadly, Elias later developed a melanoma in his eye. He traveled to Houston for treatment at MD Anderson, but it had metastasized, and eventually he died from it. A few years ago, while on a cruise in Turkey, I stopped in Mykonos to visit his widow, and we had a lovely time sharing memories of her husband.

Not all my patients were rich, famous or high-profile, however. Sometimes what I enjoyed most were the small, everyday moments—joking around a little, giving a reassuring hug, just making a connection. I remember a woman who needed Mohs surgery. I asked her age and was surprised when she said she was in her 90s. I said, "Mrs. Murphy, you don't look a day over 59." She replied, "You really think I look 59?" I said, "Absolutely." She said, "Dr. Robins, if your eyesight is that bad, I don't think I want you to do my surgery!" But of course, I did. It went well, and she was grateful.

As my son Lawrence says, "What my father accomplished was great. To me, he is a Ben Franklin or a Steve Jobs—not just because of the success he had in dermatology, but because of the kind of doctor he became. He treated the patient, not the disease. I admire the way he treated all the people in his life, even the ones who let him down. That is the most beautiful thing about him."

CHAPTER 16

Going Global

*Learning to incorporate international
adventures into all areas of my life is perhaps
my most satisfying accomplishment.*

Travel has meant the world to me. I knew it the moment my first commercial flight took off in 1953 when I was in the Army, headed to Seattle and then overseas to experience who knows what. Rather than fear, I felt exhilaration. I loved the experience of flight and, even more, that it took me to places I'd never been before.

From that point on, seeing new locales became not just a priority to me, but essential. It's a big part of who I am. I've always been drawn to people who feel the same way. Travel has defined my relationships, my friendships and my professional life. As much as I loved surgery, I would not have been as happy without being able to share my knowledge with those in other countries, and to learn from them as well.

Establishing the International Society for Dermatologic Surgery was one of the best things I ever did, not only for my chosen medical specialty but also for my own growth and quality of life, too. I loved making connections, bringing people together and sharing medical education. I also thoroughly enjoyed the camaraderie and the cultural exchange. Germany and Spain were ahead of us in dermatologic surgery in the late '70s, and we learned a lot from them. We helped the Europeans and other countries start their own skin cancer foundations and medical journals, which raised awareness and credibility for them. We were a good team, and our alliances helped the specialty explode in many countries.

As my friend Bill Hanke says, "I think the ISDS was Perry's favorite project, because it combined all of the things that he loved most: teaching Mohs surgery and the importance of prevention, early detection and treatment of skin cancer, plus international travel, meeting new and old friends, testing his foreign language skills—and, of course, eating good food." Yes, he knows me so well.

I became adept at planning international meetings, but that was only after a few missteps. In 1978, to kick off the society, I planned a founders' meeting with prominent dermatologists I knew from France, Spain, Portugal, Germany and the U.S. I had a patient who was a travel agent, so I asked him to suggest a great location for our first meeting. He said, "Well, you've been almost everywhere, but you haven't been to Morocco." I said, "That sounds like fun; let's plan it!" He suggested we have the meeting in Marrakech and then go on to Fes and Casablanca, and said, "I promise you'll have a great time."

I advertised the meeting in the *The Journal of Dermatologic Surgery* and wrote to subscribers, inviting them to attend. I was thrilled that we had about 45 people accept. We stayed at the lush La Mamounia Hotel, whose history dates back to the 12th century, and I couldn't wait to explore the area. The first day, a small group of us decided to take a tour to the 17th century sand castles of Ait-Ben-Haddou, a UNESCO World Heritage site. Our guide told us we would be back at 4 o'clock, so we posted a note that the meeting would commence at that time. Unfortunately, our guide forgot to tell us he meant we'd return at 4 o'clock the next morning!

A contingent of 14 or 15 doctors had arrived from Spain for our meeting, thanks to the support of Felipe de Dulanto, MD, a dermatologist and surgeon who had served as a personal physician to Generalissimo Francisco Franco until the dictator's death in 1975. The attendees from Spain were quite serious about being there to learn, so they didn't take it too well when we didn't return from our excursion as promised. Out in the desert, we had no way to call and inform anyone about our delay, so the doctors left a note on my door expressing their concern about how committed we were to forming this society, and they threatened to leave.

I had nothing but respect for these doctors, and I felt terrible that they thought we were playing games. But I also didn't want to travel to an exotic place I'd never seen before and spend every minute in a hotel meeting room. It was about finding the right balance of education and culture. I apologized, expressed my commitment to our mission and suggested we all stay.

They agreed to stay, and we got the meeting under way—in the hotel dining room, as I'd forgotten to ask about a meeting room. For our presentation, we had Kodachrome slides in bulky carousels we had to schlep everywhere back then. We had set up our projector and a screen, but I had forgotten about the voltage difference. I plugged it in and—*poof!*—blew it out. I was lucky we didn't blow the circuits for the whole place. We were able to rent a local projector, and we finally got the show going. But the delay made me look unprepared, and it was a lesson that stuck with me on the importance of paying attention to details, especially on timing and technicalities.

I was thrilled with our excursions to the souks and medieval architecture of Fes, and to experience the port city of Casablanca in living color, rather than just my black and white Bogey and Bergman fantasies from the beloved movie. I remember one crazy market selling everything you can imagine, including a vendor holding a stethoscope and offering medical services. He said if he placed the stethoscope on my wrist and asked me to cough, he could tell what was "wrong" with me. Imagine how well that went over with a bunch of doctors!

I had another tough lesson to learn on that trip. On one of our stops, I hosted a cocktail hour for about 25 people with local wine and cheese. The next day, I got a bill for something like $2,300, which was about three times what I had expected. I was appalled, as our budget was very tight. I had to ask all the attendees to write down what they ate and drank at the reception. Apparently our "enterprising" tour guide thought the silly Americans would never notice the 12 bottles of scotch added to the bill, even though no one from our group had consumed any scotch.

One of the doctors said his brother-in-law was a lawyer who could help us, but I knew that legal representation would cost more than the original bill. I refused to pay the bill and threatened to log my complaint into the local police register, which the *gendarmes* check periodically. The tour guide did not want that kind of scrutiny, so we reached an acceptable settlement for a one-hour event, then boarded the bus and moved on. I learned my lesson, though: Always discuss details and get an estimate in advance!

Despite the snafus in Morocco, we moved forward with establishing the ISDS. I had developed a friendship with António Picoto, MD, a prominent dermatologist based in Lisbon, Portugal, when he came to New York to train with me. He suggested Lisbon as the site of our first ISDS meeting, and I thought that was a great idea. Our first official meeting in 1979 attracted about 250 attendees and faculty from all over the world for 20 surgical symposia. Registration was $100, airfare from New York was $399, and luxury hotel rooms in Lisbon started at $86. We had fun, too, with a pig roast and a special private bullfight. (In Portugal they don't kill the bulls; they just immobilize them and drag them out. I wouldn't want to see one killed.) Our meeting was a grand success and cemented my lifelong friendship with António.

That reminds me of a slightly embarrassing story in Lisbon years later, when António invited me to be the keynote speaker at a dinner to revitalize and rebuild the Portuguese Skin Cancer Foundation. I was to talk about the importance of raising awareness about skin cancer prevention, detection and treatment in his country.

The president of Portugal was invited to attend the dinner but had a conflict, so he sent his wife in his place. She was seated at the head table next to me, with her sister-in-law on the other side of me. We had a wonderful evening. The first lady of Portugal spoke fluent English, and she told me about her niece, who was studying at Columbia University. We discussed New York restaurants and shopping, as well as our adventures in Portugal. We talked and talked. She promised that she would come and visit if she came to New York. I gave her my contact info and said, "Give your niece my name and address in case she ever needs any advice or medical attention while she's in New York. I'd be glad to help her."

At the end of the dinner, I stood up and, in typical European fashion, gave her a kiss on both cheeks, one and then the other, as I did with most of my friends. Suddenly the security guards were on me, pulling me away from her and exclaiming, *"Are you crazy? What are you doing? You don't go kissing the president's wife!"* They wanted to arrest me. I was completely shocked. Luckily, Dr. Picoto was able to calm the situation. What can I say? I'm a warm and affectionate person, and I was just being myself—but of course it's important to know when caution is warranted.

After our first ISDS meeting in Lisbon, we gathered almost every year. We went to Paris, and then Vienna. The attendees had a great time and the society grew and grew. As of 2018, we've had 39 gatherings in 24 countries, and, with one or two exceptions, I've been to all of them. We've returned a few times to some of our favorite locations (Spain, Germany, Italy, Israel), although we haven't yet revisited Morocco. Our 40th ISDS meeting in 2019 is scheduled for Manila, in the Philippines.

Once we got past the misunderstanding in Morocco, the Spanish dermatologists became enthusiastic supporters of the ISDS, and we've had more meetings there than anywhere else: in Granada in 1983, Barcelona in '87, Seville in '93, Madrid in 2000 and Barcelona in 2004. Granada was Bill Hanke's first ISDS meeting, and he remembers it as "a real happening, with tours of the Alhambra, performances by flamenco dancers, concerts by a classical guitarist and an elegant dinner in the 16th century Hospital Real." We always received a warm welcome in Spain.

We did almost all of our presentations in English. We only provided translators once in a while for a keynote speech to be heard in the home language of the host country. That didn't always make everyone happy. I recall a kerfuffle at the Granada meeting over a session on cryotherapy, which is the use of liquid nitrogen to treat some precancers and superficial skin cancers by freezing them. We had a translator for a larger session happening at the same time but didn't have a translator for the smaller session on cryotherapy. We just couldn't afford it. The attendees came out of their session complaining bitterly. So we nicknamed them the "cryo-babies" and still tease them good-naturedly about it to this day.

Why was the cryo session always the small group and not the large group? I think cryo would have been more successful if someone had developed a formal training program for it. One of the fathers of cryosurgery was Setrag A. Zacarian, MD, in Springfield, Massachusetts. A spray version of liquid nitrogen had been around since 1965, but Dr. Zacarian created a handheld device with a one-handed trigger control and special tips that would allow more pinpoint freezing to different diameters and depths of the tissue. His research, along with a few others, was very influential. But they never quite gained enough of a following to organize like we did for Mohs surgery. They would give a talk, and that was the end of it.

I loved learning languages and having a chance to practice what I knew. Or to experience being humbled by what I *didn't* know. When we had meetings in Germany or France and I needed to give a talk, *pas de problème.* My Spanish, on the other hand, was *un poco problemático.* A pharmaceutical company sponsored me to give my course in the surgical techniques of flaps and grafts to all the third-year residents in Spain, and they brought them to Barcelona from all over the country. I had become friends with local dermatologist and Mohs surgeon Alejandro Camps, MD, and he helped organize this collaboration, which we did several times. I'll never forget the first time, after lecturing for about 15 or 20 minutes, one of the braver students raised his hand and pleaded, "Dr. Robins, *please,* can you speak to us in English?" Apparently, my medical Spanish wasn't so good. I was happy to oblige but vowed to work on my skills.

During one of these sessions, Alejandro told me he was a member of the famous century-old Yacht Club in the harbor. "I made reservations at the very special restaurant there, and I'm taking you to dinner," he said. We arrived and ordered drinks while we took in the spectacular views of the entire harbor of Barcelona. I was perusing the glorious seafood dishes on the menu and looking forward to ordering, when suddenly a pack of dogs entered the dining room and began sniffing all around the place. I said, "Alex, *que pasa*? What's happening?" He said, "Oh, the king is probably coming for dinner. His security team has the dogs sniff for bombs because of the conflict between the Basque and the Catalans. They have to take all precautions."

One of my favorite memories of Spain was in 1980, when I was named an honorary member of the Spanish Academy of Medicine (with Madrid dermatologist Francisco Camacho, MD, on my right).

It was exciting, but it made us a little nervous, too. We decided not to stay for what would likely be a not-very-relaxing dinner. We had a good laugh and have remained close friends ever since. In fact, in 2006, Dr. Camps and his wife came to my daughter's wedding in Santiago de Compostela, on the coast of northern Spain. I was thrilled that my daughter married a man who was born in Madrid.

Not only is he a wonderful guy, but he (and later, my granddaughter) helped me improve my Spanish-speaking skills!

Who doesn't love Italy—the pasta, the people, the art, *la dolce vita*? It's one of my favorite places, and we had wonderful ISDS meetings in Rome in 1985, Florence in 1990, Venice in 2007 and Rome again in 2018. One of the many reasons I love going back there is my dear friend Luigi Rusciani. He would invite me to come every other year to lecture at Gemelli Hospital, which is part of the Rome campus of Catholic University of the Sacred Heart. Sometimes he would take me to the Vatican as a guest, and we could shop in a special store there that had beautiful clothing and accessories. Unfortunately, most of the priests aren't my size, so all I could buy were belts and socks.

You couldn't meet a nicer couple than Luigi and his wife, Paula. They invited me to their beautiful home in the hills outside the city center and gave me a room that was designated with a sign as the "Robins Room." I'm larger than the average Italian, and I'm sorry to say the first time I was there, I broke the bed. So they bought a new bed and put up a sign saying, *"This bed is Perry-proof."* Paula knows I love pasta Bolognese, so she always makes it for me—sometimes even two or three different kinds. We have a wonderful relationship.

Luigi's great-grandfather, grandfather and father were dermatologists, and his son, Antonio, is a plastic surgeon—that's five generations of influence in the skin surgery field. (Antonio spent several weeks with me at NYU in 2001 learning the basics of Mohs surgery, too.) Luigi came from a distinguished family in Calabria, in southern Italy. As our friendship grew, we decided my Italian name should be "Robino," spoken with a trilled "R." So I would practice my Italian and say, with the appropriate hand gestures, "My name is Robino, and I come from Calabria!" But if anyone asked me questions about the region, I couldn't answer them, as I'd never been there. One day Luigi got fed up with me and said, "We're going down there for a couple of days." Situated on the rocky coast down in the "toe" of the boot of Italy, Calabria has beautiful beaches and mountains. The region is known for its wonderful eggplant, cured meats, cheeses, bread and olive oil, and I tasted it all in the name of Robino.

My brief sojourn in Calabria came in handy on a later trip to the south of France. I was often in Cannes for meetings with my dear friend Dr. Robert Baran, who ran a very successful dermatological practice there. He is also my son's godfather. On one visit in Cannes with my sister, Irene, we drove down to Saint-Paul-de-Vence to have lunch at the famous restaurant La Colombe d'Or. Inside are paintings by Picasso, Chagall, Braque, Miró and other famed artists. The owner gave them refuge and meals in the wintertime in exchange for paintings. Today, millions of dollars' worth of their masterpieces hang on the walls of the restaurant.

On our way there, we ran into a detour, took a wrong turn or two and arrived at about 2:15. We were devastated when the maître d' told us they were closed; lunch service ended at 2 o'clock. I spoke to him in French, saying, "I hear you speak with an accent. Where do you come from?" He replied, "Me? I come from Italy. Calabria." I was thrilled to hear that and said, "*Paisano!* Me too. My name is Robino. I come from Calabria. Maybe we're relatives!" He laughed and played along. "You really come from Calabria?" "*Si!*" "OK, we feed you." Irene and I had a lovely time.

A few years later, I was with Luigi at a meeting in Nice. I suggested we go visit the restaurant at Saint-Paul-de-Vence. We arrived there (on time!) and sure enough, met the same maître d'. I reminded him who I "was" and said, "Now I want you to meet my brother, Luigi Rusciani, also from Calabria." We had a lot of laughs. As I admired the Matisse on the wall and the lobster salad, beef with potatoes *dauphinoise* and *tarte tatin* on the menu, the two real

Italians hit it off. They got along famously and even determined that they were distant relatives.

Speaking of France, I've loved Paris since I caught my first glimpse of it after hitchhiking there on my breaks from medical school in Germany. We hosted ISDS meetings there in 1980 and 1992. And we were nearby at the ISDS meeting in Brussels, Belgium, in 1989, so a few of us went on to Paris afterward. People say the French aren't very warm and welcoming to Americans, but that's not true! One of my favorite examples of this was when I was there with Mitzi, the executive director of The Skin Cancer Foundation, Iowa dermatologist Roger Ceilley, MD, who is a former president of the American Academy of Dermatology, and his then wife, Kay. We dined at La Tour d'Argent, had a great time and stayed late. When we left the restaurant, we couldn't get a taxi, as they'd all been taken by the post-theater crowd, and the buses had stopped running. Our hotel was two or three miles away, not exactly late-night hoofing distance.

We were trying to decide what to do when I saw a local woman getting into a little car, and I said, "*Je suis désolée.* Can you help us? We can't get a taxi," in my quasi-fluent French. She had a little Renault, barely a four-seater, and there were four of us in addition to the driver. But she didn't hesitate, and insisted on helping us, so we squeezed—I mean *squeezed*; I'm a big guy, and so is Roger—into the car and she whisked us away to our hotel. We learned she was a professor at one of the local universities, and we had a nice conversation. I offered her money or a gift, but she said, "Don't be ridiculous." It was nice. I want people to know there are a lot of French people who like Americans. Still, *vous trouvez plus d'amis en France si vous essayez de parler leur langue. C'est vrai!*

"Perry was at his best that night—charming and fluent in French," Dr. Ceilley recalls. "We tried to pay the professor, but she wouldn't take anything and just wanted our last evening in Paris to be fun and memorable. It was indeed a memorable night!"

It always made me happy to return to Germany and practice speaking the language (*"die Sprache zu sprechen"*) I had learned during medical school. I had many opportunities, including ISDS meetings in Munich in 1991, Berlin in 2003 and Heidelberg, where it all began, in 2011, as well as the World Congress on Cancers of the Skin in Berlin in 1993.

In addition, my friend Gerhard Sattler, MD, invited me to lecture in Darmstadt, a suburb of Frankfurt where he practiced cosmetic dermatology. I helped him start up an International Live Surgery Symposium. He arranged for us to have four or five surgical suites in a local hospital, and we brought in doctors from other European countries, plus a few Americans. We beamed the surgeries to a theater in a hotel, where a couple of moderators would ask the doctors questions. We did the sessions in English and German, using a translator. I'll never forget the first one: The hospital couldn't find scrubs big enough to fit me, so they had to send a messenger to another facility where they had more super-sized surgeons like me.

Gerhard and his wife, Sonja, knew the way to my heart was through my stomach, so they would often wine and dine me. They took me to a wonderful but rather formal five-star restaurant in the Black Forest (*der Schwarzwald*) in southwest Germany. We had two waiters in white gloves just to take care of our small group. They brought the soup course, and when I said, in German, that it was delicious, the waiter said, "Would you like to try some of our other soups? They're all very good." "Of course," I said, "Why not?" So he brought me samples of *all* the soups and then, encouraged by my enthusiasm, other specialties as well. It was an eating orgy. At the end, when I saw the chef, I pinched his cheeks and said, "You know, it's so good, I'm going to tell your mother-in-law what a great cook you are!" Apparently my style of playful enthusiasm was not the usual customer behavior in such a formal place in Germany, but I'm not a usual customer. The chef was a good sport.

We decided to have our live surgical symposia every two years in December. They were popular, and they helped Gerhard become very successful, too. He is a leader in liposuction in Germany (I tease him by saying he is the biggest fat sucker in the world). Now he is director of the Rosenparkklinik Center for Cosmetic Dermatologic Surgery and Plastic Surgery in Darmstadt, where he works with many stars and celebrities. He's even opening spas throughout Germany. He likes to call me his American dad.

I've attended these symposia many times over the years. One December was particularly memorable, when I had to stop in Belgium for another meeting on my way to Darmstadt. It was a stormy night in Brussels, with freezing rain. I had to hail a taxi to get to a dinner meeting, but when I stepped out of my hotel, I was shocked that it was so icy, I could barely walk in my leather shoes without risking disaster. I spotted a mini-mall across the street and took tiny, careful, mincing steps to see if I could buy some less treacherous footwear. There were a couple of shoe stores, but *"Zut alors!,"* none of them had any shoes big enough to fit me. My shoes are so big, my German friends call them *"Kanalboote"* (canal boats).

Luckily, I was able to catch a taxi without crashing onto the ice, attend my dinner meeting and arrive intact back at my hotel. The next morning, I was scheduled to go on to Darmstadt, but thanks to the ice storm, the airport was closed and the flights were all canceled. On to plan B: I took a car service to the train station, only to learn that the trains were all canceled, as well. I stood in a long line to check for later trains, but they were already overbooked.

I was scheduled to perform surgery for an audience of eager physicians in Darmstadt the next day, so I had to find a way to get there! I knew there were some taxis outside the Brussels train station, so I walked up to a driver and asked, "What would you charge to take me to Frankfurt?" I didn't say Darmstadt because the cab driver wouldn't have the foggiest idea. He looked at me incredulously and said, "Frankfurt, Germany?" I said, "Yes." "You really want to go in this storm?" I said, "Yes." He said, "I don't know. It would probably total about 900 euros," which was equivalent to about US$1,000. What choice did I have? I said, "OK, let's go."

I got in his lightweight little Renault (hardly the vehicle of choice for such icy conditions), and we drove *verrrry* slowly. We arrived safely in Frankfurt at twilight, and I let the driver know I was actually headed for Darmstadt. With no GPS or map, I had to ask a passerby in German for the best route. When we learned that the road was under construction and it would involve a detour, my intrepid driver gave up the ghost. In mournful French, he said, *"Monsieur, je suis désolée,* but I cannot drive anymore."

I thanked the driver, paid him and got out of his taxi. I found a local cab, which cost me another $100 to get to the hotel. The next morning, I gave my lecture to an appreciative group. Hey, the show must go on!

INTERACTIVE LECTURES
CLOSER TO HOME

I loved combining teaching and travel. Thanks to a grant from a pharmaceutical company, I did my flaps and grafts course about four times a year, and I got to visit fun places in the U.S. and Canada. These young doctors were hungry for knowledge on dermatologic surgery, and they considered me the guru. It was a time of tremendous interest and growth.

I went to Vancouver when it hosted the World's Fair in 1986, and

I went to Calgary for the Stampede. I went to New Orleans for the cuisine. But I didn't turn down any opportunity to spread the gospel of treating skin cancer. When I went to some smaller cities, like Sacramento, California, or Allentown, Pennsylvania, the attendees were nice but quiet. They didn't ask as many questions as those at the major universities, who peppered me with query after query.

I had Kodachrome slides of many of the cases I had done—thousands and thousands of them. My course included about 1,500 of these slides in carousels, and they were not easy to ship or carry. In the early days, we used flip charts as a teaching tool. I would aim a photo from the projector onto the paper, and one at a time, the students would go up with a marker and draw on the paper how they would close the wound. Then they'd flip the paper for the next one.

Everybody at their desks had a pad and pencil and would participate, too. Later that evolved so that we could project, say, a post-surgery defect on a patient's cheek onto a whiteboard. Then the students could use an erasable marker to show how they would handle the case, and then we could erase it. No paper-flipping needed.

I regret that I didn't learn Hebrew in my childhood. I never went to Hebrew school, and you may recall I had to improvise at my bar mitzvah by reading the words phonetically. I guess I hadn't developed my ear for (or love of) languages quite yet. Still, I've enjoyed my trips to Israel, where we held the ISDS in Jerusalem in 1984, and Tel Aviv in '96. Almost everybody speaks Yiddish or English, so I can get by. It is exhilarating to go there: It's bustling, there's building and construction, and a high-energy spirit. In Israel they have socialized medicine. If you want Mohs surgery, you have to wait three or four months, but if you go to a surgeon privately and have the money to pay for it, they'll take you the next day. It's universal: Money talks.

Before one of the conferences in Israel, we stopped in Cairo and went to the Egyptian Museum, which was wondrous. It was there that I learned the word *baksheesh*, which means tip, whether it's for a service you requested, unsolicited advice—or even something as intangible as more time. Visitors hear it *often* in Cairo. For example, when we went to see the Treasures of Tutankhamun exhibit, if you gave the guard a tip, he would let you stay another 30 seconds. If you wanted longer, he'd ask for more. *"Baksheesh? Baksheesh?"* Every 30 seconds he timed it for more money.

In Cairo we hosted an impromptu costume party, with me playing the part of King Farouk!

A trip up the Nile is fabulous. It's very slow, but in a good way—soothing, with no waves. The boat only goes five to 10 miles a night. You get up to Aswan and Abu Simbel and all the ruins and temples and shrines. It's really worthwhile. It made me sad to remember that my dear friend John Forline and his daughter drowned there, but it somehow gave me comfort, knowing that at least they spent their last days together traveling, adventuring and discovering new sights.

Many Americans lump together Denmark, Norway, Sweden and Finland, but there is a world of difference between them. The Swedes can be arrogant, independent and not very friendly. They were neutral in World War II and profited in dealing with the Nazis. When the Germans invaded Norway and Denmark in 1940, the Danish resisted by wearing four coins (totaling nine for the April 9 date of the occupation) tied together with red and white ribbons. Meanwhile, the Finns were fighting Russia in the Finnish Russian War for many years over territory in the northern part of Finland.

Wars help shape the character of the people, and the folks I've known from Denmark are wonderful. There couldn't be nicer people anywhere. They always seemed pro-American, enthusiastic and cheerful. I still occasionally think about Elizabeth, the smart and lovely dark-haired Danish girl I dated while I was in medical school. I also reminisce about the lavish fish buffet on the Danish ferry on my way back to school in Heidelberg! Winters were tough because it starts getting dark around 2 in the afternoon and stays that way until 10 in the morning.

In the Scandinavian summers, I loved the midnight sun, especially up in Sweden, where I lectured many times. I was excited when I was invited to lecture at the Karolinska Institutet in Stockholm, where they select the Nobel laureates in physiology and medicine. I waved at them, but they didn't pay any attention to me!

I did do a good deed in Sweden, though. While I was at the airport, I had noticed a young woman who appeared to have a melanoma on her forehead. "You should see a plastic surgeon," I told her (as I knew no dermatologists in Sweden were doing surgery yet). "This could be a cancer." She said, "Well, before I can go to a plastic surgeon, I have to see my family doctor, and because it's not an emergency, that can take a while. And then it takes several weeks to get an appointment to see a plastic surgeon." I felt that delaying could be dangerous, even life-threatening, so I said, "No, no. I'm having dinner tonight at the home of the chairman of the department of dermatology. I want you to call me at this number at exactly a quarter after nine. Not before, not after."

At the dinner, I met another guest who was the chairman of the department of plastic surgery. We discussed how the social medical system worked in Sweden, and they were bragging about how efficient it was. I told them there must be some problems at times, as I explained about the young woman I'd seen, how I'd encouraged her to see a plastic surgeon right away and she said it would take weeks to get an appointment. Without hesitation, the plastic surgeon gave me his card and said, "Tell her to call me when you see her again." I said, "She's going to call me here in a few minutes. Would you speak to her?" He said, "Absolutely." She called right on time and I said, "Here's the chairman of the plastic surgery department. He will arrange for someone to see you in the next day or two." Although I never heard about her outcome, I think of her from time to time and hope they took good care of her.

Seeing parts of China was one of my favorite experiences of all my travels. In my opinion, you can skip Beijing, which is dull with a capital D. It's a modern city with highways crossing each other and shopping centers everywhere. Shanghai is more interesting because it's on the river and on the sea. I like the way it's built with all the high-rises; they have more cranes and construction than anywhere in the world. It's impressive. The Riverside Promenade (Bingjiang Da Dao) is picturesque, with great views of the skyline. I was there in June, and to celebrate my birthday I bought a bunch of fireworks and safely set them off over the water. Within five minutes, about 300 people surrounded us, all wanting to practice their English. Of course, I wanted to learn Chinese. I did learn a bit of Mandarin, which I still occasionally practice.

Another worthy destination to see is the excavated Terra-Cotta Warriors near Xi'an. Constructed around 200 B.C. to accompany the emperor of China into the afterlife, the army of clay soldiers is an amazing tribute. The first life-size warrior was unearthed in 1974. Further excavation revealed horses, chariots and weapons. Some remain safely buried, but experts estimate there are as many as 8,000 sculptures, all different. Those figures were mind-boggling in their magnitude. But my favorite part of this trip was a simpler pleasure: touring the backcountry from a boat going down the Yangtze River. You see workers in the fields with their oxen. The boat makes stops, and buses take the passengers out and about to explore the country-side and the quaint villages of straw huts. It's a real slice of life.

Heading to South America in 1995 for the World Congress on Cancers of the Skin in Buenos Aires, Argentina, was a grand adventure. It only happened thanks to the efforts of my friend Fernando Stengel, MD, a prominent Argentinian dermatologist. Skin cancer prevention was barely on the radar in Argentina in the early 1990s, and Fernando risked a lot to form an Argentine Skin Cancer Foundation (Fundación del Càncer de Piel) and host a World Congress. He was inundated with people telling him, "No; it will never work!" I encouraged him by sending a package via DHL containing two brass balls and a note, declaring: "If you had these, you'd do it!" I don't know if that helped steel his resolve, but he organized a fantastic meeting, and 1,500 physicians attended. Plus, he was a wonderful host and guide.

I went to Rio and on to Santiago, which is probably the most modern of all cities in South America. I took a flight halfway down the coast of Chile to a place called Puerto Montt, an area that was settled by Germans. We strolled in the village, where the local newspaper was in German and most of the locals only spoke German. Of course, chatting with them was a piece of cake for me (or I should I say *kuchen*, with glorious examples to be found in every corner café).

In the Lake District of Chile, surrounded by spectacular views.

From Puerto Montt we took a ferry to the Lake District, where we traveled from lake to lake to lake. Then we took a snowcat through a spectacular scenic pass over the Andes. When we got to the other side, we arrived at a larger lake, and then a three-hour boat ride took us to Bariloche, Argentina, the popular ski resort. It was a stunning trip.

In addition to all this traveling that I did then, the mid-1990s were exciting and exhausting for other reasons, too. My son, Lawrence, had some serious problems and needed my help, support and direction. And I was soon to meet an interesting woman who would become my second wife.

CHAPTER 17

The Second Time Around

*I did my best to keep my heart open after
my divorce. Can I find love again?*

While the O.J. Simpson trial was monopolizing headlines during the steamy summer of 1995, I turned 65. For many people, that's a symbolic age for retirement and the "golden years," but for me, slowing down was not an option—even if I'd wanted to! Elizabeth had graduated from the University of Colorado at Boulder, where she was on the freestyle ski team. I was so proud of her. She was thinking about graduate school—maybe focusing on accounting, or perhaps law school. I knew she'd be great at either. We didn't have the strongest relationship after the divorce, when she needed her mother more. But when she came to me to talk about grad school, and wanted my advice (and money, of course!), it was a good opportunity to strengthen our relationship. We both wanted that. She decided on law school at Hofstra University.

As for Lawrence, he had big ideas and dreams about being a filmmaker, producer or dealmaker in the entertainment field, but could never quite make a go of it. His radio show was canceled, his film deals fell apart and he spiraled into a serious depression.

"When I was 26, everything in my life broke," Lawrence says of that time. "I was directing my first movie, but it got too big for me and I couldn't control it. After that, every other deal I was working on broke for various reasons. One partner got cancer. I had a series of major failures. I completely lost a sense of who I was, and it led to a major, major collapse. I remember waking up in bed, soaked with sweat. I hit complete clinical depression, and it took me months to get out of it."

Lawrence and I were so different. I never let failure stop me or even slow me down. It was easier for me to shake it off and just keep pushing. But Lawrence is a sensitive soul, and I tried to be there for him and help him if I could. He says:

> *"The thing about my father that was really wonderful is that he always made himself available. And he supported me financially through all my falling apart, when I couldn't support myself. He never turned his back on me when people said, 'Leave your son. He's out of his mind. The kid is just all over the place; he's smart but out of control. He's a know-it-all. Just forget it.' But he never did."*

CAPTURING ME IN RHYME?

My observant grandniece Alyssa wrote this poem to me around that time:

Uncle Perry
At most of our dinners
He sits at the head
But most of his jokes

Will put you to bed.

His son's name is Larry

And he's always on the go

Making movies is his job

Will he be famous? I don't know.

His daughter's name is Liz

And she sure likes to ski

And I'm sorry today

She couldn't be here with me.

He travels the world

To lecture and speak

In the skin cancer profession

He is the peak.

A top doctor in the world

He's usually merry

But to all of our family

He's just Uncle Perry.

Mohs surgery's reputation got a boost in 1995, when my friend and former fellow, Rex Amonette, MD, became the first Mohs surgeon to be president of the American Academy of Dermatology (AAD). It's a very prestigious position, and it was a symbolic breakthrough and sign of mainstream acceptance for our specialty.

I had done my best to help in advance of the election. I arranged a dinner with Mohs surgeons in New York to ask these colleagues to help support Rex and vote for him. There was an international aspect to it, too, which I hadn't expected. One day I received an email from my French dermatologist friend Robert Baran asking my advice on who he should vote for in the upcoming AAD presidential election. I replied, "Robert, you can't vote. You're a foreign member." He said, "Of course I can." I was happy to hear that news, as I had influential dermatology friends in many countries. I wrote each of them a personal letter suggesting that they vote for Rex: "He speaks our language and would be the best president we've ever had."

I heard that the vote was very close, but the outcome was positive. Rex Amonette was the perfect person for the job. Everybody loved him. He was humble and always very responsive in acknowledging other people and their achievements. His wife, Johnnie Amonette, says, "He's a natural leader and inspires trust. He has no personal agenda."

"There were organizations that did not want me for a long time because I was a Mohs surgeon," Rex says. "But when I became president-elect of the AAD, that changed everything." It definitely helped our cause!

I was ready to date again, and I wanted to broaden my horizons, so I perused the "Strictly Personal" ads in *New York* magazine. Sure, it was chancy, but why not? I reached out to two women who sounded intelligent and intriguing. I made plans for cocktails with one and lunch with the other. The first one? There was no chemistry. On the second try, my luck changed. I walked into the dining room of the Ritz-Carlton on Central Park South and saw a woman who looked like a princess. I thought she was stunning.

Her name was Marina. Dark-haired and elegant, she had been educated in Switzerland, Paris, New York and London, and was fluent in French, Spanish and Italian. She was divorced, Jewish, but had adopted the last name of her Italian grandfather when she began designing a line of evening wear for women, knowing a collection with an Italian name would sell better. She seemed glamorous, smart, creative—and I was bowled over.

We soon became a couple. Marina fit into my world with ease. As she says, "We shared many interests, including travel, health and education. During my first marriage, into one of the elite families of Latin America, we had five homes in four countries, and we traveled very frequently. It was helpful for Perry to have someone beside him who had an international background. My languages were helpful to him on many occasions. And I introduced him to some new things, such as Ashford Castle, in Ireland, where we learned falconry. Later we continued with the sport in Vermont."

Marina and I went everywhere together. I had stayed in touch with the patient from Istanbul whose melanoma I had treated, and on a follow-up visit to see me, she asked, "Do you ever come to Turkey?" I said, "You know, I haven't been there since I was in medical school. But I'm planning a trip with another dermatologist and her husband to go to Istanbul this summer." Her husband, who was with her, mentioned that they had a boat they kept in Bodrum and invited us to come see it. I didn't think too much about it but said, casually, "Thank you very much. Maybe we'll come by." I didn't know where Bodrum was, but I learned it's a port on the Mediterranean in the southern part of Turkey. I said we'd play it by ear.

We told them when we were coming to Turkey, and to our surprise, when Marina and I and the other couple we were traveling with arrived at the airport in Istanbul, my Turkish patient and her husband were there to greet us. He said, "Give me your ticket and I'll get you your visas. You can pick up your bags and we'll put them in the car." Outside of the airport, we saw that his car was an armored Hummer. He said, "I want you to know that I changed your hotel." I said, "That wasn't necessary." We had a reservation at a Sheraton, and we were perfectly happy with that. He said, "No, I put you in the Ciragan Palace," which is probably the most luxurious (and expensive) hotel in Turkey.

When we arrived at this magnificent Ottoman palace on the Bosphorus, they gave Marina and me an enormous suite. I told her, "Well, there goes our budget for the next three years," because it was $2,000 a night. Our new Turkish friend picked us up the next morning to show us around. He took us to his office, and we learned that he owned the high-rise building. It didn't take long to figure out he was the patriarch of one of the wealthiest families in Turkey.

Marina and I at the Blue Mosque in Istanbul.

We agreed to fly down to Bodrum to see our friends' boat. I had recently had a bad experience on another pal's vessel that had been less than comfortable, with a diesel leak, overwhelming heat, voracious mosquitoes and nonworking toilets. But I was starting to think this might not be too shabby. When we arrived at the dock on the Mediterranean, we saw the King of Jordan's sister's yacht, among others. When we got to the end of the dock, we saw the "boat": 150 feet long, with a crew of 11, in uniform, standing at attention—and a helicopter on top. They gave us a beautiful suite that was designed by Philippe Starck.

We cruised up and down the coast for a week, as they wined and dined us regally. We were accompanied by bodyguards in one speedboat, plus another boat available for water-skiing. It was phenomenal, one of the greatest tours I've had in my life. We became close friends, and they invited us back several times.

Each visit was more fascinating than the one before. We flew down to Antalya, a resort city along what is called the Turquoise Coast, and we stayed in a hotel the family owned. We visited their ranch, featuring his collection of antique cars. And we toured Cappadocia, an otherworldly region of lava and ash, forming cones and caves. Used for settlements for thousands of years, it looks like the landscape of the moon. We followed a tour guide way underground into the caves. The passage narrowed down to about four feet high, and I'm *not*. When I got a bad cramp in my leg and couldn't straighten up, I realized I wasn't able to move forward or backward! There was no room for others to pass, and no central exit. People behind me were saying, "Come on, you've gotta move. You're holding up the line. We're getting scared back here!"

Finally, after I'd rested a bit, I was able to move forward a few steps, rest again, take a few more steps, etcetera, until I finally made it out. It took about an hour. I was so relieved. I asked, "What happens when someone is truly stuck?" The guide said, "We put a rope around them, put a blanket underneath and slide 'em out." I was grateful I didn't have to be dragged out but somehow made it on my own two feet. It was still a grand adventure, and I was glad I had a chance to see this unique site.

Marina and I had a lot of fun together in those years. We decided she would move into my apartment near NYU. She wanted to keep her studio on Central Park. I was in love with her, but one thing concerned me: She was very private, even a bit secretive.

HOW I WON OVER PERRY ROBINS, MD

By Paul Sowyrda

In the year 2000, I was running Dusa Pharmaceuticals, and we had just gotten a new drug approved for treating actinic keratosis, a common type of precancer on the skin. It was a topical drug that gets activated by light to destroy the precancerous cells before they can progress into a full-blown skin cancer. I wanted to get the word out. I didn't know Perry Robins, MD, but I knew he was the most famous skin cancer doctor in the world. I decided to just call and see if I could get him on the phone. Turns out, I could.

I introduced myself and said that I wanted to get his help in launching this new drug into the United States dermatology community. Immediately he asked me, "Am I on the clock?" I said, "I guess you are." He said, "OK. When can you get to New York so we can sit down and get to know each other?" I live in Boston, but I said, "I can be in New York tomorrow."

He said, "OK, can you be in my office at 7 AM?" It was already about 5 PM, but I didn't hesitate. "Sure," I said. "I'll see you at 7 AM in your office at NYU. By the way, do you drink coffee?" He said yes. I said, "Cream and sugar?" He said, "No, just black." So I flew down that night, found a hotel and was sitting outside his door at NYU the next morning at quarter to 7, with two cups of coffee, when up he walked. "Who are you?" he asked. I said, "I'm Paul Sowyrda. We have a meeting at 7." He said, "That's interesting. I never thought you'd come." We've been good friends—and partners on a few business ventures—ever since.

Perry Robins is a unique person. He tries to help everyone. If you're sincere, a hard worker and do what you say you're going to do, he'll go out of his way to help you.

It was a glorious September sky that morning in 2001. Pilots call that kind of brilliance "severe clear." I was in my 41st-floor apartment near NYU. It is one of the taller buildings in my New York neighborhood, with panoramic views and no obstructions (until recently) all the way down to Wall Street. I looked out the window, and I could see smoke coming from the south. I heard on television that there had been an accident at the World Trade Center, and a lot of casualties were expected.

If I'd stayed at my windows, I would have had a firsthand view of the agonizing collapse of the Twin Towers, one after the other. But I hurried down to the emergency room at the hospital to see what I could do to help. The emergency response team had set up facilities at Bellevue. The staff was ready. But no one came in.

A bomb wouldn't have brought down the buildings, but because there was so much jet fuel onboard those two planes, it disbursed and burned hot enough to make the steel lose its structural strength. No one on the upper floors of those towers survived. I thought of the thousands of flights, private and commercial, I had been on since I became a physician, and I could not imagine the suffering and devastation. I also thought about how I'd hosted our first founder's meeting of The Skin Cancer Foundation at Windows on the World there more than 20 years earlier. I felt helpless. Nothing was happening in the ER, so I went upstairs to my office and just watched the news and waited.

One of my patients who owned an investment company had a scheduled breakfast meeting that morning at Windows on the World. His wife was sick, so he had to drop off his kids at school, which was a detour. And with slow traffic, he got to the building late, just after the crash had already occurred. Had he not taken his kids to school, he would have been killed. But he lost many colleagues that day. It was amazing how many of the patients I treated had connections with people who lost their lives when the Twin

Towers came down. I'd say one in four had somebody who was involved, and I heard all their stories. They included a couple of firefighters who survived. They said there was little they could do, and they lost so many of their courageous fellow first responders.

My view to the south stayed smoky for a long time. Every morning when I walked to work, I paid my respects at the wall in front of the hospital with posters saying, "Missing . . . " "Missing . . . Please Help Us." They showed photographs of fathers, mothers, sisters, brother, kids—it was heartbreaking.

It was a sad time right after 9/11. But I was happy to learn that Elizabeth and Lawrence were joining forces to use some of their contacts in the entertainment world to put together a 9/11 commemorative event in New York for 2002. Elizabeth had graduated from law school and had been working in entertainment law for Scholastic. The idea came about when Elizabeth introduced Lawrence to music producer Phil Ramone, and Lawrence was friends with singer, songwriter and producer Moby. They brainstormed, and brought in other connections, including Quincy Jones and Sting, to discuss a celebrity concert for the first anniversary of 9/11 in 2002. They worked together on it for a year, and Elizabeth remembers it as "a really cool time in our lives." But somehow it outgrew its simple premise and ultimately went sour. This was not what Lawrence needed in his life. As he recalls:

> "We had a bunch of celebrities for this project; it was a huge movement to get it done. But true to form, I had to make it bigger than it needed to be. So rather than being happy with a commemoration event, I decided we should create a nonprofit organization to run an event that was basically like the Olympics, but with music. Instead of competitions, it would be collaboration. We would set up a 'world stage' at a host city. Then all the contributing companies would build

the stage, which would remain there after the event. For 10 days we would have artists from all over the world meeting each other and playing music together, bringing different cultures together for a really cool jam fest. The king of Jordan wanted us to do it in Jordan, but we wanted to do the first one in New York City, so we turned him down. But we thought Jordan could be a future host city.

"We had millions of dollars in commitments from sponsors to do this event. We were ready to start the nonprofit foundation and plan the next one. At the 11th hour, however, the victims' families spoke up; they were against it. Maybe they felt it got too big, too international—or maybe it was just too soon. That was it; it was over.

"I ended up going through another depression, thinking, I'm cursed by entertainment. Every time I get involved in something, it seems huge and then gets killed. If I could ever hit one success, my life would be totally different."

I felt terrible for my kids who had worked so hard, and so well together, on this project that they truly believed in. I wanted to help them both find something they could do that would have a chance of success and satisfaction. I thought of my real estate development in St. Augustine, Florida, that I'd never had time to give the focus it deserved. I knew Elizabeth was looking for something more challenging, so she might like to go down there and see what she could do with the development. She agreed to move there and give it her best shot. As for Lawrence, coming up with the right project for him would take a bit more thought.

I was a guest speaker at a conference in Hawaii. During a coffee break, a young chap approached me and said, "Dr. Robins, I understand you have a lot of experience in publishing dermatology journals. I want to start a new one called *Journal of Drugs in Dermatology*, and I'd like you to be my partner." I said, "You have to be kidding! That's the last thing I want to do, after losing money for 20 years the first time I tried it. I don't think it's judicious or wise for you to start a journal."

But he persisted, saying, "No, you don't have to put money into it, but I need your help. I'll give you 5 percent of the company if you help me do it." *Sigh.* The last thing I needed was a stressful new start-up, but I couldn't resist. I said, "As long as I don't have to invest any money, I will be glad to be supportive. If you do earn a few shekels, I will donate it to The Skin Cancer Foundation." He agreed.

I cajoled some of my colleagues and friends to submit articles for this new journal. I gave them three months to do it. Three months went by and they weren't done, so I gave them another month, and then another month. Finally, we had enough articles to put together our first issue. I sold advertising at a ridiculously low rate and was able to secure about 10 pages of ads, which I hoped would cover the printing costs. To publicize it, I planned to send it to all dermatologists in the United States.

About three weeks before we were scheduled to go to press, I had the ads lined up and the articles finally in and edited when my partner called me and said, "Perry, I got my old job back, and there's a conflict of interest. I can't do the journal. We have to cancel it." I said, "Are you kidding? My colleagues who worked so hard on articles will murder me!" He said, "Well, it's all yours, if you want to continue with it." You know me; I never give up. I thought, *OK, I'll print the first issue. I'm already committed. I'll lose a couple shekels and then I'll close it or give it to somebody who will want to take over.*

The first issue of *Journal of Drugs in Dermatology* came out dated July/August 2002, with a lot of fanfare. People were excited about this new publication. And guess what? By a strange coincidence, we made money! Not because of subscriptions or ad revenue, but because of the popularity of paid reprints. We marked up the price a little, and pharmaceutical companies bought them by the thousands to hand out to doctors.

With the second issue, I doubled the price of the reprints, and everybody was elated. Hence, the journal started to take off, and I decided to keep it. I had an idea that maybe I could convince Lawrence to take over and run the publishing company.

While the journal start-up was in the works, Marina and I had taken the plunge and gotten married! We had a private civil ceremony performed by a Manhattan Supreme Court judge in January 2002 with close friends and family in attendance. That was followed by dinner at the elegant Metropolitan Club on East 60th Street, where Marina was a member. Then we decided further parties were in order. In April we threw a big festive brunch at the Metropolitan Club. In July, for all our European friends, we organized a cocktail reception at a very fashionable club, le Cercle de l'Union Interalliée, on rue du Faubourg Saint-Honoré in Paris.

What a whirlwind! In the middle of all that, in June, I celebrated my 72nd birthday. I was happy and wanted this marriage to work. But to protect my interests, just in case, I had asked Marina to sign a prenuptial agreement that would become effective after three years.

On our honeymoon, we visited five countries. Marina says one of her favorite stories was when we were in Burma (Myanmar), in a small town close to the Irrawaddy River. She recalls, "One day we went to a factory with a dirt floor and no electricity or air-conditioning, where artisans were making lacquered wooden boxes with gold leaf decorations. The boxes were quite lovely. We spent more than an hour there, choosing different shapes for sets, for gifts and for ourselves. It was clear that to ship it all to us in New York, a large crate was going to be required." The problem was that there was no relationship between the U.S. Postal Service and Burma at that time.

The tour guide had an idea: He said that in six weeks his brother, a lumber merchant in Thailand, was arriving in Burma. He could give the big crate to him to drive to Bangkok, where it would be easier to have it sent to New York. Marina says, "Well, I thought that was very far-fetched and too circuitous, but, trusting soul that he is, Perry agreed to it. I was certain we would never see those boxes again. About three weeks later, though, we received a letter from the brother. He said he had a little money left over from the $150 Perry had given him for the shipping charges and asked what we wanted him to do with the extra money. Perry suggested he give it to his brother as a tip. The crate soon arrived, with all the boxes in perfect condition!"

HOLY MOLEY!

By Paul Sowyrda

Above all else, Dr. Perry Robins truly cared about his patients. I happened to be in his office one day and he asked, "Would you mind coming to Long Island with me? I have to go visit a priest who has terrible skin cancer. Usually, one of the nuns would drive him to NYU and back, but I can't get a nun to drive him here today, and he really needs to be treated." I said, "Of course." I helped him put all the equipment in his car, including a big blue light, in order to help this priest who was in his 80s. We drove to Long Island and entered the rectory where he lived. I said, "Perry, we can't get this heavy equipment up the stairs." We had no choice: He had to treat the priest in the back of the church.

Father K. had so many areas of skin that needed treatment. The cancer was everywhere, so Dr. Robins couldn't even do surgery on him anymore. The treatment was grueling, and the priest started to cry out with pain. We didn't realize at first that there were confessions going on, and all of a sudden these other priests came rushing out of the confessional rooms, wondering what the screaming was about. Who knows? Maybe they thought it was an exorcism. I was thinking, *Gosh, this is awful.* But the bottom line was, Dr. Robins got the man treated. That's just who he is!

Through all my ups and down in life, my work has been an oasis of balance, order, collegiality and, when needed, solace. I especially valued the friendships I developed with many of the fellows I trained. I had gotten to know Elizabeth Hale, MD, during her dermatology residency at NYU, when she would grab any opportunity to come up to my office and shadow me with my patients. She was eager to learn, we got along well, and when she applied for my fellowship to follow her residency in the fall of 2002, I was privileged to offer her the spot. She was one of the final (and among the favorites) in my long line of fellows.

The fact that Dr. Hale had just given birth to a baby boy in May of that year didn't deter me in the least. If I know anything, it's that busy, curious and passionate people get the most done. I knew she'd find a way to balance it all. Plus, we loved seeing the baby at the office from time to time. Below, she says she learned a thing or two from me while we worked together, and I'm grateful we've remained close friends to this day.

> *"My fellowship was such a great way for me to transition into becoming a mother and a dermatologic surgeon. Perry Robins works really, really hard but is also such a good person and a kind soul. Yes, our days were very busy, but they ended at a decent hour. It was great for me that year as a new mom because there was so much love and support from him and his office staff.*
>
> *"Training with Dr. Robins was amazing because of the exposure to a vast number of cases. This was before dermatologists were doing fillers and Botox, so we literally did Mohs surgery all day, every day. I also was struck by how often previous fellows of Dr. Robins would fax over a picture of a defect, asking if he could draw on the piece of paper how he would reconstruct it. He had such vast experience, it was second nature to him. He could just draw it out and fax it back.*
>
> *"I also learned people skills from Dr. Robins, and how to deal with people from all walks of life. He knows, because he came from nothing*

and built his education and reputation from scratch. Throughout his career, he had famous celebrity patients and very wealthy patients, but he also had people of very humble means. He knew how to make everyone comfortable, and he treated everyone with the utmost respect.

"Dr. Robins had a perfect blend of sincerity and humor. He'd say, 'A good result requires a good patient, a good doctor and good luck.' It's so true! He'd say to the patient, 'I've done my job. Now you have to avoid working out, avoid blood thinners, etc.' Still, you can do everything perfectly, and some patients are just luckier than others.

"He makes everyone around him feel important. He loves being a role model and mentor to the new kid on the block. He is also really skilled at connecting different people and seeing the good in people. He is proof that having passion and drive are more important than just about anything.

"Every day in my interactions with patients, I think about Dr. Robins and what I learned from him. I'm so grateful for the role he played in my life."

By 2004 my little publishing company was making about $200,000 a year, but I just didn't have the time to devote to the day-to-day details or nurturing its growth. Lawrence needed something to focus on, and he needed a salary. I thought some responsibility (and being a taxpayer) might ground him a little. I knew this wouldn't be his dream job, but I also knew he had the smarts and skills to do it if he tried. I asked him to meet me at my office one afternoon.

We sat down together, and I said, "Lawrence, I want you to take over the publishing company. I've been supporting you financially, but it's time for you to pay your own way." His reply? "I don't want to. I don't know anything about it, and the answer is no." I did what I had to do. I had a colleague there, and I said, "Here is my witness.

If you don't try this for six months, I'm going to disinherit you." He looked at me and said, "Papa, why are you blackmailing me?"

"So, of course, I took the magazine," Lawrence says. "And within a few years, the company, which we expanded, was doing between $3 million and $5 million, with my father partially involved. He did help us start with some of our original big sales. Then we pretty much learned how to do it on our own. I hired my best friend, Shelley Tanner, as CEO/president, and made myself the chairman. My heart really wasn't in it to manage all the details, and she learned how to do that well.

"We built the company up to 30 people, overseeing many physicians and producing content in other areas in addition to dermatology. We also developed complimentary conferences for residents. Still, I was always looking at more entrepreneurial things while Shelley was managing this. I also ended up deciding to invest time into my own personal growth—I mean, really deep, inner work."

I was doing a little soul-searching myself. *Was my marriage everything I had dreamed?* I wanted it to be, I really did, but no. I feel like I'm an open book, and it really bothered me that Marina was so private and secretive.

Our final adventure together was to Ecuador and the Galápagos Islands. I thought it was a wonderful, romantic trip. The mountains were beautiful, but we both had a bit of altitude sickness in Quito. Marina's fluency in Spanish was especially helpful there. She spoke with the locals and made changes to our travel schedule, so we could get down to Guayaquil, on the coast, as soon as possible and wait there for the group we were traveling with to catch up with us. Then we departed together for the Galápagos Islands. It was a magical place; we were passionate on the boat, and I never felt closer to her.

Imagine my shock when soon after we returned to New York, I came home from work and found her in the lobby of our building, saying she had moved all of her things out. "I want a divorce," she said. She wanted to move to Paris and write books. I was devastated, like I'd been sucker punched.

CHAPTER 18

True Love at Last

*After my second divorce, when I least
expect it, my soul mate, Marcia, walks into
my life, and it feels just right.*

I did not expect to be divorced again at the age of 75. I felt like a victim and a failure, but I was never one to wallow in self-pity for long. I was lucky because I was still energetic, seeing patients and performing surgery in my busy practice. I felt young at heart. So, in my usual way of dealing with troubles, I threw myself into my work. And it didn't take long before I felt like dating again.

I honestly don't know what the secret is, but I never had any trouble meeting women. I was seeing a talented teacher named Barbara, who worked with young children who had difficulty reading. She had created a technique to help these kids and wanted to start a foundation to share her knowledge and curriculum. The cause was close to my heart because of my own dyslexia as well as my love of pediatrics, so I couldn't say no. I raised some money and, in 2006, helped her set up the Foundation for Children with Learning Disorders, Inc.

Around that time, a patient was referred to me for a small red spot above her right eyebrow that was bothering her. I could see immediately it was not skin cancer, but a benign growth called a cherry angioma. I could easily remove it and take my fee, but it would leave a little divot. If I sent her to a physician who had a certain type of laser, it could be zapped with no scar. I did the ethical thing and referred her.

As we were chatting, I learned her name—Marcia Robbins-Wilf—and that she had a doctorate in education. Since she is Dr. Robbins with two b's and I'm Dr. Robins with one b, I made a little joke: "Two b's or not two b's? That is the question!" Of course, I appreciate anyone who laughs at my jokes, and she did. I told her I had recently started the foundation to help preschool-age children who have difficulty in reading and wondered if she would like to help. When she said she would be glad to, I said, "Can you wait in my office? I have to see the next patient, and then I'll have a chance to chat with you."

Marcia told me a little about her background. After college, she taught in elementary and nursery schools for a few years, then went back to school to receive two master's degrees and then a doctorate in education from Yeshiva University, with an emphasis on remedial developmental reading. She also owned a nursery school, taught and ran a day camp.

I told her that I thought Barbara's method was effective. I had spoken to a woman whose child was tutored by this method, and she thought it was very successful. I asked Marcia if she would like to meet the executive director of the new foundation, and she said she would be pleased to do so.

I thought Marcia was impressive, but I wasn't thinking romance at that time; I was thinking credentials. Besides, I had also started seeing a very nice woman of Italian heritage named Vicki. I had recently gone to a dermatology convention in Israel with her. She had family in Rome, so I had arranged for her to stop off and visit there for a few days on our way back to the States. She had extended her visit, but I knew she'd be back soon.

A few days later, Marcia, Barbara and I met for dinner. Marcia made a number of valuable suggestions, such as producing a video of some children learning the technique. We agreed that we would meet again to further our goals.

We wanted to create a one-day free summer "boot camp" course for teachers to come and learn Barbara's technique for improving reading skills. But we found that teachers were reluctant to attend during their vacation time, and some requested that we pay them. Unfortunately, we didn't have enough money in our budget to rent a venue, provide meals and pay for attendance. As I was already on extracurricular overload with The Skin Cancer Foundation, my lectures and my businesses, I reluctantly decided I didn't have time to spend on this project. I also felt like our dating relationship had run its course. I gave Barbara the money we had raised for the foundation and said, "Run with it."

A few evenings after that, I called Marcia to tell her and said, "I want to thank you for coming in from New Jersey and taking the time to help us. It was supportive and wonderful of you." She said she had been pleased to offer her help, then surprised me with some personal flattery. "You're such a wonderful doctor. You have a stellar reputation, and you help so many people." I hadn't been expecting that!

I was starting to get the idea that Marcia was smitten. I may have been a little slow on the draw, but she says that she knew right away. "I knew the minute I saw him that I was going to fall in love with him," Marcia says. "He was standing outside his office in his scrubs, reading my chart. I took one look at him and thought, *I wonder if this guy is married?*"

She invited me to attend a fundraiser as her guest, and I said I really didn't have time. She probably thought I was rejecting her, but honestly, I thought, *She is much younger, attractive, accomplished, educated. What the heck would she want an old guy like me for? Even though I am special!* Maybe I was guarding my heart a little, knowing that I hadn't always made the best choices in the past. Fear of getting hurt again is a powerful emotion.

I resisted for a short time, but I was intrigued and soon said, "Let's get together for dinner." We met at the Water Club, a floating restaurant on the East River with romantic views of bridges and the Manhattan skyline. (Since it opened in 1982, the Water Club had been one of my favorite spots, but as of 2017, it's an event space for weddings and such.) Marcia and I had a fantastic evening. We talked for hours, until the staff finally chased us out.

We learned that we were both born in Newark, although, yes, 19 years apart. Marcia's paternal grandparents, like mine, emigrated from Russia to escape the pogroms against the Jewish community and settled in New Jersey. Marcia's father, Saul Robbins, cofounded the toy company Remco with his cousin in 1949. The name stood for "remote control." Marcia says, "He and his partner took walkie-talkies from the war and made them into toys. I mean, who does that? He was smart, creative—a visionary ahead of his time."

I learned about giving back from my mother. Marcia learned about giving back from her mother and father. As soon as he became successful, Saul Robbins started supporting local charities. "When I was in my teens, he took my younger brother, Ralph, and me up and down the East Coast to look at Jewish Community Centers," Marcia says. "Then he started one in West Orange, because he saw so many kids who needed help." That planted the seed for her own philanthropic projects later, many of which focused on children and education.

I found out Marcia had been married for almost 20 years to Leonard Wilf, whose father and uncle founded Garden Homes, now one of the largest real estate development companies in the world. Their divorce was hard on her son, Orin, who works for Garden Homes, but the exes have remained friendly. Orin is also president and founder of Skyline Developers, which owns, manages and develops luxury rental and commercial properties in New York City.

Marcia and I discovered we both love dogs, art, musical theater, traveling and wonderful food. "I knew that was it," Marcia says about our evening at the Water Club. I definitely wanted to see her again.

I said, "In two days I'm lecturing to residents at Stony Brook University Hospital. Would you like to come and hear me talk?" She said, "I would love to." She was living in New Jersey but came into New York with her driver, and he dropped her off. We had a gentleman product manager from a pharmaceutical company who drove us to Stony Brook on the North Shore of Long Island. After my lecture, I said, "You know, I have to go on to Albany for another meeting, but the man who drove us will take you back." She said, "No, no. I'll come to Albany with you." *Really?* I thought. This fascinating woman wanted to hear me lecture students and was willing to accompany me to decidedly unglamorous Albany? That was impressive.

On our drive upstate, we smooched once or twice, and it was clear that our connection was real and special. Most people probably don't think of Albany as a place of romantic dreams, but for us it will always be a beautiful memory of the start of our relationship.

While we were there, however, Vicki, the other woman I'd been seeing, returned from her visit to Rome and let me know that when I arrived home, she would be cooking dinner for me at my place. *Uh-oh.*

When the gentleman driving us pulled up to drop me off at my building in New York, Marcia asked, "Can I come up?" I had to confess that my soon-to-be-ex-girlfriend was probably up there whipping up some pasta for me. Marcia put her foot down and said, "If you don't get rid of her in 24 hours, we're history." I said, "OK."

When I got upstairs, the conversation wasn't pleasant. But I knew what I had to do. Marcia was different from anyone I had dated before. We shared many common interests and a passion for philanthropy. She was exciting, enthusiastic and supportive of my work. I felt like we were wonderfully compatible.

Marcia says, "I remember Perry called me on Monday and said, 'I did it.' I asked, 'Are you sure about this?' He said, '*Absolutely.*' I knew that we were meant to be together. Isn't that funny? I just knew."

When Marcia told her son, Orin, about me, he asked her, "Does he play golf?" She said, "No." "Does he play tennis?" "No." "Does he love baseball or football?" "No." "What do you do together?" "Shop." He said, "You've found your match."

I *do* like to take her shopping! Marcia will often buy expensive gifts for other people, from Tiffany & Co. or Bergdorf Goodman, but for herself, she leans more toward T.J. Maxx and Marshalls. I love going with her to stores like Escada in Palm Beach to help her pick out clothes that look great on her. I enjoy seeing her look stunning, getting compliments and knowing that I helped. We share similar taste in things about 80 percent of the time.

Marcia has such a tender heart about people in need—and animals. Oh, how she loves animals! If we're watching a movie that shows, say, a deer being killed by people stranded in Alaska who have no other option for food, she has to walk away from the TV. She can't watch an animal being hurt, even if she knows it's fake and no animals were harmed shooting the scene. One day in the middle of a rainstorm, she saw a turtle on the road and screamed to her driver, "*Stop, stop—don't hit the turtle!* Please move it to the side of the road. I don't want anyone to run over his shell!" She truly loves all creatures great and small, and she supports many causes that help animals, too.

Marcia was very close to her mother and father. Her father suffered from health problems, so he sold the business and retired when he was about 49 or 50. Marcia looked after them for many years. She had bought a couple of apartments in the building next to where her parents lived in Verona, New Jersey. When we became a couple, Marcia bought another apartment and blended all three together, and I moved in with her. I still kept my apartment in New York for when we wanted to be in the city.

Marcia and I were having a lot of fun, and it suddenly hit me, at the age of 76, that maybe it was time to stop and smell the roses, slow down and enjoy life more. I turned in my resignation after more than 45 years at NYU, although I didn't move out of my long-time office there until March of 2007. It wasn't an easy job, as I had records for 13,000 patients, plus more than 125 certificates, plaques and awards on the walls.

My friend and former Mohs fellow, Deborah Sarnoff, was practicing in two offices: a large one on Long Island and a smaller one on Park Avenue in New York City. She was very generous and said, "If you have any favorite patients that you would like to see, why don't you book them at my Park Avenue office one afternoon a week?" I thought that was a wonderful idea.

I told a couple of patients that I was closing my practice and gave them some names of other doctors they could go to. When they heard I was seeing patients in Dr. Sarnoff's office on the Upper East Side, they wanted to come see me there. Soon others heard and wanted to come there, too. The half day grew to a full day. Then some of them wanted me to do surgery and wouldn't go anywhere else. So I added one day to do surgery, and I loved it. One day soon became two, and I thought it was terrific.

Early summer in Italy—what could be better? A vacation seemed like a good idea. I had so many friends in the dermatology world, and Marcia meshed with them beautifully. "I felt absolutely compatible in his world," she says. So in June 2007, we planned a fun trip to Tuscany with a group of physicians and friends, including Bill Hanke, Debby Sarnoff and her husband, plastic surgeon Robert Gotkin, and Martin Braun, a respected cosmetic physician in Vancouver.

Marcia, Bill Hanke, Debby Sarnoff and I were careful to use sunscreen under the Tuscan sun—and everywhere else we went, of course!

Marcia says, "Martin's wife, Susan, found a house for us all to stay in. She'd never seen it in person and was worried that we wouldn't like it. But we loved it! Every room was a suite. We had two swimming pools, and we ate breakfast on the terrace every morning, surrounded by beautiful views. The weather was gorgeous, and we all got along famously." Bill Levis, a longtime friend and melanoma expert, and his wife, Georgia, were with us. Georgia painted the scenery each morning before we headed out for the day's adventures. We visited the leaning tower of Pisa, we went to the Prada factory, we shopped for shoes. We attended an outdoor opera in a beautiful setting in the mountains over dinner. We ate the most fantastic steaks Florentine. It was a wonderful trip!

After I returned from Italy, I plunged back in to seeing patients.

By 2008, my patient load in Dr. Sarnoff's office had grown like an explosion, and the facilities were too crowded. I realized I really wasn't ready to stop and just smell the roses quite yet.

Before the holidays that year, I learned that my New York apartment building had some commercial space available. I went to see the realtor about constructing an office space for my practice there ASAP. He said, "Yes, we can arrange this, and we can probably have it ready for you in about four to six weeks." I said, "No, I'm moving in one week." He said, "That's unheard of. We wouldn't even have the contract done by that time." I said, "Screw the contract. I want to start in a week or I'm not taking it." He said, "Well, we'll see how much we can get accomplished." I said, "That's fair enough." In a week, I was up and running.

When I was in Vienna to scout facilities for the World Congress we held there in 2005, the travel agent I was working with said it was a shame I wouldn't be there in the wintertime to attend the world-famous New Year's Eve ball at the Hofburg Imperial Palace. For more than 600 years this magnificent palace was the seat of the Holy Roman Empire and the Austro-Hungarian Empire. He whetted my appetite with his descriptions: "Celebrities come from all over Europe to attend this extravaganza," he said. "Many different orchestras perform, and there are entire companies of ballet dancers, singers, opera stars. Elegant formal dress, jewels, waltzes. Chefs work for months to prepare the cuisine." He got me excited about it, then crushed me when he said, "It's been sold out for years. It's impossible to get tickets."

I had never forgotten about this. One weekend in 2008, Marcia and I were reading the newspaper and she said to me, "Oh, look! Here's an ad for a cruise line doing river tours on the Danube during the holidays. It travels from Nürnberg to Vienna to Budapest, and it includes the New Year's Eve Ball in Vienna." I said, "Book it instantly!" I was so excited. I figured the cruise line had been running this tour for years and probably was able to reserve a number of tickets for its customers.

A few weeks before we were to leave on our flight to meet the boat in Nürnberg, we received a message with more details about the ball. We learned that there are quite a few New Year's Eve balls in Vienna, with varying levels of price, luxury, grandeur and exclusivity. I called the cruise line immediately and asked, "You mean we're not going to the Hofburg Palace?" The agent said, "Of course not; that's way out of our league. We don't have the budget for it. Besides, you can never get tickets for that. Do you want to cancel?" I said no, since I'd already bought the airline tickets, blocked time off from my office and arranged for someone to cover me, thinking, *You win some, you lose some.*

However, Tom Chin, a business colleague, knew a lot of people in Vienna and, by coincidence, was planning a holiday trip there in early December! I challenged him to see if he could pull any strings to get us in. Tom says, "I knew the master ticket dealer in Vienna for every cultural event in the city. Through him, I was able to score tickets. I even got a discount, but they were still thousands of Euros. The broker didn't want to risk mailing the tickets, due to their value, and this was still before electronic tickets were in use. So when I arrived in Vienna, I delivered an enormous bundle of cash from Dr. Robins and picked up the tickets in person at the broker's office by the Albertinaplatz, not far from the palace. While the less fortunate folks on the cruise would be attending one of the lesser balls, Dr. Robins and Marcia would be at the best ball of all."

Before Marcia and I left New York to head to Europe, though, I learned there was another complication: arranging transportation to the ball from where our boat would be berthed in the Danube, away from the city center. Because of the multitude of events, crowds, packed hotels, traffic and security, getting anywhere near the palace on New Year's Eve is extremely difficult and often impossible. I called several resources suggested by the cruise line. One said they could arrange something if we could get them a ticket to enter the palace area, too. Another source said they could get us there for $400. I was prepared to pay that, but they called me back and said, "I'm sorry, we have to cancel, because we cannot get closer than a mile to the palace. It's all roped off. No one is allowed closer, and you probably don't want to walk a mile to get your taxi to take you back to the boat." It was time to head off to Nürnberg for the start of our cruise. We decided to just wing it on the transportation to the palace. We figured we'd find a way.

Sure enough, once on the boat, I went to see the concierge, who said, "Dr. Robins, you're so lucky because the venue that many of our passengers will be going to on New Year's Eve is very close to the Hofburg Palace, and we have a bus pass to get there. You can travel on our bus; you go to the left, we go to the right. No charge. Just be sure that after the bell strikes midnight, 30 minutes later you're back on the bus." We felt like Cinderella and her prince!

After that, we relaxed and enjoyed the journey. It was cold, but the experience was great. River cruises are lovely because they're slow and smooth. There's a big, heated Mercedes bus to deliver you to excursions. The food was fantastic, and while we were cruising in Germany, the cuisine was German (spätzle, stollen!). When we were in Austria, we feasted on Austrian specialties (Wiener schnitzel, Sacher torte!). When we went to Hungary, we savored Hungarian dishes (goulash!). There were experts onboard to teach us the different styles of waltzes. We had a ball.

We don't know why, but we were invited to the Captain's Table one night to celebrate our "seventh anniversary." We'd only known each other two years, and we're not married. But there we were at the Captain's Table with some celebrities and VIPs, celebrating anyway. I don't know where they came up with that. We just went along with it, and considered it a bonus on this great, great trip.

Once we had berthed in Vienna on New Year's Eve, we dressed up, bundled up, boarded our appropriate bus and arrived intact at one of the grandest events we'd ever seen. It was truly an extravaganza—platinum plus. The whole place was bedecked with banners and flowers. There were military generals in full regalia, costumed dancers in enormous hoop skirts. In each room two orchestras played classical and popular music. They had entertainers rotate through, performing ballet and opera. We even took a photo with the chancellor and his wife. It was fantastic.

At dinner we sat with some fascinating young Russians who'd made a fortune in oil. Afterward, Marcia and I took to the dance floor and waltzed like a couple of old pros. With beautifully dressed and bejeweled couples swirling around us, we felt like we were in a movie. At midnight there was a 21-gun salute with cannons: *boom, boom, BOOM!* I flashed back to that special night nearly 50 years earlier in Heidelberg, when I had graduated from medical school and watched the spectacle of lights, flares and fireworks at Ludwig's castle, and a German word popped into my head, just like it did on that special night long ago: *Erlebnis,* a once-in-a-lifetime experience.

What a thrill it was in 2008 to attend the world-famous New Year's Eve ball at the Hofburg Imperial Palace in Vienna with Marcia.

Back in New York, I had started seeing patients two days a week at the new office in my apartment building, which grew to three days and then to four. One day early in 2009, I felt fed up with it all and said, "You know what? This is ridiculous. I love my patients, but I'm sick of fighting with the insurance companies. I don't want to be the richest man in the cemetery. I have enough. Why don't I just stop and enjoy things and travel?" I talked to the last fellow I had trained, Ritu Saini, MD, and said, "How would you like to take over my practice?" She said, "I'd love it." My decision was a little impulsive. I hoped I wouldn't regret it.

In March 2009, Marcia and I flew out to San Francisco for the American Academy of Dermatology annual conference, as well as the roast to celebrate the 30th anniversary of my founding of The Skin Cancer Foundation. (Remember, I described the evening in the Introduction to this book? Wow, now we've come full circle! And what a journey it's been—both living it *and* writing about it.)

That night, as I prepared to face my panel of roasters, I felt so grateful—for my family, friends and colleagues. I was also overwhelmed with gratitude to have met Marcia, my soul mate, at last, and to have her by my side.

When I stood up to say a few words that night, I said, "Life is not a dress rehearsal, so enjoy it!" I realized, then and there, that my impulsive decision to sell my medical practice was the right decision at the right time. I also blurted out, "Marcia told me that in spite of all the things said tonight, she still loves me." At that moment, I felt like I had it all.

CHAPTER 19

L'Chaim, to Life!

*Finding our way home, literally and
figuratively, Marcia and I savor our life
together, with friends and family,
philanthropy, travel, dogs, music, theater,
good food and so much more.
What a journey!*

I had met my soul mate, and I was ecstatic when my daughter, Elizabeth, met hers. She had always been fiercely independent. She went to school at the University of Colorado at least partly to get away from her feuding, divorcing parents. (And partly for the ski team, too.) Elizabeth and I didn't always see eye-to-eye, but we made up many times over. I admired her adventurous spirit. For example, she once told me she was going to climb Mount Kilimanjaro. I asked, "Why?" She replied simply, "Because I want to." And she did—all 19,341 feet of it. She and a girlfriend traveled there, trained hard and made it to the summit.

Elizabeth dated quite a few men and was deservedly picky, but one she met at a party turned out to be the right one—and a wonderful romance. Originally from Madrid, César Sanchez went to school in the States, and Elizabeth couldn't have found a better person or a better match. They married in March 2010 at the Council on Foreign Relations office on New York City's Upper East Side. Both Marcia and Ingrid attended, and it was a beautiful night. They followed that with a beautiful reception in Santiago de Compostela in northern Spain.

Just three months after that happy occasion, Marcia lost her beloved father, Saul Robbins, and then a little more than a year after that, she lost her mother, Ruth. Her sorrow was tempered with gratitude for all the years they were able to spend together, although Marcia had been their caretaker for a long time. She says, "After my parents died, I would visit the cemetery in Iselin, New Jersey, and when Perry went with me, we discovered that his parents' grave sites were also there, just 50 feet away! We have so many common threads in our background, and we thought that was an amazing coincidence. Now we go to the cemetery together once a year before Rosh Hashanah to visit them all. Then we go out to lunch in their honor."

Every few years I was invited to lecture at the Florida Society of Dermatologic Surgeons. For years, after my father remarried and retired to Florida, I had negative feelings toward the state. I would dutifully visit them there, but without my mother, it just wasn't the same. After my father died, Florida started to grow on me as I was dipping my toe into real estate developments there. Once Marcia and I were together and traveling to Florida for meetings, we began to like the state more and more. We decided that spending a month or so there in the wintertime might be a pleasant diversion from frozen New Jersey. We couldn't do that while her parents were ill, as she wanted to be nearby to attend to them. But now we were free to travel more often.

A friend referred us to a realtor named Eva, who showed us a house in Palm Beach Gardens that was available for rent. It was in such poor shape, it looked like it was furnished with early Salvation Army rejects. I said, "Marcia, that's not for us." The realtor said, "There's another place in this development that is pricey, but you may like it." We drove about 10 minutes to this other home, and it was like a palace—the cat's meow. I took two steps in and said, "Marcia, this is more like it!" It was decorated to the hilt and had a large pool. Marcia said, "We'll take it." We only wanted to stay a month or maybe two. The real estate agent said the minimum was four months. We settled on three. Marcia was a little skeptical at first, and said she missed her friends. After one week she said, "I'm sorry we came and took the place." The second week she said, "It isn't so bad." The third week she said, "Let's buy a house down here!" We fell in love with the place, the people, the environment and the atmosphere.

We started looking for the perfect house to buy. One of the first we looked at was a palatial home that was owned by Russian tennis star Anna Kournikova's mother. Marcia liked it. It had an enormous family room the size of a gymnasium. It was big enough that she could envision entertaining and hosting major fundraising events there.

Second opinions were in order, so my son and daughter came down and looked at it. Marcia's son, an expert in real estate, checked it out and said it was fine. We had a builder inspect it. Everybody said it was a beautiful house. But I *did not* like the place, because from the family room to the kitchen, all you looked at was the house next door. I would have preferred something open and airy, with expansive views of the pool, the golf course, flowers and scenery. Who wants to look at a brick wall? Marcia was determined, however.

We gave the real estate agent a check. When we went to bed that night, Marcia was excited about getting this house, and I was mute about it. I kept my feelings to myself because if she loved it, I could survive. When I woke up the next morning, though, I said, "Marcia, I had the craziest dream. I dreamed that I spoke to your mother, and she kept saying, 'Don't let Marcia buy that house. Please don't let Marcia buy that house.'"

Marcia said, "Really? You spoke to my mother in your dream and she said that?" I said, "Yes." "Do you feel that way, too? You don't like the house?" "I don't like the house." "OK, we'll get our check back."

Remember "Tevye's Dream" from *Fiddler on the Roof?* Tevye tells his wife, Golde, that he dreamed that her grandmother Tzeitel came back from the grave. She wanted to warn him not to let their daughter (also named Tzeitel) marry Lazar, the wealthy, older butcher that the matchmaker arranged for her, but to let her marry Motel, the young tailor she loved. This was my version of Tevye's dream. And it worked.

We looked at more houses, but nothing was quite right. We wanted everything on one floor, no stairs. There was always a problem: too big, too small, not enough bedrooms for guests. The day before we were about to give up and go home, we looked at two last houses. At the first one, we walked in and saw a grand staircase going up to the second floor. I saw a baby grand piano in the magnificent sunken living room. Marcia said, "This is a home for people with a lot of kids." We walked out the door.

Marcia was getting tired of the endless search and said, "I don't want to see any more houses." I said, "Well, there's one more down the street, and it's one floor." The real estate agent said she hadn't shown it to us because it was way above the price range we had set. I said, "Let's see why they want so much money for a single family home." We walked several houses down and stepped inside. Marcia looked to her right, looked to her left and said, "We'll take it." It was like "Goldilocks and the Three Bears": This one was *just* right.

We were crushed when the real estate agent said, "I'm sorry, but another couple already has a contract on it." The wife had signed the contract, but the husband hadn't. They were in the process of divorcing. Our real estate agent said, "You know what, we're going to increase the bid. We're going to go to the lawyer's office first thing in the morning where the husband is supposed to sign it, and they'll have to take the higher bid." The other agent should have been there, but he was playing in a golf tournament and he was winning, so we asked the listing agent to represent him and she said, "I can't." As luck would have it, they accepted our bid, we got the house and we absolutely love it.

Everybody who has seen this house loves it because it's open, expansive, light and airy, and it has a big pool. I can make it from the bedroom to the office (or from the bedroom to the refrigerator!) in 15 seconds. We're north of Palm Beach in a gated community. It's in an area that is absolutely lush and plush. There are people of all ages and backgrounds. It's clean and fresh and everything is, well, idyllic.

We have made many friends there. We belong to the local country club, even though we don't play golf (a game that, to me, seems like a waste of time). But we can eat at the club very often, and the food is fabulous! We're always out and about, meeting people for dinner. We have a clique of about 15 couples that we're very friendly with. Many of them are from New Jersey and belong to the same club there as we do.

I'm surprised by how often I run into people in Florida who come up to me and tell me I did surgery on them years ago. It's often awkward because I can be in a hardware store, a theater, a black-tie gala, and someone will come flying at me, saying, "Dr. Robins—it's me! Do you recognize me?" Unfortunately, I often don't (except for the ones who have deep pockets and made generous donations to The Skin Cancer Foundation). Of course, my patients remember me, because who doesn't remember the face of a physician who performed surgery on you? And hey, I am big and jolly and memorable, right? But while I loved all of my patients, my poor, overworked gray matter didn't transfer and store all of their faces and life details into my long-term memory. Since I performed about 47,000 surgeries on people who often basked in the sun too much, I guess I shouldn't be surprised that many of them ended up in Florida. I'm happy to see them and renew our acquaintance. I hope I taught them a thing or two about the importance of sun protection.

Marcia and I are social animals, and we love to entertain. We've had some large parties. Marcia is very generous; she invited our neighbors over and we made many new friends. We've had as many as 80 or 90 people in the house. One New Year's Eve we had a three-piece orchestra and brought in a dance floor. We hired a valet service and cooks to help prepare the food, and we had a fabulous time. Entertaining isn't easy. It's a big commitment, and it's disappointing when not that many people reciprocate. Still, it's worth it.

We love our part of Florida. I'm mostly happy all the time. I get up every morning and bounce up. I'm always cheerful. If I knew how good retirement was, I would have done it years earlier. It's wonderful!

THE (WEIGHT-LOSS) STRUGGLE CONTINUES

I've been lucky that as I've gotten older, my health has remained textbook quality. I'm mostly healthy as a horse. The only thing is that I still fight with my weight, and the reason is that there's not a day that goes by where Marcia and I are not out for dinner or lunch. When we're in Florida, we go with many people to their country clubs. The hors d'oeuvres arrive immediately, and then you head to the buffet. As I've said many times, I still haven't met a food I didn't like, and I haven't learned to keep my mouth shut. So occasionally, I will take a break from the buffets and go on a diet to lose a few pounds. I've tried 'em all: low fat, low carb, high starvation!

continued

The late Phil Casson, the wonderful mentor and Australian plastic surgeon who once trained me, said that he loved working with me all those years, but his only regret was that he couldn't keep my weight stable. He would keep track of my losses and gains and once calculated that I had lost between 565 and 600 pounds over a period of 30 years. Can you believe it?

I had a brilliant idea to monetize that for the benefit of The Skin Cancer Foundation. As former executive director Mitzi Moulds explained it, "He put his money where his mouth was! His weight-loss regimens, which occurred rather frequently over the years, were used as a means of getting a potential donor to make a bet with him. If he could meet a goal of losing 10, 15, maybe 20 pounds in a certain period of time, then that donor would agree to contribute a substantial amount of money to the Foundation. You can bet our budget got some big boosts!"

I never really did retire, however. At least not in the traditional sense. My semi-retirement includes quite a lot of work. I can't help it. I love creating new projects. I don't really want to run them, but I like to use my entrepreneurial savvy to get them started. For example, I partnered with Joseph Sant'Angelo, who has a doctorate in chemical engineering and about 30 patents and counting, on a new type of polymer liquid bandage. It's a clear, thick liquid that helps wounds heal beautifully. When you put it on, it stays on for five or six days. Then it dissolves and you can wash it off with soap and water. It kills fungi, viruses and bacteria, even MRSA. I helped him fund a company called MedPak. We published articles and went through the process of getting FDA approval on the product, which took a couple of years, on an extremely small budget. Eventually, we turned the company over to people with expertise in the field.

I've also invested in projects with my inventor friend Paul Sowyrda. One business went belly-up, but I stick by him because he needs a partner like me, and I believe in his insight and ability to tap into the kind of research that could win a Nobel Prize. It's inspiring to take a chance on ideas that could change the face of medicine and make a positive difference in the world.

For example, in early 2014, Paul started a biotech company called Novellus in Cambridge, Massachusetts, with three other people. At its core is a breakthrough technology for regenerative medicine, using gene editing technology that they invented to permanently correct mutations for any genetic disease. This includes many types of cancer, including skin cancer.

Paul called me and said, "I want to tell you about my new company and the technology we have. I would like your help in putting together a world-class dermatology medical advisory board for it, and I really want you to be on it."

I said, "Paul, that sounds very exciting and I wish you luck with it, but I don't want to take on any new projects. In fact, I need to get *rid* of projects! I really appreciate you asking, though."

I could tell Paul was incredibly disappointed. And I couldn't stop thinking about it. So the next day at 7 AM, I called Paul and said, "I've been thinking about your new company, and I want to give you a list of names that I think should be on your dermatology medical advisory board." He said, "That would be fantastic, Perry!" He arrived at his office and saw my email with a list of prominent physicians—including mine. He called me immediately to ask if I had changed my mind. I said, "Well, of course, I have to help out with this." Paul was thrilled. From that point on, we would speak about the business almost every day.

In 2015, Novellus scheduled a meeting with top executives from Galderma in Switzerland. Paul called me and said, "This is short notice, but is there any way you could come to Boston for this important meeting? They love you, and it would bring a lot of credibility to what we're doing to have you there."

I said, "I'm sorry, but I can't. Marcia and I have a commitment that night. I just can't do it." But I couldn't stop thinking about it, so I juggled a few things, then called Paul back and said, "I can make it. I'll be at your meeting."

Paul says, "That's just the way Dr. Robins is. He does not know how to say no. (And when people tell Perry no, he gets even more motivated.) His motivation comes from the heart. He wants Novellus to work on the problem of hard-to-treat forms of basal and squamous cell skin cancers. He wants us to make a difference. With his help, I believe we will."

The publishing industry has had more than its share of hard times in recent years thanks to lots of mergers and acquisitions, plus downturns in advertising revenue. Under Lawrence's guidance, the publishing company SanovaWorks is seeing good results from creating more online CME programs and other educational tools for physicians.

I'm always looking for new projects for the publishing company to do, and I came up with the idea of special training for nurses to become dermatology or Mohs surgery nurses. For many who have just graduated from nursing school, they have to pay their dues to gain experience by working night shifts, weekends and holidays for low pay. But if they have some experience being a dermatology nurse, then they have a much better chance of finding a job that is 9 to 5, five days a week, with holidays off and vacation time, plus better pay. I've been working on a 40-hour program to help train these nurses.

Debby Sarnoff is doing a great job of carrying on The Skin Cancer Foundation's mission into the future as its current president. But it is like a beloved baby to me, and as its founder and chairman of the board, I have stayed involved in doing what I can to help it grow. Each fall, I always bring my extended family and many friends to support our major fundraising event, the Champions for Change

Gala. Marcia established an annual research grant for young physicians in the field of skin cancer, and she has persuaded her son and friends to make contributions to the Foundation. I love helping to plan our annual International Dermatology Exchange Program trip each spring. We pick a place (such as Costa Rica in 2019) where our group can share medical insights and cultural discovery together. I'd also like to see the Foundation forge a stronger relationship with the American College of Mohs Surgery. The two organizations have so many things in common—including me!

I didn't become a grandparent till I was 82, but oh, was I thrilled when little Heidi came along that September of 2012! She is personable and sweet. She is extremely bright and a bit precocious. She started out not babbling but speaking in full sentences. We adore her. We didn't think there would be another baby, so in 2014, when Elizabeth announced at my birthday party at Debby Sarnoff's house that I was going to be a grandfather again, it brought tears to my eyes.

Lucas was born on New Year's Eve that year, with Elizabeth nervously saying, "Come out, come out, little one, before the doctors start drinking!" Elizabeth says Heidi is extremely witty, verbal and adventurous, and Lucas is loving and pensive. Marcia says, "Perry's grandchildren are so cute. Lucas looks exactly like him—the spitting image. It's so funny; he's like a clone of Perry. Heidi's adorable. They're good children. And they live right across the street from where I used to live in New Jersey. We usually see them once a week."

You know how much I love to learn and speak other languages. Before she met César, Elizabeth spoke French and had taught herself German, since her grandparents were from Germany. But she didn't speak much Spanish. Neither did I. But we're learning! I started practicing with Heidi when she was about 3 years old and could speak Spanish better than I could. I have put in a lot of time to improve my Spanish. And it doesn't come easy. Anyone who says,

"You just have a natural aptitude for learning languages," doesn't know how hard I have to work at it. I don't have a photographic memory. I work my tush off! The kids have also learned about their Jewish heritage, studying holidays, culture and Hebrew expressions. I'm proud that Elizabeth serves on the board of directors of The Skin Cancer Foundation. I respect her judgment and advice. I'm so happy she is raising a family and also putting her law degree to good use with a fund she owns and is running.

To date, Lawrence has not followed the traditional route of marriage and kids, and that's OK. "I don't think I need to procreate to validate my life," he says. "I don't think making a 'mini me' means anything. I think anyone can be a dad, but not everyone can be a *father*. Until a few years ago, I had not been living a very responsible life, financially or otherwise. I felt defeated, inadequate, like I failed at so many things—even though they weren't really my fault. I believed I wasn't capable of financially supporting a family properly, so I just hid from all that."

My boy is feisty and independent. He led a very fast life at a young age, and he sees things differently from most people. He's twice as creative as I am. He seldom admits that he's wrong— although as he gets older, he's getting better about that. I believe he'll find his match eventually.

Lawrence says, "I think on some level, my father never quite knew how to handle me. I think there is some part of me that he very much appreciates.

"But now," he continues, "I think I've matured and am becoming a more evolved person. I think I can *matter*. And I think I can make a better contribution to our relationship. I hope my father will live long enough to see the benefits of all this work-in-progress I've been doing. That would be my only regret: if he misses the time frame and understanding that what he created was something good. I think the best is probably yet to come."

STAMP IT OUT!

Besides my business projects, the Foundation's needs, our social commitments and professional meetings to attend, what else was I going to do in my golden years, sit around and work on my stamp collection? Why, yes!

I started my stamp collection as a child, and since I "retired," I have resurrected it and am building it up at a ferocious rate. I'm going to leave it for my granddaughter and grandson, Heidi and Lucas. It's a nice collection, and it will be worth something.

My collection includes every major stamp since 1930. Pre-1930, I have about half of the important stamps, but not the most valuable ones. I have many plate-number blocks, in which the stamps are still attached to their original sheet and include the serial numbers. I have a great Israeli collection. But I don't want to accumulate a lot more because it's just too much, and I don't know if the kids or grandkids will be interested in something so hands-on—and not electronic.

I want to tell them, though, about the famous Inverted Jenny, a 1918 24¢ U.S. stamp in which a biplane was inadvertently printed upside down. Almost all of the 100 or so of the infamous misprints have been found. One sold for more than $1 million! I thought I had an original inverted Jenny, and I told an expert about it. He came over to examine it but determined it was a copy, which was printed in 1952, worth about $20. Darn. For a few hours that day, though, I thought I might have a potential windfall. Hey, you win some, you lose some!

My years with Marcia have been the best of my life—unequivocally. I have been my happiest and most lighthearted self since we met. And we have never felt the need to get married. Maybe that's the secret? "We never really even talked about marriage," says Marcia.

"We weren't having kids. We didn't have to worry about money. This way we have to be on our good behavior at all times, because we could just say goodbye and walk away. It's really good the way it is; it works out perfectly."

We're still in Europe often, and we visit other countries when we can. Recent trips have included Italy, Panama, Cuba, Colombia and Costa Rica. Marcia says she is a different person since she met me, too. "I never liked flying before," she says, "but Perry gets me to go everywhere. I never wanted to go *anywhere* when I was married. But with him, I just say, 'OK, we're going!' What else am I going to do—stay home while he goes off to have fun and adventures in exotic places? I don't love flying, but I go and he holds my hand. I'm always nervous; he's always calm. He doesn't get excited; I get excited over everything! We balance each other. And when we arrive, friends are always there to meet us and everyone has a good time. We've been to 20 or 30 countries together. I love learning more about the foods, people and traditions of each one. We never stop being fascinated by other cultures."

Marcia and I love our time at home, too, with our chihuahua, Salsa. She travels on planes with us when we shuttle between Florida and New Jersey. She also likes to visit New York and other places by car. She is absolutely terrified of thunderstorms, however—and you know how especially stormy Florida can be. The little worrywart sits on the bed every night, looking out the window to see if there's lightning. She likes to sit on my desk while I'm working, too.

I still love the excitement and energy of New York City. It's alive and pulsating 24 hours a day. We love going to fundraisers, theater and museums. It's convenient to be able to stay in our apartment overlooking the East River and eat in our favorite restaurants. But New Jersey will always feel like home to both of us. Marcia's on the Board of the Paper Mill Playhouse, a very successful theater in Millburn, New Jersey. About 25 percent of the shows there end up going to Broadway. The plays are just as good as the ones on

Broadway, and many of the stars perform there. We love supporting our community there, too.

Here I am in May 2018, speaking at the 50th anniversary of the American College of Mohs Surgery in the Grand Ballroom of the Palmer House Hilton in Chicago, back where it all started.

Marcia and I headed to Chicago in May 2018 for a special event celebrating the 50th anniversary of the founding of the American College of Mohs Surgery. Grant Park was in full flower under a brilliant blue sky on the day we arrived at the Palmer House Hilton, that grand, historic hotel dating back to 1873. (Did you know the brownie was invented at the Palmer House more than a century ago? They still make the same gooey recipe, with walnuts and apricot glaze!) But back to the serious topic at hand. I felt like I had come full circle, since I had been one of the founding fathers of the group that first gathered in the Wabash Room at the hotel back in 1967. I had been invited to say a few words to the many physicians and friends celebrating in the Grand Ballroom that night—along with a few other speakers who had been instrumental in the growth of the organization.

It felt like an important night for me. I was pleased to see such a big turnout in the ballroom, including a large number of young doctors (and no, this wasn't a free event for them) as well as many old friends. Fred Mohs himself died in 2002, but many of his family were there. The crowd, gathered around the central dance floor, which would be packed later when the band tuned up, grew silent as I walked to the microphone. The first line of my speech was: "The reason most of you are here is because I did not know the meaning of the word 'No.'" That got a big round of applause, and I relaxed and told my tales of the early days and the obstacles we overcame to make the field of dermatologic surgery what it is today. I made a few jokes and bragged a bit about what we have been able to achieve. I wanted the aspiring young doctors there to know who came before them to pave the way. I wanted my family, friends, students and colleagues to be proud of me. When I finished, the crowd rose for a standing ovation and I even heard a few cheers.

As I sat down, I thought back to those days on the farm in high school when I would get home so late from working after school that I could barely keep my eyes open at the dinner table and had trouble concentrating on my homework. I had never been on an airplane or ventured outside of the state of New Jersey. I did not think I would ever go to college, let alone see the world and achieve things beyond my wildest dreams. My mother died at 62 and my father at 67, and their lives were hard. Here I was at 88, feeling great and knowing that these were absolutely the best years of my life.

At the end of the evening, as Marcia and I walked out with friends toward the elevators, I was thinking that life couldn't possibly get better than this. Then we saw that a table had been set up near the exit with giant canisters of the famous Chicago popcorn, plus utensils so we could shovel our own mix of luscious cheese corn and caramel corn into big bags to take with us. Yes, indeed, life *can* get better. And it does. Make the most of it!

CHAPTER 20

Appendix

The Perry Robins, MD, 10 Commandments for a Good Life

I used to give a lecture I called "The 10 Commandments for Dermatologic Surgery." It was very popular with the doctors who heard it. But it's not for patients. After all, a good magician never reveals his secrets, right? So now I have created my "10 Commandments for a Good Life." This one I'm happy to share! I hope these recommendations will inspire you.

1. Do it!

I am proud that I am a doer, and you can be one. When people ask me how I accomplished such a huge tally of places I've visited, people I've known, patients I've seen, businesses I've created, things I've learned and obstacles I've overcome, I say that it's all about action. Dreams, wishes, bucket lists—they're not for me. Hoping and doing are two different things. Doors didn't magically open for me; I opened the doors myself! Sometimes there was a brick wall, so I went over it, around it or hammered my way through it. Don't overthink, and don't let fear stop you. Make things happen! Do it with honesty, integrity, compassion, knowledge and hard work (see below). Win or lose, the key is in the doing.

2. Put in the work.

Don't be lazy, mentally or physically. Success is not about luck or magic. It's about hard work. There are no shortcuts. I learned that from my parents at an early age. My mother toiled in a bakery. My father worked at a gas station and then, during World War II, a night shift in defense for the Pennsylvania Railroad. (My father was Jewish; his supervisor was Polish and would only hire Catholic people for the day jobs.) My parents did this to give me a chance they never had: to go to college. The harder you work, the smarter you get. Find a way to go to school. Do the research. Solve the problem. Find the answer. Burn the midnight oil. Take the job and give it your all to make the money that will let you do the next thing you want to do. As my good friend in Portugal, António Picoto, MD, says, "Perry Robins has so much energy. I remember when I was training with him in New York, I would work at maximum level hour after hour, and at the end of the day I would be so tired I would have to sit down for a moment. He would always catch me just then and ask, 'Why are you sitting there doing nothing?' That was frustrating at the time, but it makes me laugh now. I'm so grateful for everything he taught me.'"

3. Have fun, too.

Going to medical school in Germany was an opportunity beyond my wildest dreams and also the hardest thing I've ever done. I worked my tush off. Even though I had to study harder than I ever had while learning a new language, with almost no money, I also had the time of my life. I hitchhiked to Paris and Rome, made friends and met wonderful women, visited museums, explored the countryside and sampled all the local foods. Don't waste time, but find a way to fit in the important things. Become a well-rounded person. I made time for fun throughout my entire career, and I still do. You can, too.

4. Do what you do best.

I was really excellent at performing Mohs surgery on skin cancer. I was always booked up and often had 100 patients waiting for surgery, so I never took up lasers or cosmetic surgery. I wouldn't be the richest man, but I was happy, and I was able to share my deep experience by teaching it to others around the world. You can't do it all. Focus on what you do best. Then hire good help.

5. Try to see ahead.

Look at the horizon, broaden your focus and anticipate consequences. In my lectures to medical students, I would drum into them the importance of taking a thorough medical history of every patient. No cutting corners. Ask the right questions; for example, the patient may not think aspirin or fish oil are medications they need to mention, but during surgery they could lead to bleeding problems. This concept extends to any endeavor: Anticipate what might lead to complications, and then do what you can to prevent them.

6. Say yes.

Accept invitations, even if you have to go alone. Do you know how many great friends and contacts I've made by just saying yes? When people ask for money or my time or expertise, I am a softie, and sometimes I don't know when to say no. I trust people. It hasn't always been to my advantage, and sometimes I've lost my shirt. But sometimes losing my shirt helped somebody who needed it more than I did. And that's OK.

7. Don't be a putz; be a mensch.

Stepping on others on your way to the top is not an acceptable way to get there. I am not a traditionally religious man, but I do believe in treating others as you like to be treated yourself. I always tried to be an empathetic boss, a compassionate doctor and a helpful friend. I've had business and personal relationships go wrong. I've had investments that looked like sure things fail miserably. I've been scammed. I never sought retribution and always tried to shrug it off and let it go. If you accept that you win some and lose some, you will have a much happier life.

8. Make peace.

Don't let anger control you. I happen to be an easygoing person, but you can cultivate that trait, too. I compromise or meet people halfway. If you tell me, "You're wrong, you're crazy," I might say, "Yes, you're right, but I'm right too. So let's take a little of your right and my right and amalgamate them together into something good." Don't hold grudges against the naysayers who once tried to hold you back. Maybe you were just ahead of your time. Prove them wrong, then bring them around to your side and see if, together, you can do some good. As my close friend C. William Hanke, MD, says, "You would think a person with a vocabulary as big as Perry's would have understood the words 'no' and 'can't,' but fortunately for us, he didn't. He accomplished so much in the face of naysayers who said these things couldn't be done or didn't need to be done. And he's friends with many of them now. He has my admiration and gratitude for that."

9. Give back.

Do the right things for the right reasons. You can never really go wrong. Donate time, money or influence to something you believe in. Or raise money. Back in the 1970s, some of my grateful patients asked what they could do to help The Skin Cancer Foundation. I would occasionally joke that my fantasy fundraising strategy was to raise a scalpel and say, "What's it going to be: a donation or a scar?" But only if they knew me well enough and would laugh! Seriously, I told them that giving to the Foundation would help them save lives. And it did! As my son, Lawrence, says, "One time I was speaking to a celebrity friend. We were talking about the definition of success, and we came to the conclusion that the highest level of success to anyone, no matter how rich or famous, is philanthropy. It doesn't get any higher than that. My father has always tried to do that in every way that he could."

10. Be grateful.

As I finish writing this book, I think of all the mentors and people who taught me and helped me throughout my life. I feel proud and humble to have worked with so many great physicians, such as New York City plastic surgeon Daniel C. Baker, MD, who took me under his wing and helped train me back when dermatologists were not considered surgeons. Dan says, "You never see Perry down. There must be times where he's a bit miffed, but he never shows it. His energy is unbounding. He's done more for the treatment of skin cancer than almost anybody I can think of."

I appreciate him saying that, and I've done my best to pay it forward and train others. I regret that I didn't have more time with my children when I was younger, and I hope I've worked hard to make it up to them. I love my son, daughter and two beautiful grandchildren more than anything. I'm so thankful I found my soul mate and partner in Marcia Robbins-Wilf, EdD. I'm grateful for my good health. I've had a rich and satisfying life. I always wake up with a smile on my face, and I always look at the glass as half full. You might as well, too. It's way more fun than the alternative!

Acknowledgments

This book would not have happened without the unrelenting persistence of my dear friend C. William Hanke, MD, who always believed I had an inspiring story to tell. I could not have told it so well without my coauthor, Julie Bain. She has an uncanny knack for capturing my voice and spirit, as if she were channeling me! Working together felt like magic at times, and I truly believe our partnership was *bashert,* or meant to be.

I want to thank Eileen Cope, my agent, for helping us turn this book from a dream into a reality. I'm amazed at the skills of copyeditor Grace White, our wizard of grammar, punctuation, continuity and style. I'm also eternally grateful for all the support of my friends, family and colleagues in contributing to this story. They've enriched my life in so many ways. Marcia and I would also like to throw a treat to our chihuahua, Salsa, whom we love like family.

Any success I've had would not have been possible without the inspiring mentors who encouraged me on my sometimes rocky path to becoming a physician and then a dermatologic surgeon—especially Donald B. Strominger, MD, at Tokyo Army Hospital, and Alfred W. Kopf, MD, at NYU. In addition to all those who trained me, I'd like to thank the physicians I had the privilege of training in dermatologic surgery at NYU between 1969 and 2007 (in chronological order, next page). Some of them are no longer with us, while many continue to thrive in their practices across the U.S. and around the world, from Canada, the U.K. and Switzerland, to Israel and Australia. I learned something from each of them, and I remain close friends with many of them. I raise a toast to all of the young doctors my former fellows have trained as well. Our family tree already extends to four "generations." It will continue to branch out and grow. I am immensely grateful for the countless lives we have saved, and for all the passionate, dedicated people who will carry our mission toward a bright future where skin cancer may become only a distant memory.

I started The Skin Cancer Foundation in 1979 and served as its founder and president for 38 years. In 2017, I passed the torch to one of my former fellows, Deborah S. Sarnoff, MD, who now serves as its president, because I believed she had the drive, the brains and the passion to carry it on. I entrusted my baby to her and am grateful it is in her capable hands.

It would be remiss of me not to encourage you to visit **SkinCancer.org** and use it as your trusted source for useful, compelling, medically reviewed information about prevention, early detection and treatment of skin cancer, or to make a donation to its good work. This book is published in 2019, as the Foundation celebrates its 40th birthday. In the spirit of giving back, I'm donating proceeds from this book to its worthy cause.

MY FELLOWS, 1967 TO 2007:

Henry W. ("Bud") Menn, MD

Günter Burg, MD

Marc Chabanon, MD

Bernard Tapernoux, MD

Rex A. Amonette, MD

Luis S. Suarez-Reyes, MD

Michael J. Albom, MD

Willis Cottel, MD

Richard G. Bennett, MD

Ricardo G. Mora, MD

Sheldon Pollack, MD

June K. Robinson, MD

Leonard H. Goldberg, MD

Leonard M. Dzubow, MD

Harold S. Rabinovitz, MD

Calvin Day Jr., MD

Roy G. Geronemus, MD

David J. Goldberg, MD

Deborah S. Sarnoff, MD

Carl Vinciullo, MD

Blas A. Reyes, MD

Isaac Zilinsky, MD

Mark H. Hassel, MD

Robin Ashinoff, MD

Vicki J. Levine, MD

Lisa Renfro, MD

Maritza I. Perez, MD

Yardy Tse, MD

Bonnie S. Ross, MD

Kishwer S. Nehal, MD

Keyvan Nouri, MD

Marina Kuperman-Beade, MD

Brian Jiang, MD

Elizabeth K. Hale, MD

Sherry H. Hsiung, MD

Ritu Saini, MD

About the Author

Perry Robins, MD, is a world-renowned surgeon and medical pioneer who changed the way people think about the sun. He's also a teacher, mentor, philanthropist, entrepreneur, publisher, adventurer, father, grandfather and joke-teller.

Robins grew up in New Jersey during the Great Depression, where money was scarce and undiagnosed dyslexia rendered his schoolwork an upward battle. Despite that, he became the first person in his family to attend college. It wasn't until he was drafted into the Army, though, that a mentor saw his potential and planted the seed for a big dream: to become a doctor.

And he did, with some assistance from the GI Bill, at Heidelberg University School of Medicine in Germany. Dr. Robins returned to New Jersey for his internship, then did a residency at the Bronx VA Hospital and completed his dermatology training at NYU.

During what would become the turning point of his career, Dr. Robins studied a type of skin cancer surgery invented by Frederic Mohs, MD, at the University of Wisconsin and recognized that this technique had great potential for the field of dermatology. Dr. Robins established the first formal training program for the technique, performed more than 47,000 surgeries during his 40-plus years of practice at NYU and saved many lives. He taught Mohs surgery in nearly 50 countries and in four languages.

In his spare time, Dr. Robins created an international society and two dermatology journals to spread the word among physicians. He fought the long-held belief that tanning was healthy, started a foundation and raised millions to educate the public about the world's most common cancer.

He also learned to fly, invested in businesses and real estate, traveled the world, made lifelong friends, married and divorced twice, had two kids and found the love of his life at the age of 76. Now retired from practicing medicine, Dr. Robins invests in start-ups and splits his time between New Jersey, New York City and the Palm Beach area.